THE AUTOBIOGRAPHY OF
CHIEF OBAFEMI AWOLOWO

AWO

THE AUTOBIOGRAPHY OF
CHIEF OBAFEMI AWOLOWO

CAMBRIDGE

AT THE UNIVERSITY PRESS

1960

B
Aw 61

PUBLISHED BY

THE SYNDICS OF THE CAMBRIDGE UNIVERSITY PRESS

Bentley House, 200 Euston Road, London, N.W.1

American Branch: 32 East 57th Street, New York 22, N.Y.

West African Manager: P.O. Box 33, Ibadan, Nigeria

©

CAMBRIDGE UNIVERSITY PRESS

1960

PRINTED AND BOUND IN ENGLAND BY
HAZELL WATSON AND VINEY LTD
AYLESBURY AND SLOUGH

TO
A NEW AND FREE NIGERIA
WHERE
INDIVIDUAL FREEDOM
AND
A MORE ABUNDANT LIFE
ARE GUARANTEED
TO
ALL HER CITIZENS

CONTENTS

PREFACE

'ANYTHING, though ever so little, which a man speaks of himself in my opinion is still too much.' So says John Dryden. In writing an autobiography, one can only observe in the breach, without necessarily being disrespectful, this *ex cathedra* dictum of a Poet Laureate and one of the greatest English men of letters. In my case, I have undertaken this task for three reasons.

First, three firms of publishers of international repute have paid me the compliment of offering to publish my autobiography. When approaches were made to me in 1957, I felt somewhat flattered, and made up my mind to accept the best of the three offers, which I did in February this year when a contract was entered into between me and my present publishers. Under the stimulus of the offers made to me, I started work on this book on 18 July 1957, on board m.v. *Aureol* when I was going on holiday to the United Kingdom. But from that time up to the end of 1959, I only succeeded, in the midst of my multifarious official and political duties, in making a draft of the first four chapters, and assembling much information and data on which I have drawn for the completion of this work. Having lost the last federal election, I am able to devote more time than ever before to writing, which is one of my few hobbies. On 8 February of this year, I resumed work on the book, starting with a revision of the first four chapters. Secondly, I believe that some of the things which I have to say in my autobiography will help to refresh the memories of my contemporaries, and supply to the younger generation some facts about our political evolution. Thirdly, I also believe that certain events in my life and the manner in which I have faced them may serve as a source of inspiration and hope to some struggling youth. The usual recipe for success is not wanting in the story of my life: a single-minded definiteness about one's object in life; an intense concentration of all the energies of one's body and of all the forces of one's brain and mind on the attainment of one's chosen objective; and finally, in the pursuit of one's aim, perseverance. 'Per ardua ad astra'. Those who desire to reach, and keep their places at the top in any calling must be prepared to do so the hard way.

I now want to express my gratitude to all those who have been of assistance to me in the writing of this book. I am indebted to Miss Frame Smith of Messrs Buffalo Books, London, who helped me to tidy up my old Nigerian Youth Movement and other files, by classifying their contents into 'important' and 'not important', thus making references to them much easier for me. Unknown to each other, she and Mr W. Foges (also of Buffalo Books) on the one hand, and Mr P. J. Harris (of the Cambridge University Press) on the other, have been responsible for stimulating and sustaining my zest for this work. Mr Harris has also kindly agreed to assist me in correcting the proofs. The measure of my indebtedness to him and to Miss Frame Smith and Mr Foges, is the conclusion of this humble enterprise.

A good deal of material had to be obtained from old newspapers in the Nigerian National Archives at the University College, Ibadan. I knew what I wanted, and remembered either the exact date, or the month and year, or just the year. But I owe the search for and the collection of the required informations to the ready and willing co-operation of my friend, Mr Latif Jakande, formerly Managing Editor of the *Daily Service* and now Managing Director and Editor-in-Chief of the Allied Newspapers Limited. He was assisted in this tedious task by Mr Akintunde Emiola, Editor of the *Nigerian Tribune*, Mr S. A. Adejumo my Political Private Secretary, and the *Daily Service* photographer, Mr Wahab Saba, who made photostats of many newspaper articles and reports. Because of the size of this book it has not been possible for me to use more than a small fraction of the mass of material which they have helped me to assemble. The heavy strain of typing the tiny prints of the photostats fell upon Mr K. A. Lawal who is one of the most thorough and painstaking shorthand typists I have met. I am immensely grateful to them all.

In the course of writing this book, I have had to dodge members of the public some of the time in order to have peace and quiet for concentration. In this regard all praise goes to my wife Chief (Mrs) H. I. D. Awolowo who tactfully screened me from those who wanted to see me at inconvenient times. None of these people, however, was left unanswered and unattended. As is her wont on similar occasions, she stood in admirably for me. I am profoundly grateful to her.

My very warm gratitude also goes to my typist Mr A. O. Onafowokan. He is efficient and exceedingly industrious. He has had to work at odd hours and at different places to type my manuscripts which, I must admit, were not often written in legible hand: but in all the circumstances he remained a cheerful worker.

OBAFEMI AWOLOWO

AKURE
5 *June* 1960

When all thy mercies, O my God,
  My rising soul surveys,
Transported with the view, I'm lost
  In wonder, love and praise.

JOSEPH ADDISON

Once to every man and nation
  Comes the moment to decide,
In the strife of truth with falsehood,
  For the good or evil side. . . .

Then it is the brave man chooses,
  While the coward stands aside,
Till the multitude make virtue
  Of the faith they had denied.

JAMES RUSSELL LOWELL

If ever this free people—if this government itself
is ever utterly demoralized, it will come from this
incessant human wriggle and struggle for office,
which is but a way to live without work.

ABRAHAM LINCOLN

CHAPTER 1

HOW IT BEGAN

IKENNE, the place of my birth, is a small town. You will not find it on most maps of Nigeria. As towns go there, however, it is the fourth in order of population in the Administrative Division of Ijebu Remo of which it forms a part.

The marriage between my father and my mother did not take place at the time originally fixed for it, and indeed it only providentially managed to escape complete frustration. A few weeks before the time scheduled for the wedding, both father and mother were, at different times, fugitives respectively from an angry pagan community and from a British punitive expedition which had been despatched to Ikenne to protect its small Christian community by strengthening the police force there.

In accordance with custom, mother had been betrothed to father, and the latter had paid the prescribed dowry in full. It was the custom in those days—and this custom still lingers in various parts of Ijebu—for those who belonged to the same age-group to get married during the same period. An annual festival is the most appropriate occasion for wedding ceremonies. During the festival, it was customary for the brides-to-be to stage street dances for a number of days in succession, using the same kind of apparel, displaying their charm, and singing songs of love and praise to the beat of drums. On the last day, the brides-to-be, after receiving the blessings of their parents, wended their ways, accompanied by friends and relatives, to the houses of their respective bridegrooms, amidst the melodies of songs and drums.

All the customary procedures having been completed by father, the day for the wedding was fixed. As part of the preparation for the great day, mother had gone to Lagos in company with many other members of her age-group to buy new apparel for their weddings.

About three months before she left for Lagos, a tragedy had occurred. A group of Christians who had gone fishing in the dead of night in an Ikenne river called Uren had been waylaid and violently attacked by a group of pagans, and one of the Christians, a young man in his early twenties, had been killed. The only reason for this murder was that the Christians had greatly provoked the pagans by catching some of the fish in the Uren, thereby violating a cardinal article of Ikenne pagan faith. When I was a little boy in school it was still forbidden to catch or kill any of the fishes in this river. They were regarded as sacred. Furthermore it was claimed by the pagans that the fishes if caught could never be successfully cooked, and that in any case evil was sure to befall anyone who caught or killed any of them.

The new Christian converts doubted the validity of these claims, but refrained from putting their scepticism to the test. As a result of centuries of absolute safety, the fishes in the Uren had waxed big, numerous, sluggish and contemptuous. If you entered the river, they rushed clumsily at you and nibbled at your clothes or legs or anything around you. They lived their lives unmolested and unafraid.

Then in 1905 a vaccinator from Lagos, who was posted to Ijebu Remo and who visited Ikenne in the course of his duty, had occasion to go to the river for a bath. He was astonished at the quantity of fishes in the Uren, and at their sluggish motion and contemptuous behaviour. It may be mentioned in passing that the water of the river Uren is very clear—so clear that you could see the river's bed as well as its contents quite plainly. The vaccinator from Lagos was not used to that type of behaviour on the part of fishes towards man, and he was compelled to ask questions. The answer came; and it was to him, as it had seemed to the Christians of Ikenne, arrant nonsense. He decided to catch some of the fishes. It was clearly realised that if attempt was made to catch the fishes in daylight, the pagan elements would be provoked to violent action. So it was decided to execute the project at night. The first attempt was made without a hitch. Many fish were caught, and what delicious dishes they must have made! No special skill or exertion was required to catch the fishes in the Uren. You merely had to dip your hands into the river and pick them out. When I was a child, we used to pick any one that we fancied out of the water, have a good gaze at it, and then drop it back into the river when it began to struggle.

The second attempt, made a few days after the first, was a tragic one for the zealous iconoclasts, and fatal for one of them. The pagan elements had been apprised of the first attempt. Not knowing when a further attempt would be made, they had posted some two or three hunters along the footpath leading to the river to keep vigil for successive nights. Their efforts were rewarded when the band of fishermen, including among others the vaccinator, the Catechist, Chief Adelana (who later became my father-in-law) and Sonubi who was killed that night, passed by. The hunters on duty sent word to their colleagues. On their way back, the fishermen were attacked. They threw away their catches and ran into the forest. But Sonubi fell, and he was done to death. My father-in-law had some injuries, but escaped with the others.

The following day, on the receipt of a report, a number of police constables came to Ikenne. The man who dealt the fatal blow, with a few others, was arrested. The statements made to police implicated the War Chief who held the title of Balogun (i.e. the equivalent of a General), and who was also ex-officio Head of all hunters in the town. The Balogun was, therefore, wanted by the police. But he was nowhere to be found. In the meantime, whilst search was being made for him, those who had been arrested were remanded in custody in Lagos prisons. Time dragged on, and it was after three months of search that the Balogun was apprehended. On his arrest, he was handcuffed. But he refused to go with the police unless he was carried by them. As the police were not inclined to carry him, a stalemate ensued. In a flash, news of the Balogun's arrest reached the

3

hunters. They quickly assembled and demanded the release of their leader. The police refused, and the hunters forcibly took him away. They later broke the handcuffs, and gave complete freedom to their leader.

After the Balogun's forcible release, and the departure of the police who found themselves excessively outnumbered, the Christians were terrorised by the pagans, and had to flee for refuge in neighbouring towns or in some hideouts in the forests. Father fled to Ilishan where his own father was born and which was the home of his grandparents. On 6 January 1906, a punitive expedition arrived in Ikenne, and all the Christians were called upon to return home. They did, and it was the turn of the pagans to flee. Mother left for Lagos about two days before the apprehension of the Balogun. She was still in Lagos when the soldiers were despatched to Ikenne. In the course of their peregrination around the shops along the Lagos beach on the Lagoon at Ebute Ero, she and the others of her age-group did see some soldiers embarking, but their destination was unknown to them.

The brides-to-be concluded their purchases in Lagos and left for home. In those days, it was roughly twenty hours' journey from Lagos to Ikenne—ten hours on the lagoon by canoe, and about the same number of hours on foot, with stops for meals and a bit of a rest, to cover the distance from Ikorodu beach to Ikenne. It was the fashion for the brides-to-be to sing at their best during their journey. Singing lightens the ennui of a long journey by foot, and in their case they had cause to be gay and cheerful. But the melody of the songs was rudely jarred and terminated, and their high spirits gloomily damped when, at Shagamu, about four miles from Ikenne, they learnt that Ikenne was already occupied by soldiers and that all the pagans had fled the town.

At this time, mother, with many others of her age-group, had not become a Christian. After her marriage to my father, even though she attended church regularly with my father and discharged all her financial obligations as well as rendering voluntary services to the Church, she remained unbaptised, and

4

a mere proselyte at the gate. It was a condition precedent to the consent to her marriage with father, stipulated by her parents, that she should not be baptised and admitted to the Christian fold. Her mother worshipped the river god (Oluweri, i.e. Owner and Ruler of the Rivers). When she gave birth to my mother, she had dedicated her to this god of the rivers, and she was not going to break her vow under any circumstances. Though mother, after her marriage, learnt to read in the vernacular and was, therefore, able to read the Bible, the Prayer Book, and to sing hymns, and though she continued to attend church after father's death, it was some years after her own mother's death that I succeeded in getting her to break her mother's vow to the river god, and become a baptised Christian.

Being non-Christians, my mother and her fellow brides-to-be decided not to go to Ikenne but to seek refuge elsewhere. Apart from the news of the occupation of Ikenne, and of the hostility of the soldiers to pagans in general, a distasteful story also reached them that some pagan girls who had had the misfortune to fall into the hands of the soldiers had been severely assaulted and violated. The happy band of brides-to-be dispersed in sorrow and dejection. Mother, in company of some, went to Ilishan. Unknown to her, father had been to Ilishan and had left before she arrived there. She was compelled to move from there to Ode Remo and then to Iperu, where she stayed with her relations.

After some days at Iperu, she heard the good news that all was back to normal in Ikenne. All those (including the Balogun) who were wanted by the police had been arrested; the soldiers had left, leaving behind sufficient police to ensure the maintenance of law and order; the pagans had returned and were living peaceably with the Christians.

Mother returned home. A few weeks later—much later than the time originally scheduled for it—father and mother were married. The first child of the marriage, a son, died five months after birth. Then on 6 March 1909, I was born. Father's name was Shopolu and mother's was Efunyela. Father became a

Christian in 1896. It was the fashion in those days, and this fashion still obtains in most parts of Nigeria, for baptised Christian adherents to adopt Biblical names. And so, on his baptism about a year after his conversion, father took the name of David, thus becoming David Shopolu. I was baptised when I was three months old, and father gave me the Biblical name of Jeremiah in addition to my other names: Obafemi Oyeniyi. Following the same fashion, when mother was baptised some ten years ago she was named Mary, thus becoming Mary Efunyela.

The society into which I was born was an agrarian and peaceful society. There was peace because under the Pax Britannica there was a total ban on intertribal as well as intra-tribal war, and civil disturbances of any kind and degree were severely suppressed and ruthlessly punished. There was peace because there was unquestioning obedience to constituted authority. There was peace because the people lived very close to nature, and she in her turn was kind and extremely generous to them. And there was peace because the family life was corporate, integrated and well regulated. The order of pre-cedence in the family and in the community as a whole was essentially in accordance with age. The little ones were given every legitimate indulgence. The parents, grand-parents, and, more often than not, the great grand-parents, were all there— living in one and the same compound, sometimes under one and the same roof—to pet them. Discipline, when occasion called for its application, was severe and spartan. The sturdy members of the family were also there to cater for the aged parents or grand-parents as the case might be. The land was fertile, and the rains fell in their due season. At that time there was more than enough land for everybody. Land was and still is owned not by the individual but by the family. This is the custom in Ijebu as well as in other parts of Yorubaland. Every member of the family is entitled to cultivate any portion of his family land either on the paternal or maternal side. Because of the fertility and sufficiency of farmland, only a minimum amount of effort was required to satisfy the sparse

6

wants of the individual. Until western civilisation began to make its inroad into the lives of the people, it did not require too much exertion to provide food, shelter and clothing. Food was obtained with the minimum of effort from the farms. Shelter was easily provided by erecting mud walls and covering them with thatch or certain kinds of leaves for a roof. Friends and relatives usually helped one another in building one another's houses in turn. It was one of the obligatory duties of a son-in-law to help build the house of his father-in-law, and annually to help repair the roof thereof. The amount of clothing required was limited to the demands of a peasant farming life and of the annual festivities. There were many annual festivals, all of which were and still are held during the period of harvest. There was plenty of leisure.

Notwithstanding its ostensible mirth, peace and tranquillity, the society into which I was born was one which was riddled with fear, uncertainty and suppression. There was the fear of the white man who was the supreme lord of any area placed under his jurisdiction. His word was law, and his actions could never be called in question by any member of the community. Those Africans who dared to criticise the white man lived in Lagos, and they went by the un-Biblical English names of Williams, Macauley, etc. There were one or two westernised and politically conscious individuals in Ijebu Remo who played the role of champion and defender of the people's rights. But apart from being somewhat oppressive themselves, they were not quite so effective. The barriers between the people and the white official were language, and the latter's undisguised aloofness. The sources of the people's fear of him were his strange colour, his uncanny power to shoot people down at long range, and his obviously unimpeachable authority. There was the fear of the white man's carriers and messengers who were a law unto themselves.

There was the fear of the local chieftains who were more or less the agents of the British Government, and who, as a result, acquired new status, prestige and power. The form and the system of government in Ijebu Remo, before the advent of

British rule, were respectively monarchical and gerontarchal. At the head of each town in Ijebu Remo, as in other parts of Yorubaland, there was a king. Under British rule all the Yoruba kings were designated Obas, since there could only be one reigning monarch at one and the same time in the Empire. The fact remains, however, that the English equivalent for 'Oba' is 'King'. Apart from the Oba, there are Chiefs in each town. It is the prerogative of the Oba, in consultation with his Chiefs, to confer a chieftaincy title on any citizen who in his judgement possesses the necessary qualities. The candidate for a chieftaincy title must be an outstanding person in the community, possessing good character and integrity, and fairly well-to-do. It is a maxim among the Ijebus that 'A rascal or a poverty-stricken person is not qualified for a chieftaincy title.' He must also have a reputation for tact and wise counsel. He must be of a very ripe age. The appointment of educated, enlightened, well-to-do or prominent young persons as Chiefs is a modern innovation, and it is an eloquent proof of the importance attached to western education and culture in present-day Yoruba society.

The affairs of each town were administered by the Oba and his Council of Chiefs, subject to such checks and balances as were provided by the reactions of the populace to any given measure. In the days before British rule, an unpopular Council would not remain long in office. In Ijebu, the younger elements under the Balogun would attack the houses of the guilty Chiefs and completely destroy them. If the Oba was the guilty party, he would be advised by the Chiefs to retire, and this might take one of two forms: suicide or voluntary exile.

Under British rule, these methods were no longer applicable, and as there were no popularly elected Councils at the time, the Oba and Chiefs, instead of regarding themselves as being responsible to their people as before, considered themselves responsible to the white man who in the view of the people was unapproachable as well as unassailable and invincible. In due course, therefore, the word of the Oba and his Chiefs also became something of a law. If they chose to be tyrannical there was nothing that anyone could do about it, unless there was an educated or semi-educated person around to advise on and help in writing a petition to the white man. But it required a good deal of guts to write petitions criticising the Oba and his Chiefs. It was regarded by many white men, then in the Administrative Service, as gross impudence bordering on sedition to write critical letters, petitions, or remonstrances about an Oba. During the first five years of this century, two educated citizens of Ijebu Remo who summoned up enough courage to call attention in a petition to what they regarded as glaring cases of injustice and misrule on the part of one of the Remo Obas, were arrested, tried summarily, and sent to gaol for some months for their impertinence.

There was the fear of innumerable gods, and of the medicine-men who claimed and were credited with all manner of supernatural and magical powers. Every natural phenomenon, like drought, unusual flood, or thunder, was attributable to the anger of one of the gods. Every serious ailment or disease or organic disorder like severe headache, ulcer, tuberculosis, elephantiasis, barrenness, or mental malady, never happened to man save through the agency of an irate god or a malevolent and offended medicine-man. Whenever someone had fallen on bad times, or was seriously ill, it had always been because he had offended one or more of the gods or medicine-men in some inexplicable manner. The well-known remedy in any one of these cases was the offering of sacrifices as prescribed by the medicine-man who was the earthly accredited intermediary between a given god and mortal beings, supported by the taking by the patient of an indiscriminate quantity of various assortments of herbal preparations and medicinal powder.

The newly converted Christians were in a quandary. They believed in one God as against a multiplicity of gods; they believed that all the graven images or idols which they previously worshipped were nothing but the blind, deaf and dumb things that they really are; they believed in Jesus Christ as a Saviour and Redeemer and as an Intercessor between them and God; they believed also in hell with its brimstone and un-

9

quenchable fire; and in short they believed in the Apostle's Creed, and in as much of the teachings of Christ as were imparted to them. But in spite of their belief, they suffered from serious ailments and diseases whose causes were unknown to them, in the same way as the pagans. At best, they ascribed the cause in each instance to the work of Satan, whose agents, according to them, the medicine-men were. They believed in the efficacy of certain herbs in the cure of ailments and diseases, but their belief in this connection had not always been justified by results. They believed in the potency of prayer.

In a society where most people did not have anything at all like a bath more than half-a-dozen times in a year, the Christians were in a class by themselves. They cultivated the habit of having a really good bath, and of putting on their best apparel, at least every Sunday. Christian men and women had to co-operate in maintaining the church and the Mission House in a state of perfect cleanliness. This in its turn had some influence on the way the Christians looked after their own houses. As time went on, the Christians looked cleaner because they lived more hygienic lives, and in consequence many of them and their children became immune from some diseases like yaws. In this, they saw some evidence of the triumph of their faith. But as they still suffered from other diseases in the same manner as the pagans; as there were no hospitals and trained doctors around; and as the medicine-men continued blatantly and garrulously to claim to possess the power of dealing with such diseases, the occasions when the faith of a new Christian convert was shaken were much more numerous than now.

They were, however, immensely sustained in their faith by the activities of the missionaries of those days. These Christian missionaries were intrepid pioneers, and conscientious and selfless evangelists of a great doctrine. They reflected the spirit and teachings of Christ as much as any human being could, in their day-to-day contact with their new flock. They lived more or less with the people, and conducted constant visitations. They cared for the flock in sickness, helped them in times of trouble, and, through the instrumentality of the administrative authorities, protected them against attacks or unnecessary buffetings and threats from the pagan elements. In spite of the prevailing fears, therefore, I was made to realise quite early in life that Christianity was, of a surety, superior in many respects to paganism.

CHAPTER 2

PARENTAGE

UNTIL I visited Abeokuta in 1921, I had thought that the white man was a superman. To me, his colour symbolised delicacy, innocence and purity, because it resembled very much the colour of Ikenne children at birth. Why he remained white and we grew black beat my little imagination. I don't think I saw more than half-a-dozen white men before I went to Abeokuta. There was a Rev. G. Henry Lester—a Wesleyan minister of religion. I saw him fairly often—on Empire Days and when, during my pupillage at the Wesleyan School, Ikenne, he came there for inspection. There was a Rev. L. C. Mead—another Wesleyan minister. I saw him only once, but I vividly remember him. He came in the company of the Rev. Lester to inspect our school.

On a number of occasions, I saw white officials who passed through Ikenne at different times. The first white official I saw was carried in a hammock by two hefty Nigerians. His luggage was carried by a number of Nigerian carriers. He was ministered unto by a number of messengers and police constables. We were told that a white man used to sleep in the hammock in the course of the journey. But the one I saw did have an open book on his chest whilst he was being carried through Ikenne. Presumably he had been reading the book before he reached our town. Almost all the little urchins in the town flocked around to have a glimpse of him. What a mighty man I thought he was, so specially favoured by God to have a white skin and to occupy such a position of exalted superiority. The second one I saw spent about two days in Ikenne. His tent was pitched in the market place. The children—particularly school children—were there to have a look at him and his carriers, messengers, police constables and interpreter. A few days before his arrival, the Oba of Ikenne had caused a public proclamation to be made for firewood, yams, chickens, water and other necessaries to be provided in plenty in the market place for the use of the *Ajele* (Administrative Officer). Certain specified age-groups were saddled with the responsibility. But apart from the Oba and his chiefs (aged people all of them) who must visit the Ajele to pay their respects, no other adult or able-bodied person—man or woman—would dare to come too near to the Ajele, especially when his carriers and messengers were about to depart, or when they were actually on their journey. It was the practice for the messengers and carriers to impress anyone forcibly into the service of the Ajele as a relief for themselves. Those who had the misfortune of falling into their hands had been forced to carry the Ajele's luggage until the messengers and carriers could get hold of other persons as substitutes, or until they were about to reach their destination. The forced carriers were entitled to neither money nor thanks for their labour.

In the midst of a multitude of external influences, our home was to me a veritable haven. I felt completely secure there, and impregnably insulated against the mysteries of life which perplexed the community of Ikenne. I was perfectly confident that, ensconced within the four walls of father's house, the invisible arrows and agencies of death and evil which were said to be constantly in the air could never touch me. Three persons provided this impenetrable bulwark of my childhood days: father and mother, and my father's own mother.

Father's mother, by name Asefule, was the virtual empress of our home. As a child, I thought the world of her. She died when I was thirty-two. At different times I spent about sixteen years of this period living under the same roof with her; and for the rest we were in regular touch with each other. Over the years, I have had no cause to alter my estimation of her, and even now, I think she must have been in a rare class by herself. She was clean, elegant, self-confident and dominating. She regarded me as the apple of her eye, and fondly referred to me as

13

her 'father'. Up to a point she tolerated corporal punishment being inflicted on me, but only in connection with my education. Father believed and used to assert categorically that physical affliction was indispensable to book learning. Outside this limited orbit, I could, with impunity, be as naughty and troublesome as I pleased when granny was about. Once or twice she caught father in the act of flogging me. He quickly threw the whip away. She chided him and caressed me. I felt very pleased and triumphant. As for mother, I don't remember her ever flogging me. There appeared, however, to be perfect understanding between granny and my parents on one thing: I was always made to suffer the consequences of my acts. For instance if, out of sheer naughtiness, I refused my food when offered to me, then there would be no food for me until the next meal, even if I tried to cry my head off to win their sympathy.

Granny did not share my father's belief in one God and faith in Jesus Christ. But unlike many a pagan parent at the time, she and her husband Awolowo displayed an exemplary tolerance. Father was left free to practise his new faith without let or hindrance or even as much as a threat or opposition from his parents. Granny had an undisguised contempt for the so-called medicine-men, the witches and wizards, and thought they were charlatans. Her attitude may be summed up in her repeated saying: 'He who does no evil, need not fear any evil.' Another saying of hers which impressed itself upon my young mind is: 'Little bits of evil-doing sooner or later accumulate to bring disaster on the evil-doer.' She confined herself to the worship of only one of the pagan gods, and the adoration of the Ifa Priest.

In spite of my father's views in the matter, our home had been visited by an Ifa Priest on a number of occasions at the invitation of granny. Each visit had invariably been followed by some modest sacrifices: the killing and cooking of one or two chickens and/or pigeons. Father had warned me not to partake of sacrificial meat or food. But I could not resist the temptation, especially when the tempter was the formidable and unassailable granny herself. Father had punished me once for my disobedience in this regard, when granny was not in. Mother advised me not to report the incident to granny on her return, and I kept my peace. For if granny learnt of it, father might be in trouble.

It was the practice with granny to get the Ifa Priest to consult the Oracle on certain occasions, especially when a child was born to or by one of her own children. She did so, to my knowledge, when my sister Olufunmilayo was born. I understand she did so seven years after I was born. Father always made sure that he was not in the house when the divination took place. In my case, the Oracle declared that I was the re-incarnation of granny's own father. I am told that granny had a profound admiration and affection for her father, and I can never help feeling that she had transferred these emotions to me from the moment I was authoritatively declared his re-incarnation. Granny was also very proud of her father. He was a warrior of note and fortune who held many chieftaincy titles in his lifetime.

My mother is a gentle and an unobtrusive housewife: hard-working, kind-hearted, affectionate and unquestioningly obedient to granny and father. She was very much beloved by both granny and father; the former took mother under her protective and soothing wings and treated her like her daughter. Mother has a sharp and sarcastic tongue. Granny and father were totally exempt from this verbal weapon; but I was an occasional victim of it when I proved naughty. On the occasions when I had fallen victim, I would have preferred some strokes of the whip, which she never used against me, to her biting invectives. Mother worshipped no other god to my knowledge. My first sister Victoria Olufunmilayo (Olu for short) was born in 1915, the second sister Bolajoko in 1919, and my third sister Idowu, by another father, was born in 1923.

Mother, like father's mother, has a distinguished military ancestry of which she is also very proud. Her father, Awofeko, held the military title of Are (Generalissimo) at the early age of about forty-three. Mother is very fond of telling the stories of her father's prowess and exploits, and of his matchless courage. Another story which she never tires of telling with nostalgic emotion is that of her Egba ancestry. Her own maternal great-grandmother was a full-blooded Egba. She was married to an Ijebu Remo husband, and had two daughters, the first of whom was mother's maternal grandmother.

My father was to me the very embodiment of an ideal parent. Granny before her death, mother, and many of father's friends and contemporaries, with whom I have been communicating of late, have testified to his outstanding qualities and virtues. He was truthful, forthright, fearless, and unyielding in his detestation of any form of hypocrisy and dishonesty. Of medium height, he was robust both in physique and in health. He was famed in Ikenne for his tireless energy and industry, and for being an ideal parent and husband. He was accommodating and generous to a fault. His house was a dumping-ground for helpless relations. On one pretext or another they came in from time to time, stayed for as long as they liked, and lived on father's resources for the duration. In my childhood days, I saw in this unfailing concourse of relations staying in our house an excellent social arrangement. I enjoyed their company because they all tried to pamper me. But as I grew older, and still more as I write now, I have come to realise that it is an excessively burdensome social system.

On me and my sisters father lavished the utmost affection and devotion. He did the same on mother. He was highly respected and trusted by all and sundry in Ikenne, and he was long before I was born and until his death, the organiser and president of a number of thrift societies. (In Yorubaland a thrift society is called *Esusu*.) A great optimist who was never known to say die, he had a buoyant and magnetic personality. He was a farmer as well as a sawyer, and apart from his two brothers, he employed about a dozen other people in his lumber business.

After the day's work on the farm or in the lumber camp, he indulged himself in animated conversation and hearty laughter. Night after night, when he was not out to visit his friends and relatives, he was surrounded by friends and conversationalists

16

who more often than not had meals with him. He therefore always made sure that food was prepared for more than the household required. As far as I can recall, these nightly conversations, or, on Sundays, when father did not work, afternoon conversations, usually centred round agriculture and the state of the weather in relation thereto, harvest prospects, the prices of farm and lumber products, and a host of other matters of general interest. They were also in the habit of discussing the white man's regime, often referring to it with awe and admiration. Occasionally there was some criticism too. I cannot recall the full details of their discussion. As for the praise, however, I remember that the white man's suppression of intertribal war, his abolition of slavery and the slave trade, his sense of justice and fair play—all these, I remember, were warmly eulogised. As for the criticism, I remember quite vividly that father in particular and some of his friends strongly condemned what they used to describe as '*Mashai-Lo*'. My understanding was that *Mashai-Lo* was a Yoruba phrase the English rendering of which is: 'It is compulsory to go.' Father held the strong view that with all he had done in suppressing intertribal war, slavery and slave-trade, and in introducing Christianity, it was a blemish on his record for the white man to introduce '*Mashai-Lo*'. My childish brain and imagination could not quite puzzle out what the compulsion was about. When I grew older and became literate in English, however, I understood the phrase to mean 'Martial Law'. But the phrase had been used by father and his friends in an entirely inappropriate context.

From 1894 to 1914, Ijebu Remo was administered as part of the Colony District of Lagos, and Remo people were regarded as British subjects. During this period, there were no Native (now Customary) Courts, and justice, in criminal cases and civil causes which could not be settled by arbitration, was administered by the white man. The people liked this arrangement very much. Then in 1914 the Indirect Rule System was introduced into the Southern Provinces. Ijebu Remo was detached from the Colony District and merged with Ijebu Ode for administrative purposes. The Awujale's suzerainty over Ijebu Remo was restored, and native courts were introduced. The Oba and his chiefs acquired a more enhanced status and authority. It was this new system that was described as 'Martial Law'.

Father was a handsome and well-dressed person. He loved clean surroundings and always had a bath every day after the day's work (an unusual thing in those days in Ikenne Community). Mother always saw to it that father's tastes were catered to. She washed and ironed his clothes regularly (only fairly well-to-do Christians indulged in this luxury then); and she swept the house and its surroundings first thing in the morning, and if need be once again during the day. Father's chief quarrel with me was that I was extremely untidy. I liked to be left alone without a bath. But as often as she could, mother insisted on my being bathed. In this connection, she had never hesitated to invoke the authority of granny whom I feared and respected above all else. If granny gave the order, I had to obey. Otherwise, I would lose my only protection against father's just indignation. I hated to be gorgeously or well dressed even on Sundays or during Christian festivals. I regarded all the shoes, clothes and caps which father had ordered from Lagos for me as burdensome, and felt miserable and uncomfortable whenever I had them on.

By the then prevailing social standards, father was descended from an illustrious and noble ancestry. His great-grandfather held the double chieftaincy titles of Oluwo and Losi. In Ijebu Remo the instrument of authority, which was the equivalent of the British Parliament and Cabinet, was the Oshugbo. The Oba and his Chiefs could hold deliberations as a Council; but any decision taken by the Council must receive the imprimatur or approval of the Oshugbo before it could take effect; and such a decision would not in any case be executed save by the Oshugbo. The Oba was the king and head of all the community and he presided over the meetings with his Chiefs. In Ikenne, as in most parts of Ijebu Remo, the Oluwo is next in rank to the Oba, but it is the former who presides over the meetings of the Oshugbo. As a rule the Oba does not attend the meetings of the Oshugbo. When he does, he takes precedence after the Oluwo. On the demise of the Oba, the Oluwo acts in his place. The Oluwo title which was held by father's great-grandfather is a public title, whilst the Losi title, one of the chieftaincy titles which I now hold, is a family title. The former could rotate from one recognized ruling family to another, whilst the latter remains in our family to be held by any worthy successor on whom the Oba may confer it.

Father's great-grandfather was reputed to be an outstanding statesman. He was also said to be a wealthy man, possessing many slaves. His wife was also a wealthy woman and a chief in her own right. She held the family title of Ligu. Father's own father Awolowo lived with his own grandfather from a very early age. He accompanied him to most public meetings and functions, and carried his bag and other paraphernalia of office. As a result, after a comparatively brief spell as a farmer, Awolowo took to public life as a career, doing farming as a sideline. He stopped farming altogether after his grandfather's death. When his grandfather died, the title of Oluwo passed to another family whose turn it was. But Awolowo was made an Iwarefa and soon became the head of it: the Iwarefa consisted of only six members and was the inner circle or the executive council of the Oshugbo. It was the equivalent of a cabinet. In those days, it was even more than a cabinet. It was the highest judicial body in the town to which appeals could be made, and it alone could pronounce a sentence of death, and order execution subject to the consent of the Awujale conveyed through the Akarigbo. Awolowo held the key of the Oshugbo House and of the Inner Chamber (the meeting place of the inner circle), and no meeting could be held there without his knowledge and consent.

During his long tenure of office, Awolowo acquired the reputation for being a very firm and impartial administrator and for being resentful of the overlordship of Ijebu Ode. On one occasion, about 1887, a relation of Awolowo (a distant one by modern conception) committed adultery with the wife of an Ijebu Ode Prince. It was a capital offence. The offender was arrested, and was detained in a cell in the Oshugbo House. He was tried, found guilty of the offence and sentenced to death by the Iwarefa under the presidency of Awolowo. Without waiting for the necessary approval from the Awujale, Awolowo ordered the execution of the convict. The Awujale considered his authority seriously slighted and ordered his Balogun—the general of his army—by name Kuku to despatch a punitive expedition to Ikenne. The Iledi was burnt and utterly destroyed as an indication that the executive authority in Ikenne had been abrogated.

Awolowo escaped to Ilishan which was his own father's home. Some of the Iwarefas were arrested and taken captive to Ijebu Ode. Representations were later made to the Awujale, who imposed a heavy fine on the Oshugbo of Ikenne. This fine was paid, the executive authority of Ikenne was restored, and the Iwarefas, including Awolowo still at their head, were rehabilitated.

Father did not follow in his own father's footsteps. He took to farming early in life. At first he worked under his father. But when the latter became a full-time politician, he had to stand on his own as a farmer. With him were his four uterine brothers, three of whom were also Awolowo's sons, to wit: Jacob Kujore, Michael Onanuga, James Oye and Adebajo. They worked together under father's leadership and direction.

On the advent of Christianity to Ikenne in 1896, father was one of the first few to embrace it. He succeeded in bringing all his uterine brothers by Awolowo into the Christian fold. At their baptism they also adopted Biblical names. He was responsible for many other converts outside his family circle. He quickly learnt to read and write in the vernacular, and taught his three Christian brothers and others (including mother at a later stage) to do likewise. I did not and do not know what pagan god father worshipped before then. But from the moment of his conversion, he never looked back. He was a conscientious Christian and an unfailing church-goer. He abhorred paganism, together with all its innumerable rites, rituals and festivals. He impressed it upon me to shun anything

20

connected with paganism. He had contempt for the medicine-men and he openly pooh-poohed belief in witchcraft and wizardry.

He was a monogamist up to the year 1919. Up till that time, I never knew him to quarrel with granny or mother or even to exchange hard words with them, or to question the authority or dominance of granny. Early in that year, however, he married a new wife. With her advent into the house, there was a re-alignment of relationships among the members of the household. Father was less intimate with mother. Before then, father, granny and mother had more or less a common purse, and did things in common. This was no more. The new wife did not accept granny's authority as mother did, and granny was resentful of this. The new wife set herself up as a custodian of father's belongings and would not allow anyone to make use of even the smallest of them without her consent. She was exceedingly kind to me and treated me with a respect which, now I look back on it, was beyond my age and standing; but I did not reciprocate it. She appeared to me as an intruder, someone who had come without any just cause to mar the harmony of our home.

One day, a big quarrel flared up between father and granny on account of the new wife. Mother took sides with granny. It was a terrific and terrible affair and I will never forget it. For the first time to my knowledge, father and the new wife on one side, and mother and granny on the other, exchanged harsh and unkind words at the tops of their voices. The new wife set the pace in this battle of verbal virulence. The incident shocked me badly and I wept bitterly as the disgraceful scene was being enacted. For the first time in the history of our home as I knew it, neighbours came to intervene in our internal affairs. Later on, the elders in the neighbourhood got together in the house of granny's uncle, a very aged man, to settle the matter. But granny was never herself again. She had been deposed from her high and hitherto unchallenged pedestal, and she knew it. Shortly after this quarrel, she left Ikenne for Abeokuta where she stayed and carried on business as a trader dealing in poultry. When granny left the house, I had a sure feeling that the soul of the home had departed. In any case, the home was not as it had been: mother was deprived of a most considerate and affectionate mother-in-law and companion, and my city of refuge from father's anger was irredeemably shattered.

Early in 1920, there was an unprecedented ceremonial in connection with the worship of a certain idol in Ikenne. It is the god of small-pox. A large number of male and female devotees of the idol gathered at the shrine, and for twenty-one clear days they worshipped most reverently—dancing, singing, offering sacrifices and oblations, and performing all other rituals pertaining to the idol. One month or so before this revival of the Oluwaiye worship, there had been an outbreak of small-pox epidemic. It was said that many others who were not originally devotees of the idol joined in the course of the twenty-one day ceremonial, attracted chiefly by the promise of immunity from small-pox which devotees of Oluwaiye were said to enjoy. It was the first time for many years, so the elders said, and the only time within my memory, that the idol was worshipped in such a magnificent manner, and it was the last of its kind. But in spite of this gargantuan ceremonial and propitiation, the small-pox epidemic raged on, choosing its victims without any discrimination. As the epidemic persisted, the rumour gained ground that the priests of the Oluwaiye were responsible. It was the custom that if a pagan victim of small-pox died, he could not be buried except by these priests who, before undertaking their task, demanded exorbitant sums of money, in addition to declaring as forfeit to themselves all the moveable property of the deceased.

Under the leadership of my father, a group of young Christians got together, and decided to destroy the shrine and the idol of Oluwaiye in order to demonstrate their revulsion against the callous though age-old practices of its priests. The night after the conclusion of the twenty-one day ceremonial, this group of Christians carried out their plan. They removed the idol and all its paraphernalia, together with all the sacrifices

22

that had been made to it during the twenty-one days, piled them up, poured kerosene on them, and burnt them to ashes. When on the following day the news of this act reached the populace, there was a great sensation. The pagans felt outraged, but they did not know who the perpetrators were. In any case, the epidemic raged on with unabated intensity, and the Oluwaiye priests were said to be pleased that their god was losing no time in avenging itself. Vaccinators had come into the town not long after the outbreak, and our entire household had been vaccinated. Eventually the epidemic came to an end, after it had probably spent its force. Several hundreds of people including many devotees of Oluwaiye had died.

One day in March 1920, whilst the epidemic was still raging, father appeared ill. The second day he appeared, to me, well again. In the evening of that second day, shortly after sunset, he called me and my sister Olu, and told us that he was going to Lagos to buy things for us. He would stay there for some time, but he would not be long in coming back. That was good news for us both. Whilst I detested new clothes, I very much loved the 'Tiger Biscuit' which was then only obtainable in Lagos. My second sister, Bolajoko, was too little to understand anything and in any case she was already asleep when father talked to Olu and me. So father left the house ostensibly for Lagos. That was the last I saw of him.

Some weeks later, I learnt that father had died—a victim of the small-pox epidemic. The date was 8 April 1920. I did not know it at the time; but I was told that there was jubilation among the Oluwaiye priests when they learnt of my father's death. The god had done well, so they rejoiced, not to have spared the person who had had the effrontery to organise and carry out the violation of its sanctity. My father was said to have been given a decent Christian burial. On that evening when he finally left the house, he had simulated good health to lend credence to the story he told Olu and me. He had left the house to stay with a friend in an isolated place so that we, his children and the other members of the household, might not contract the small-pox disease. Mother tells me, however,

23

that Bolajoko my second sister, who I knew had small-pox, had contracted the disease the day father died. She had carried her on her back once or twice when she visited him.

At the time of father's death I had a strong suspicion that something untoward was in the air. Granny had returned from Abeokuta. She treated me as usual with tenderness and affection, but she was at times moody. Then suddenly she appeared grave and sad. Two of father's uterine brothers Jacob Awolowo and James Awolowo who lived in Lagos and Abeokuta respectively came back home. Before then, both had only been home in Ikenne once to my knowledge. All my uncles and aunts, together with granny and some other relations, were assembled in father's house. At the same time, mother moved to her parents' house. The whole atmosphere was charged with gloom and restraint. There were hush-hush discussions. Later, I learnt the reason why I was not told of father's death at the time it occurred. It was forbidden and regarded as anathema for anyone to weep when a victim of small-pox died. My fondness for father was well known and no one could predict what my reaction to the tragic news would be. I was therefore kept out of the picture, in order to make sure that the grim taboo was not broken.

At the time I learnt of father's death, the news did not seem to make much impact upon my mind. I remember that I did not weep. But as the events of my life rapidly and remorselessly unfolded themselves, it dawned more and more upon me that by the death of father a most tragic incident which was to shape the course of my life in a most decisive manner had happened.

CHAPTER 3

SCHOOLING AT IKENNE

LIKE other ardent Christians of his time, father sent me to school when I was about five years of age. I remember that I intensely hated the project. First of all it very severely curtailed my period of play. It was no longer possible for me to romp about with children of my age from dawn till dusk with inevitable and delectable intervals for food and, if I so desired, for an afternoon siesta as well. Secondly, there was too much regimentation about schooling. You must be tidy in appearance coming to school, which meant either a complete ablution or the washing of face and limbs to present at least a good façade. I did not normally relish the former: I tolerated the latter. You must be punctual in coming to school, which opened at 9 a.m., on the pain of corporal or some other form of punishment. I thought the scheduled time was too early. We broke up for lunch at 12 noon—good show; but we were expected back at the tick at 1 p.m. On arrival at school, we lined up outside and later marched in to the tune of a school song. Then—prayer. This would have been a pleasurable item but for the rigid rules attendant thereat. You must close your eyes, and must not talk or whisper to your neighbours whilst it lasted. To break any of these rules was to invite one form of punishment or another. After prayer, there was physical exercise. I would have enjoyed this, but for the manner in which it was conducted. The entire school lined up in order of height, and the lone teacher stood in front of us and rapped out the orders: 'At-te-e-n-tion! Right turn! Left turn! Ab-a-a-out turn! Hands up! Hands down! Expand! Fold! Fist! Chest! Right turn—Quick march! Halt!' After a few repetitions of these orders, it was all over. Thirdly, I dreaded the corporal and other forms of punishment which were frequently applied in the school. No offence or lapse was allowed to go unpunished: lateness in coming to school, opening your eyes or whispering during prayer, turning left when the order was 'Right turn!', inattention in the class, or quarrelling with another pupil—all these and others were promptly punished. Forgiveness was rare, and it was the exception that proved the rule.

Corporal punishment might be applied to you on your back-side, or on your palms, or on any part of your body, all depending on the whim of the teacher. Strokes of the cane on the palms of the hand were, to me and to many pupils, preferable to those on the back-side. In the latter case, the teacher would start by shouting the order: 'Upon the table!' or 'Back him!' The one meant that you would be laid on the table flat with your face downwards by two or more hefty men who abounded in the school in those days as there was no age limit to admission; and the other meant that a tall and sinewy pupil would carry you on his back while the ordeal lasted. Apart from this form of punishment to which I was not accustomed at home, there was another one which I dreaded most—of all the types of punishment in the armoury of the teacher. When the teacher ordered you to 'stoop down', it meant that you had to bend down, touch the ground with your right fore-finger only, put your left arm on your back, and raise your left leg up in the air. You were expected to keep this posture unchanged until the teacher was satisfied that you had sufficiently expiated your offence. If your body wavered and you allowed your left foot to touch the ground, you would be promptly visited with a volley of strokes, in order to compel you to resume what was indisputably a painful and unbearable torture.

Occasionally I could not help having the feeling that father was less considerate and less concerned with the well-being and happiness of his son than the parents of my playmates. When I reported my first experiences at school, granny shed tears and caressed me; mother remained apparently unmoved by my tale of woe; but father declared, in his rich voice, that it was good for me. 'Those teachers, clerks, and interpreters that you see,' said he, 'have had to pass through similar experiences to become the important people they are today.' In my part of the world at that time, the élite of society were the pastors, catechists, teachers, clerks and interpreters. They were respected, admired and adored. The *summum bonum* of a Christian parent's ambition was that his son should, after leaving school, be like one of them. I too thought the teachers and clerks were wonderful and wanted to be like them; but I definitely did not like to tread the path which according to my father led to the heights attained by them. My own dominant yearning at that time was to be left free to play about to my heart's content, and to be outside the reach of the teacher's whip or cane or other forms of punishment.

Failing to secure support from my parents and granny, I started to play truant. As and when opportunity afforded itself, I went to farm with Osinoiki who stayed in our house. In addition to occasional truancy, I had a habit of losing my Yoruba Primer. Father must have bought me about half-a-dozen of it. I made no progress in my studies. When father, therefore, discovered that there had been times when I deliberately absented myself from school, he decided to give himself a holiday in order to teach me at home how to read and write in the vernacular. Inside one week, under father's instruction, I mastered the First Yoruba Primer. I tackled the Second Primer and found it easy. Father was happy at my progress; he congratulated me, and sent me back to school with words of encouragement. I did well at school on my resumption, most of the time at the top of my class. The teacher and the senior pupils who assisted him showed admiration for my performances. I received much less caning and punishment; I began to like schooling, and ceased playing truant.

As time went on, father developed an extraordinary zeal for my educational progress and decided that school instruction alone was not enough for me. He wanted me to study at home as well so that I might permanently be the best pupil in my

27

class. To this end he employed one of the senior pupils in our school. My home instructor was Soyebo Sotire, now a chief and a barrister-at-law. He came over to our house twice a week in the evenings to do his assignment. I did not like this arrangement at all, nor did granny or mother or Osinoiki like it either. I did not like it because it interfered unnecessarily with my time of play with the other children in those two evenings in the week, and because Chief Sotire was in the habit of caning me. Father himself provided the whip and, apart from paying him a small fee, he occasionally gave him food as well.

Before father's death and, indeed, before I left for Abeokuta, I attended two schools in Ikenne. I started at St Saviour's Anglican School and, after about three years' stay there, transferred at father's direction to the Wesleyan School. In each school there was only one teacher at a time to instruct about seven classes. But of course, the population of the school itself was very low, say 60 to 70 pupils in all. In order to cope with his task, there was a device common to each of them. In the mornings, the lone teacher gave instruction to the senior classes, that is, Standards IV and V and sometimes Standard III as well. In the afternoons, the senior pupils were released to assist the teacher in teaching those of us in the junior and infant classes. These senior pupils were, I thought, horrible. They were not allowed to use canes; but it appeared they had a licence to slap you on the cheek or to knock you with all their might with a clenched fist on the head. If you cried, the teacher would fall heavily upon you with his dreaded whip without asking any question as to the rights and wrongs of the situation. One unforgettable feature of my early school life was that in the mornings when the teacher was busy with the senior pupils we in the lower classes were expected to learn a few things by heart and to repeat them aloud so that the teacher might be certain that we were well and truly doing our stuff. More often than not the best pupil in the class, on the previous day's assessment, was charged with the responsibility for conducting this assignment. As I was most of the time the best in my class, I often played this role. At such times, I always felt right on top of the world. I stood in front of the class and shouted 'Are you at it?' and the response came: 'Are you at it?': 'I am at it'. 'I am at it', and so on and so forth. As the school-room consisted of only one unpartitioned hall, and as the same vocal demonstration went on in the other junior classes, I now regard it as a veritable marvel, looking back upon it, that the instructions imparted in the school were at all imbibed by the pupils. What was more, in later life when I met some of these teachers. I was staggered by their own utter scholastic inadequacy. One of them had only a niggardly acquaintance with the English language. The miracle of this ill-organised and badly supervised system of instruction is that it did produce results. Many of my schoolmates at the time are now occupying important positions in different spheres in the life of this country.

As a boy I loved wrestling, which was a very popular sport in Ikenne. Father encouraged me in it, and always complimented me most warmly any time I had worsted other contenders. In my age-group I was among the best wrestlers. Father always warned me against entering into a quarrel; but once in it with any of my age-group, he, like many a father in Ikenne, strongly disapproved of my disengaging myself from the fight or retreating. As a matter of honour to the family, I was expected to fight on until I had either worsted the other fellow, or had been so worsted myself that I could no longer stir a limb in my own defence. On this policy, father and granny were in perfect accord. Mother has told me that she never liked it. One day I was confronted with what at first appeared to be a difficult situation. A playmate of mine had been to Lagos, spent some six months or so there with an uncle of his and returned to Ikenne. It was a belief in Ikenne that Lagosians were much better wrestlers than Ijebus. Consequently, anyone who had been to Lagos, and then claimed to have learnt wrestling there was avoided by his compeers, in order that the latter's own reputation at home might not be seriously jeopardised. So this fellow returned, and claimed perfection in Gidigbo (wrestling). He challenged a group of us one after another to a contest and we all declined. Then he became rather swollen-

29

headed and started to beat us one after another. We tried to run away from him. But as I was trying to do so, I saw my father from a distance. It became imperative that I should stand my ground, and I did. Father took cover behind a tree. I clinched with my assailant, and down he went. Again—down he went; and again—down he went. According to the rule of the game, having floored him thrice, I became his superior. I was cheered. The others challenged him to further fight and he declined. I did not see my father again until I got to the house. He was very pleased with my performance and he told me so. As a result of father's and granny's encouragement, I became very tough, fearless and defiant as a boy, and acquired an Ikenne-wide reputation as such. I always stood my ground against anyone even if he was older than I.

Outside the field of my physical activities, father resolutely objected to my dabbling in anything other than my school lessons. He maintained, and he said it repeatedly in my hearing whenever occasions called for it, that he wanted me to be a man of consequence in accordance with prevailing civilised standards. To this end he was determined to give me a good education. After I had completed my schooling at Ikenne, he always declared he was going to send me to a high school in Lagos, after which he wanted me to become an outstanding clerk in Lagos. Under no circumstances was he going to allow me to embark on farming or the lumber business as a career. Nonetheless, during the holidays or on Saturdays I always like to go with father to his farms. These were located in different places, and in different directions from Ikenne town, due, as I discovered later, to certain factors. Father was a relatively big farmer—one of the biggest in Ikenne; but there is a limit to the quantum which an individual member could cultivate in a particular parcel of family land. Furthermore, the system of farming was, and still is, extensive cultivation which necessitates the shifting of farm holdings from place to place. At first, if the distance was not more than a mile or so, and, as I grew older and stronger, if he was favourably disposed, he might take me along. Whenever he did, he had always insisted that I should stay back in the hut to assist in attending to the cooking of food which would be required for lunch. Father never spent a night, to my knowledge, on his farm; but he might go away to his lumber camp from Monday to return on Saturday. He took me there once at my own insistence and on granny's intervention when I was about six or seven. I had to be brought home by one of my uncles after two nights there. There were too many insects and snakes, and life in the camp was so uncongenial, that I did not want and in any case was never allowed to repeat the experience. But I very much wanted to have the experience and sensation of tilling the ground. But I had neither a cutlass nor a hoe which was the main implement of farming, and which I repeatedly asked father to make for me. About two years before his death, he was persuaded by granny to make me a cutlass only.

I was thrilled at my new possession, and very much cherished it. On my next visit to the farm with father, I asked to be allowed to assist him with my new implement. He reluctantly agreed; and so for the first time in my life I bent down my body after the fashion of a farmer. It was a proud and exciting moment for me.

In my father's lifetime, I lacked nothing that I desired as a little boy and a scholar. School fees were promptly paid, and books were bought well in advance of the resumption of school. Though I was not very co-operative in this regard, father always wanted me to present a clean and impeccable appearance. I had plenty of clothes from which to make my choice at any time. There were no school uniforms in those days. The possession of chalks was the exclusive preserve of teachers. But I got father to buy them for me as and when I wanted them, for use at home. With their use, I defaced the walls of our house. I wrote all sorts of words, phrases and sentences thereon. Father had no objection, because he regarded these writings on the walls as a useful medium of practising what I had been taught. I do not now remember all the things that I was in the habit of writing. But one of them has stuck in my memory, partly because I liked its pedantic pomposity, and partly

31

because father liked it very much and frequently asked me to repeat and translate it to him. Here is the sentence: 'To laugh at infirmity or deformity is enormity.' Father, I think, liked this adage because it accorded with one of his moral codes. I was strictly enjoined never to behave like other children by laughing at any infirm or deformed person. Before and after I learnt this adage in 1918, father had often said 'A person is not infirm or deformed of his own choice. It is God's doing. And whilst we still live, we never can tell what may befall us. It is unwise and sinful to laugh at other people's misfortunes.'

I was present, in January 1920, when father discussed my future educational career with a townsman who worked in Lagos as a teacher, and who had previously been a student of the Lagos C.M.S. Grammar School. Father told him of the sort of career he wanted me to pursue. He was advised by this gentleman to send me to the Grammar School by January 1921. Four or five years there, he assured father, were enough to equip me for the post of a good and well-paid clerk in a government department in Lagos. Father wholeheartedly welcomed the idea and asked the gentleman from Lagos to help in making arrangements for my admission to the Lagos Grammar School. It was a rosy and fascinating prospect for me. I had been longing for some time to pay a visit to Lagos, but father ruled that I was too young to undertake the journey. Lagos had been depicted by travellers as a city with wonderful shops, houses and people. Many thrilling tales had been told about the sea and the lagoon, and of the singing fishes in the latter. The composition of some new melodious songs had been attributed to canoe-pullers who had claimed to have heard them from a 'choir' of fishes. Besides, it was the height of the ambition of a schoolboy of my age in Ikenne to attend a secondary school in Lagos. Now, I was to be allowed to visit Lagos, to attend the Grammar School there, and later become a clerk in a government department there.

By this time, I had begun to develop some ambition. I had seen a car, and wanted to ride in one. But as it belonged to the Akarigbo, the Paramount Chief of Ijebu Remo, and as I had

32

heard that even in Lagos only a lawyer, doctor or a wealthy trader rode in one, I was not sure whether so marvellous and expensive a thing would ever be within my reach. I had seen a motor-cycle owned by a native court clerk in Ijebu Remo. The two catechists in Ikenne as well as a number of Ikenne traders owned bicycles. Some Ikenne sons working in Lagos also owned bicycles and occasionally brought them home. I felt confident that when I became a clerk, I too could own a bicycle or a motor-cycle. In the circumstances, I strongly desired the accelerated arrival of January 1921.

But the January 1921 of my dream never arrived. With the death of my father in April 1920, there was an abrupt cessation to my schooling, and all the hopes and aspirations which father had systematically and relentlessly instilled in me were remorselessly dashed. At the time of his death, my father had more than enough property to cater for my schooling at least up to Standard V, and for our sustenance and maintenance for some two or three years thereafter. There was a large quantity of unsold planks and joists. There were outstanding debts due to father which were later collected. There were at least five parcels of farmlands planted with yams and other crops which were doing well. There was some money too. Notwithstanding all these, mother and we her children were left destitute immediately after father's death. We were the victims of a native law and custom which gives precedence to the deceased's younger brothers and sisters, and to the children of his elder brothers and sisters in the disposal of inheritance. The unwritten maxim of this unwritten Law may be stated in English thus: 'Brothers and sisters of the deceased had been before his children ever were.' A few days after father's death some of his friends together with some elderly members of his relations on the maternal and paternal sides congregated to administer his estate. Nothing came to me, except a big gown. This was given to me by the administrators, not because I was entitled to it, but as a token of the profound affection which my father was known to have had for me. I sold it in 1929 to swell my meagre savings in order to pay for the correspondence

33

courses which I took in that year in English, commercial knowledge, shorthand, etc.

In the course of the administration of father's estate, mother was assigned to one of father's brothers. But she did not favour the arrangement. So she moved to her parents' house and took us with her. It was an uphill task for her—to maintain us and herself unaided. She was unable to pay my school fees, and in fact, for a time, I felt as free as a lark and did not think of going back to school. Then two of my father's brothers made representations to mother and her parents, and as a result I was taken back to my father's house to live with them. Instead of sending me to school, they took me to the farm to assist them. This arrangement did not at all appeal to me, and father's repeated remonstration came constantly rushing into my mind: 'Femi is not cut out for farming, I want him to be an outstanding clerk in Lagos.' I endured the situation, and did what I considered to be my best on the farm. But my uncles thought I was a failure as a young farmer. One day, I felt so maltreated that I left them in the farm, and came to stay with my mother. For the first time since I learnt of my father's death, the irreparableness of the loss overwhelmed me. I wept and bemoaned my fate. Why did father die so early? If he had lived, I would not have suffered so. From this moment on, I made up my mind to resume schooling and told mother so. She told me quite plainly that she could not afford the school fees. One of her brothers could afford very easily to pay my school fees of 3/- a quarter if he was minded so to do. I asked mother to appeal to him to help me. She did, and he promised to think about it. Trusting that my maternal uncle would be favourably disposed to render the required assistance, I packed my books one morning and went to school. As the fees were not forthcoming, I was sent down. In course of time, I discovered a few things that perplexed and shocked my young mind. All those friends and relations of father who used to flock into our house to enjoy his hospitality and kindness, and all those brothers and relations of mother who had great respect for her during my father's lifetime and who had had occasional assistance from my father, did not appear to care at all for my mother and her three children. And those who had inherited my father's properties were indifferent to our privations. For a while I assisted my mother's step-father (her father's younger brother to whom her mother passed on the death of Awofeko— mother's father) on the farm. I did what I considered my best in his service, but he too did not think much of me as a young farmer. One day, he and mother's brothers who worked with him, mocked my agricultural incompetence so much that I decided not to work with him any longer. I was now beginning to wonder what sort of future lay ahead of me. I was no good as a farmer, and I had no means to learn enough at school to become even a junior teacher or clerk.

Then in April 1921, Uncle James who had returned to Abeokuta in 1920 after harvesting the crops on his own share of inherited farmlands, and disposing of his own share of planks and joists, visited Ikenne. He spoke to my mother and me and told us that granny, who had returned to Abeokuta a few days after father's death, wanted me to come and stay with her. I welcomed the news with mixed feelings. In our part of the world at that time, Abeokuta was next to Lagos in order of importance and renown. I would have loved to go there provided I had some assurance about my schooling. I also had a feeling of delight at the prospect of a reunion with granny: but it was going to be a granny in Abeokuta—sans my father, sans my mother, and sans the happy atmosphere of our home in Ikenne in the days before father had a second wife. My mother stoutly objected, but I remember making my reaction unequivocally clear during the discussion. I wanted to resume schooling, and was prepared to go wherever it was possible for me to do this. Uncle James gave the assurance, but mother maintained her objection. The day after this discussion, I asked mother for permission to spend the night with Uncle James at my father's house where he was staying. Mother gave the permission, unaware that I had agreed secretly with Uncle James to go with him to Abeokuta, and to leave Ikenne in the early hours of the next day. And so, on 20 April 1921 (I

35

have never forgotten and will never forget the date) I arrived with Uncle James in Abeokuta.

On the approach to Abeokuta on the narrow footpath by which we came, we got to a hilltop. From this vantage ground, one is able to see a good view of a section of Abeokuta town. The sight staggered my imagination, and even energised my very weary legs. The largest town I had seen before I came away was Shagamu. I had heard reports of Abeokuta's immense size, but I had never imagined it to be anything like what I saw. There, in the distance, lay a sea of zinc roofs—stretching as far as the eyes could see. On entering the town, I was astonished at the size and beauty of some of the houses. It took me four days to recover from the weariness and exhaustion of the journey on foot from Ikenne to Abeokuta from about 4 o'clock in the morning to about 6 o'clock in the evening of the same day. Granny shed tears on seeing me, embraced me, and bewailed the tragedy of my father's untimely death. She poured on me a profusion of parental affection. Uncle James reported to her the circumstances surrounding my departure from Ikenne, and granny sort of guaranteed Uncle James's assurance that I would be sent to school. I rejoiced inwardly at the prospect of resuming schooling again. But as I lay there in granny's lodging recuperating from the rigour of the journey—with legs aching and tiredness in all my limbs—my dominant thought was to do as much sight-seeing as possible before I started schooling. As soon as I got on my feet again, I roamed round Abeokuta town in company of some of the children and grandchildren of granny's friends and fellow traders. Most of the things that I saw were so different from what I was used to at home. There were good and wide roads; there were many more than one car; there were lorries too; there were steam-rollers used for making roads; there were street electric lights, and there was pipe-borne water supply. Every day, save Saturdays and Sundays, many students of the Abeokuta Grammar School passed along the road in front of granny's residence to and from their school: how neat, how smart, and how self-confident in their bearing! If father had

36

not died, so I pondered, I would have been like one of these. Along the same road—i.e. Shapon-Ibara Road which was the most important highway in Abeokuta at the time—passed, every day save Sundays, to and from their offices and shops at Imo and Ibara in Abeokuta, immaculately dressed people, in cars and on motor-cycles and push-bikes, who were employed in various categories such as clerks, traders, salesmen, book-keepers, cashiers, etc., etc. I greatly admired them. If father had been alive, so I mused regretfully, it would have been only a matter of time for me to become one of these! I visited the Olumo Rock—which is a landmark as well as a most popular object of sight-seeing for any visitor or tourist to Abeokuta to this day. I saw the River Ogun—wide, muddy, and fast flowing. I visited the railway stations at Ibara, Aro and Lafenwa, and saw the trains coming and leaving. I saw mercantile houses, shops and government offices, and in every one of them there were white men to be seen. I saw some of these white men on push-bikes and motor-cycles, and some as train drivers in jet-black and soot-covered suits. None of them was carried in a hammock; and they behaved more naturally, like ordinary human beings.

CHAPTER 4

I FENDED FOR MYSELF

AFTER about a fortnight's stay with granny, I was transferred
to Uncle James who stayed at Ibara, Abeokuta, some three
miles away from granny. I had hoped that all was set for my
resumption of schooling. This, however, was not the case and
was not to be. Instead of sending me to school, and I had no
doubt he could afford to pay the fees, he made me work for
him in all sorts of capacities. Uncle James was a man of many
parts: contractor for all manner of petty works, a farmer, a
firewood seller, and proprietor of a palm wine bar. As a contractor he had a number of labourers under him. He did his
farming and firewood fetching partly with hired labour, and
partly by his own direct labour when there was no contract
work on hand. I was employed chiefly as a labourer to till
his farms and to fetch firewood; and partly to call the roll of
his labourers and to join them afterwards in executing the
particular work in hand. I took part in constructing two important roads in Abeokuta—one inside the town leading to the
government reservation at Ibara, and the other from Idi-Aba
to Ajebo (then Asha), now on the new Lagos-Ibadan Road.
Though I did not like the types of work I was being made to
do, yet I gave of my very best in the hope that my conscientious
efforts would attract the much needed school fees. I was
prepared to do any honest work however hard and distasteful,
provided I would thereby be enabled to pay my school fees.

But my ambition remained unfulfilled and I made repeated
complaints to granny and Uncle James. One excuse or another
was from time to time given for postponing my schooling. At a
certain stage, I felt I was being deceived and cheated, and I
told granny so. I had no courage to say this to Uncle James

38

who could be very bad in his temper, and who on two occasions had shown me, to my painful discomfiture, that once he started to wield the whip the more you cried the more and severer flogging you got. Granny on the other hand, had implicit confidence in Uncle James and never failed to assure me that all would soon be well with my schooling. As for herself, she made it clear that she was not in a position to pay my school fees. In the meantime, however, I had discovered from some of my playmates who were circumstanced as I was, and who were attending school, that it was possible to live with masters who would pay the pupil's school fees in return for domestic services rendered by him outside school hours. I decided to try this experiment. After consultation with granny and Uncle James the proposed experiment was approved. But unfortunately it was an unmitigated failure. I worked for four masters in all from 1922 to 1923. In the intervals between my peregrination from one master to another, I employed my time in working for Uncle James as usual.

My first master was the official driver to the then Resident of Abeokuta Province. I did not stay long enough with him for him to pay my fee for one quarter which in those days could be paid in arrears. Because I broke a plate, his wife abused me to her heart's content—well and good; but she also made derogatory references to my parents and my tribe. At this point I was constrained to retort and I did so in such a rude and sharp manner as to provoke her to take up a stick in order to beat me. I got hold of a stick too, ready and determined to give blow for blow. At this stage, the husband emerged, returning from work. I ran for it, and he chased me until I got to a stream. As the stream could easily be jumped by him, and as he was already close on my heels, I ran along the course of the stream instead of across it. He had shoes and long trousers on, and was obliged to give up the chase. Granny later went to him to collect my books and clothes.

My next master was a drunkard and could not have cared less about my fees. He neglected his wife and an aged mother, and was always dead drunk for the greater part of the day. He

39

was a public letter writer! and was sober only in the mornings when he strove hard to earn enough money for food and for the next bout of drinking.

My third master—a very genial and kind-hearted man—was a photographer. It was during my service with him that I first visited Lagos in 1923 to buy photographic materials for him from a Mr Freeman who was himself both a photographer and dealer in photographic materials, at Tokunbo Street. He sent me to school, paid one quarter's fee, and later decided to make a photographer instead of a teacher or clerk of me. He refused to pay further fees and employed me in carrying his camera along to the places where he was called upon to practise his profession. He taught me focusing. I enjoyed the adventure at first, but after some two months of enforced training as a photographer, I took French leave. My stock of clothing was now becoming attenuated, and my books—some old books bought by father with some new additional exercise books— were becoming rather ragged. I left them behind in this photographer master's house, and I owed their recovery to granny.

My fourth master, a Lagosian by the name of Gladstone Coker, was a surveyor under the Egba Native Authority. I came under his charge in 1923 in accidental circumstances. Uncle James had a sub-contract for the construction of the road leading to the government reservation at Ibara. I was there to call the roll as well as work with the labourers. Mr Coker came there one day, as he had done on previous occasions, on supervision. He came immediately after I had concluded the roll call. A short and robust man, somewhat corpulent and handsome, he looked at me with a stare. He approached me, asked what I was doing there, and I told him. He then turned to my uncle and told him it was wicked of him to bring a young and intelligent-looking lad like me to do road work. The boy should be in school, he asserted. Without waiting for a reply, he declared that if my uncle and I did not mind, he would like me to go and live with him, and he would send me to school. Uncle James had no objection, I was happy at the unsolicited generous offer, and it was agreed that I should report at Mr Coker's house the following morning. Mrs Coker was a beautiful and charming woman. The couple had two children—a son and a daughter. My arrival brought the number of their domestic servants to three, but I was the only one who was to attend school; the other two were employed full-time as domestic servants, and were paid wages as such.

Mr Coker was very much in earnest about me and my education. It did not take long for me to realize that he regarded me as an adopted son. He sent me to the Roman Catholic School, Itesi, where, after a test, I was placed in Standard III. He bought me all the prescribed books and school materials. He bought me two suits of clothes for use when attending school. On my books, in his own hand—a flourish of calligraphy it was—he wrote my name as 'Jeremiah Obafemi Owolowo Coker'. I had no objection to being addressed as 'Master Coker'. In those days, an English name was a *prima facie* passport to important and exclusive circles which formed the upper strata of the then social structure. But I pointed out, not without some hesitation, that he had wrongly spelt my surname. He promptly rejoined that 'Awolowo'* sounded too pagan in its import, and that 'Owolowo'† was not only as good as any other name, but it was also more in keeping with my Christian profession. At the same time he expressed a strong desire to convert me to the Roman Catholic confession. Mr and Mrs Coker were themselves devout Catholics. All this did not appear to me to matter at all. What mattered was my schooling. In this connection, I was not only impressed by Mr. Coker's sincerity, I was deeply touched and moved by his affection for me. Here at last was another father who was determined to ensure the fulfilment of the aspirations which my late father entertained for me. Unfortunately, however, Mrs Coker did not share her husband's fondness for me. Mr Coker was in the habit of going out of Abeokuta town for several days on end in the course of his duties. When he was in town,

* Awolowo means Cult or Fetish deserves respect or honour.
† Owolowo means Money deserves respect or honour.

I had nothing to fear or worry about. I was made to feel perfectly at home, and was treated by him as the eldest child in the family. But as soon as he was out of town, I was in trouble. On such occasions, I was put in my proper place. During one of Mr Coker's absences from home, a series of events happened which depressed and saddened me so much that I left the home of the Cokers without notice. Again, as on two previous occasions, I owed the recovery of my scanty belongings, which I had left behind, to granny.

In the course of this chequered period of my young life, I attended four schools, namely: Ibara Anglican, Ogbe Wesleyan, Itesi Wesleyan and Itesi Roman Catholic. In the same period my clothes were reduced almost to tatters and rags, and there was a brief period when all I had for a decent apparel was a pair of shorts and a shirt (called 'Buba'). In spite of my indigent plight and scholastic set-backs, I was on the whole as light-hearted and happy as my playmates. I took part in all healthy juvenile activities which came my way. I wrestled as brilliantly as ever; I joined in playing a form of soccer—using a tennis ball for our purpose but with no regard whatsoever to the number of players or to all the rules of the game. Any ground was good enough for a field; two pieces of stones or bricks at each end marked the goalmouth; and all the players acted the part of a referee. In case of dispute, the strongest and boldest lad in the field was the final arbiter. I invariably played this role.

Towards the end of 1923, I unaccountably felt home-sick. I told granny and Uncle James about it. But I had nothing in the way of clothing other than my pair of shorts and Buba, and, for shame, I shrank from the thought of returning to Ikenne in that state. Granny, who wholeheartedly supported my proposal, bought me one new suit of clothes. In company of traders returning to Ikenne, I went back home on foot. At Ikenne, I was distressed to find that some of my classmates had become teachers and were busy preparing for entrance examinations to teacher training colleges, some had gone back to farming, and others had gone to Lagos for further studies.

Those of my schoolmates who were junior to me, were already doing better than I. Unlike most of my townspeople who had gone abroad on an educational adventure, I had nothing to offer the stay-at-homes in the way of advancement, save my Egba dialect which was admired and which I have now lost for good, and the story of the great city of Abeokuta and its illustrious people. But most of my classmates and schoolmates did not scruple to embarrass me by asking me questions about my educational progress. I told them quite truthfully that I was still in Standard III, and added, also truthfully, but more in defence of my good name, that standards in Abeokuta schools were higher than those in Ikenne schools. On my saying this, two or three of them felt provoked to put arithmetical and grammatical questions to me to test the accuracy of my contention. I came out of these impromptu tests fairly well. Because, in spite of my vicissitudes, I kept my arithmetical knowledge at Standard IV level by self-study and constant revision, and my grammar was roughly within the Abeokuta Standard III level. As a result of my experiences at Ikenne during this visit, I returned to Abeokuta with my mind made up to make a clean break with Uncle James, stand on my own, and pay my own way through school. After all, three of my acquaintances, though much older than I, were doing precisely this. I also resolved never to pay another visit to Ikenne until I felt able to hold my own, and resume my former stature educationally among my classmates. Before I left Ikenne, my mother, who had been married to another husband, and who was financially better off than before I first left home for Abeokuta, was able to buy me a suit of clothes, and to give me £1 besides. I resolved to spend every penny of this money on my school fees and school materials.

On my return to Abeokuta, I went straight to granny and told her of my new plan. She welcomed it, and promised to feed me and buy me some clothing as and when she could afford it if I could earn enough for my fees, etc. Before the schools opened in January 1924, I paid a visit to Ibara to see Uncle James. I told him also of my plan. Apart from making

43

some discouraging remarks, he was indifferent. I then called on a Mr G. O. Mould to spend two nights or so with him before returning to granny. Mr G. O. Mould was literate in English, and was a very clever man. But he became totally blind some five years after he left school, when he was in the employ of the then Nigerian Forestry Department. After all known efforts had been made in vain to cure him, he decided to stand on his own as a public letter writer. He prosecuted this profession by dictating to someone who took down whatever he said in good handwriting. By reason of his profession, therefore, he encouraged schoolgoers who could pay their own fees to live with him to help him, on the understanding that he would give them tips and/or supper, and assist them in their lessons, especially in arithmetical and grammatical problems at which he was exceedingly good. You only had to read the problem slowly to him and the answer together with the method of arriving at it was forthcoming. At the times that I had stayed with Uncle James, I had slept most nights in Mr Mould's house. It was his habit to ring the bell for all his Christian neighbours to assemble in his house (built by his father) for prayers, in the morning at about 5.30, and in the evening at about 9 p.m. More often than not I was fast asleep by the time the night prayer was over. After morning prayers, he assisted scholars under his auspices with their problems. In the evening before prayer he used to give them tests in English and mental arithmetic, all of which were formulated by him. I had often taken part in these exercises, and in the course of them Mr Mould regarded me as a talent, and spoke several times to Uncle James to do something about my schooling.

During my stay with him, I disclosed my new plan to him. His prompt reaction was that, if I could work for my fees, he would give me supper and occasional tips in return for the usual services which others of my type rendered to him. There were four schoolboys staying permanently under his roof, and there were about four others who visited his house daily. I felt that the atmosphere of Mr Mould's house and the comradeship of other pupils available there, would be more conducive to my

44

educational progress and personal happiness than staying with granny. I told granny of my new idea, and as usual, she readily agreed.

When schools opened in January 1924, I secured admission to the Baptist Boys' High School. I told the Headmaster that I was promoted to Standard IV in 1920 and considered myself still good for that class; and though he appeared a little sceptical about my claim, he placed me in the class without a test. As time went on, however, I knew I did not make the grade except in arithmetic. I was poor in the other subjects. I resolved to work very hard at my studies to make up for my deficiency. School fees were paid weekly in advance there—1/- per week I believe—and I paid mine promptly. But before the second quarter was over, I was involved in an accident. A motor vehicle used to come to the school, which was situated on a high hill, to fetch water. Some of us were in the habit of boarding the vehicle, and jumping down again before it began to descend the very steep slope down the hill. The Headmaster had given repeated warnings against what he described as a dangerous prank. In spite of those warnings, about five of us repeated our escapade. The others jumped off the vehicle in time before it got to the declivity. But I wanted to try getting off when it was actually going at greater speed down the slope. So I did, and was badly bruised and wounded in the process. Apart from bruises on various parts of my arms and legs, I had a ghastly wound to my right knee-cap, and blood flowed down my right leg profusely. I tried, without success, to cover up the just reward for my disobedience, but the Headmaster could not be deceived. He discerned blood trickling to the ground where I stood; he questioned me, and I told him exactly what had happened. At his instance, the Principal of the school promptly gave me first-aid treatment. At the end of the treatment, the Headmaster remarked that I deserved severe punishment for my disobedience, but he thought I had got more than my full deserts by the injuries that I had sustained. It was with great difficulty that I limped for about two-and-a-half miles to Ibara. I did not return to the school again, for

45

two reasons. In the first place, I was very ashamed to be the only one singled out for exposure by fate, from amongst a number of fellow-culprits, for an act of flagrant disobedience. In the second place, I considered myself unequal to the requirements of the school's Standard IV, and I did not want to face the mortification of being demoted or of having to repeat the same standard in the succeeding year.

In July 1924, on the advice of some of my friends and playmates, I sought and gained admission to the Salvation Army School in Abeokuta. The school was housed in an old derelict produce store. Unlike the Baptist Boys' High School where there was a teacher to every class, there was only one teacher for the whole school. I was not unused to this feature: it was like what obtained in Ikenne in my days, and in Ibara Anglican School when I attended it. Those friends of mine to whom I have made reference, were themselves pupils of the Salvation Army School, and they too worked for their own fees by fetching firewood for sale. Hitherto I had been engaged in carrying, for hire, sheaves of dried elephant grass, which was used by local potters in firing their earthen-wares. For a full day's work, I used to make as much as 6d., and for less than half-a-day's work after school hours, I could make 2d. I also sometimes worked for the potters in pounding raw clay with a pestle on a flat bed made of closely arranged, flat and smooth-surfaced stones. This was a gruelling piece of occupation. Each time I did it, I had sore palms. Because of its exacting nature, I only did this work when there were no sheaves of grass to carry. Occasionally, I also worked as a farm labourer on a piecework basis. My friends, however, told me, on hearing of my occupational experiences, that firewood fetching and selling was not only a comparatively easier occupation, but also that it was more lucrative. I decided, therefore, to leave Mr Mould and to move to Shapon to stay with granny. I did this for certain reasons. The Salvation Army School was only a few yards from Shapon market, and my firewood-seller friends lived very close by granny's lodging. Besides, apart from wanting to keep their company in this venture, they con-

46

vincingly argued that Shapon market which was much bigger and more popular than Omida market, Ibara, and which was in operation every day, was a much better place for the disposal of firewood than the latter market, which was mainly in operation only once every four days.

The standard of instruction at the then Salvation Army School was poorer than that obtaining at the Baptist Boys' High School. I could easily have been placed in Standard V there if I desired, but I decided to repeat Standard IV for another year. I had to do a good deal of work on my own at home at nights. Every day after school hours on Saturdays and during holidays, I went in company of my friends out into the adjoining forests to fetch firewood. For a full day's work I made as much as 9d. and on other occasions I made as much as 2d. or 3d. Granny fed me, and bought me a few clothes. She made me two Salvation Army uniforms which I wore on Sundays and on other important occasions, like Empire Day celebrations. I was now really getting on. But by April 1925, I discovered that my acquaintance with the three R's was much better than that of our teacher. I therefore decided to seek admission at the beginning of the school year in July to Wesleyan School, Imo, which was very near to where I stayed. Three of my classmates decided to join me. Before we went on vacation in June 1925 our teacher at the Salvation Army School had promoted us to Standard V—the highest standard in most primary schools at that time. We sought and gained admission to Imo Wesleyan School on this basis. Imo School was a much more reputable school. Each class had its own teacher, and the Headmaster, a Mr J. A. Keleko (now deceased) was a trained teacher—a product of Wesley College, Ibadan. He was a very clean and handsome man, with a superb sartorial taste, and an open and relentless contempt and ridicule for untidiness. If a pupil was untidy either in his looks, dress or his work, he might get two or more lashes of the whip on his palms or back, and at the end of the punishment the Headmaster would exclaim to the hearing of the entire class or school as the case might be: 'Ingorgeous!' For this reason the

47

pupils nick-named him, in spite of his impeccable elegance, 'Ingorgeous'! In diametrical contrast to my attitude in the matter during my father's lifetime, I was not punished or even blamed once for untidiness. Shortly after my arrival in Abeokuta I cultivated the habit of having a bath daily. I washed my own clothes—and pressed them by folding them, wrapping them up carefully, and using them as a pillow. My Sunday wear was pressed by me with a press iron borrowed from neighbours. Imo Wesleyan School was one of the best primary schools in Abeokuta at the time, and it was with great reluctance that the Headmaster admitted us without a test, on the clear understanding, however, that if we failed the first weekly test he would either demote us or expel us from his school. I came third in the class in the first weekly test; I came second in the second weekly test; I came first in the third, and kept this position almost permanently throughout my career in the school. My only rival was a girl—a Miss Eunice Afisunlu, now happily married I believe. Unfortunately, my three classmates from the Salvation Army School fell by the wayside. One was demoted to Standard III—he was about ten years older than I. The other two were demoted to Standard IV— they were both about five years my senior. At the end of the school year they all failed the promotion examination, and gave up schooling for good.

During my tenure at Imo Wesleyan School, I stayed for a quarter with granny, and for the rest with Mr G. O. Mould. With my return to Ibara, I gave up firewood selling and reverted to my former occupation minus the pounding of raw clay. A very lucrative occupation which came my way, at this time, was the sale of water at a farthing a gallon to leisurely wives of civil servants and mercantile clerks. I entered into partnership with a friend. I used to force my way to the public standpipe, and stay-put there, to fill our receptacle (a four-gallon kerosene tin), which my partner carried to our customers until they were fully supplied, or it was time for us to go to school if it was in the morning. At that time in Abeokuta the public water standpipes were kept open only during certain hours of the day, and during such period the standpipes used to be hopelessly jammed. Most of the time, therefore, it was a feat of physical endurance for anyone to get water from any of the standpipes. My partner was a quiet and non-aggressive character. Hence the arrangement.

Furthermore now that I was in Standard V, Mr Mould considered me more qualified than ever before to take down a letter or petition to his dictation. For my services, apart from giving me supper, he also gave me occasional tips. For the same consideration, he paid my school fees once for a whole quarter. I can never forget his kindness to me. He is now gone to the place beyond, but I am happy that I had an ample opportunity of richly requiting, in a way which he very much appreciated, the valuable help and encouragement which he gave me during one of the most critical periods of my life. At the beginning of my last quarter at Imo, Uncle James came to me in Mr Mould's house, congratulated me for my educational progress, and offered to pay my fees for the quarter. I refused the offer.

At the end of my time at Imo, that is in June 1926, I passed the government Standard V examination. But I did not go to collect the certificate from the Manager of our school, because I did not feel so proud of passing, in 1926, an examination which some of my classmates in Ikenne had passed in 1922 or 1923. I was pleased with myself, however, that at last I had attained one of the objectives which my father had steadfastly and fervently set before me in his lifetime, and which I had been yearning after and striving to achieve for upwards of five years.

During the June holidays, I continued to work as water drawer, and to assist Mr Mould in return for tips. I did not now have to carry sheaves of grass. The first phase of my life's struggles was over. What was I going to do next? I could be a shop attendant, a junior clerk, or what was then known as Pupil Teacher. But I wanted to pursue my education much further. In Abeokuta, I had seen lawyers in court, and from the moment I set my eyes on their wigs and gowns, I was

49

possessed by an overpowering desire of one day becoming a lawyer. I sometimes thought I was being silly, for I was told it cost several thousands of pounds to study in England to become a lawyer; and, as it was, I had neither the parents nor the guardians to sponsor me for such an expensive career. Nevertheless, the desire remained with me. After finishing at Imo, therefore, I thought the best thing for me to do was to devise ways and means of finding money to pay my fees at the Abeokuta Grammar School. I reckoned that with some luck I could manage the fees up to Form IV. It only meant that I would have to work much harder than ever before to earn a lot more money than hitherto. In the meantime, Mr Mould had assured me that he would assist me to secure admission to the Grammar School. In the midst of my cogitation, Mr Keleko, my former Headmaster, sent for me early in July 1926. He offered me a place on his staff. I told him of my plan, but he advised me to accept his offer, and then work for admission to Wesley College, Ibadan, in 1927, where I would be educated free for four years, to become a Certificated Teacher afterwards. In those days, Wesley College was a very famous Institution among the Ijebus. It was an honour, second only to being a Grammarian in Lagos, to be a student there. I accepted the offer, and about the middle of July 1926, I became a Pupil Teacher at Imo Wesleyan School. I was in charge of Standard III Class and my salary was fixed at 12/6d. per month. I was profoundly filled with gratitude to God the day I took my place before the class under my charge. I continued to stay with Mr Mould who was very happy at my appointment, and at the prospect of my entering Wesley College. At the end of July, I was paid 6/3d. I invested this first salary on the 'Tutorial Arithmetic Book', which cost exactly 6/3d. and which was recommended to me by Mr Keleko, in order to prepare myself in arithmetic for Wesley College entrance examination. At the end of August, my salary was raised to 15/- and it was on this scale that I remained up to December when I finally severed my connection with Imo Wesleyan School.

50

But for Mr Keleko, I would not have been allowed to take the entrance examination to Wesley College in 1926. The Manager of our school, a very conscientious but fastidious pastor, wanted to send the strongest possible team from his circuit for the entrance examination, as only sixteen students were going to be admitted in 1927 from the Wesleyan Western District of Nigeria. He did not consider me strong enough. After all, I had only just recently passed the Standard V examination, and had been a teacher only four months—no, it wouldn't do. Mr Keleko however pressed my case, and, very grudgingly, the Manager entered me as one of the eight candidates from Abeokuta circuit. It was the practice for the mission to pay the fares of the candidates to and from Ibadan where the examination took place. Our said Manager, the Rev. E. K. Ajai-Ajagbe (of blessed memory), insisted that I must work for my fare, as he did not think it right that the mission should be made to bear the risk of my gamble. A portion of the Wesleyan cemetery at Ogbe Abeokuta which had been overgrown with weeds was allotted to me for clearing. It was generally considered *infra dig* for a teacher to till the ground; but I did, and after about a week's hard work, I earned my 5/- fare to and from Ibadan. Over eighty of us from different parts of the Western District of the Wesleyan Church sat for the examination. I was the only successful candidate from among the eight candidates from Abeokuta. The Rev. E. K. Ajai-Ajagbe invited me to his office, and most warmly congratulated me for bringing honour to Abeokuta circuit. He expressed his deep regret at having doubted my ability, and gave me 5/- out of his own pocket as a reward for my performance. This was a proud moment for me. I felt myself on the brink of success. My father's dream was being realised at last, though in a different form. For be it remembered that my father wanted me to be a clerk in a government department in Lagos; and at the time in question, and indeed until recently, a civil servant enjoyed a higher status and recognition in our social and political set-up in Nigeria than a teacher. For my part, it was enough that the days of firewood-selling, water-drawing, and journey-

51

ing from school to school without school fees were over. I spent the Christmas of 1926 in Ikenne (my first visit since 1923), and was immensely gratified that only one of my former Ikenne classmates had attained the same educational height as I. He was being admitted to St. Andrew's College, a sister institution to Wesley College, the same year as I was being admitted to the latter. I was enthusiastically congratulated by all my former schoolmates, no arithmetical or grammatical questions were asked to taunt me, my scholastic equality or superiority was readily conceded, and I felt truly triumphant.

CHAPTER 5

WESLEY COLLEGE

At Wesley College, everything was free: tuition, books, board and lodging, uniforms as well as travelling expenses to and from the student's home during vacations. This was the policy of the institution from its inception in 1905 and for upwards of thirty years thereafter. When I entered the college in January 1927, I was expected to do a four-year teacher training course, leading to the Higher Elementary Teacher's Certificate. But I spent only one year and left.

Within a week of my sojourn at the college, I became acquainted with certain aspects of its set-up which were revolting to my nature. In return for free tuition and so forth, the students were under obligation to do practically everything for themselves. The final-year students were the big noises in the place. They monopolised all the important offices in the college, and constituted a powerful and authoritarian hierarchy. It was safer to offend a tutor than to rough any of them up the wrong way. They saw to it, in accordance with traditions, that the 'new boys', that is the first-year students, bore the brunt of any menial and distasteful job that was to be done. The fetching of firewood under the leadership of one of the third-year students from among whom chief cooks were appointed; the cutting of grass; the drawing of water, sometimes during the dry season from a stream about one mile away; the removal of latrine and urinal pails; the digging of night-soil trenching grounds; the washing of plates—all these were reserved for the 'new boys'. In addition, each 'new boy' was expected to act as a fag and drudge-of-all-work to one of the final-year pundits. I did not mind firewood fetching: it was my specialty. I did not mind the other manual occupations in the college either.

But I abhorred the removal of latrine and urinal pails, the digging and tending of night-soil trenching grounds, and being capriciously ordered about by a fellow-student!

The monitor of the college, as the head of the final-year hierarchy, was the most puissant functionary in this educational dominion. In him was vested the power to pronounce and inflict punishment on any 'new boy'. He could make the offender do extra manual labour, or in addition 'gate' him on a Saturday. The offences might vary from alleged dereliction of duty to alleged insubordination to or contempt of a senior student. A 'new boy' was never given an opportunity of being heard in his own defence, before he was punished for an alleged offence. If the offence was of such a grave nature as to warrant the offender's suspension or expulsion from the college, he would be brought before the college 'court' consisting of five of the final-year students with the monitor as the permanent chairman, unless the latter was the complainant. The verdict of the court was subject to the ratification of the Principal who also constituted a court of appeal. I was once brought before the court. I raised a point which brought an impasse to the proceedings.

I was accused before the court of insubordination to all the final-year students. The particulars of the charge were that (*a*) I refused to fag for any of the final-year students, (*b*) I would not salute these senior students whenever I passed by them, as was the established custom, and (*c*) I was sometimes rude in the way I addressed them. When I was brought before the court I refused to plead on the ground that the judges were among my accusers. I also argued that since they were interested in the case, they were bound to be biassed against me. The 'judges' threatened that they would proceed though I refused to plead. I rejoined that I would appeal to the Principal against their judgment unless it was in my favour. The case was adjourned. I was cheered by all the 'new boys'. The court did not sit again in 1927.

I was very popular with the 'new boys' and with most of the second-year students. Because of my peculiar style of hair-cut which I copied from the Ghanaians and Ibos resident in Ibara,

54

Abeokuta, I was popularly called 'brush-up'. The 'new boys' saw in me and my activities the outward manifestation of their suppressed rebellion to the powers-that-be. My only companion in open rebellion was Mr S. A. Oshuntoye of Ago Iwoye, who has ever since been my intimate friend. By the same token, I was thoroughly unpopular with the senior students including those in the third year. The tutors appeared at first to be somewhat unsure of what attitude to adopt towards me. My performances at games and sports were praiseworthy; and I had in fact been frequently commended for them. At football, I played centre forward in the college's second eleven. I was fairly good in high jump and long jump. I was a star in games and sports in Freeman House of which I was a member. Because of my activities in these spheres, the Rev. W. Eric Hodges, who was Vice-Principal of the college and also the games' master, took some liking to me. I was very good in my class-work except in geography, dictation and handwriting and drawing. Geography lesson was something of a soporific to me. It was always taken in the afternoon, after a heavy lunch which was in itself an incentive to slumber. To make matters worse for me, the subject of the lesson was the Iberian peninsula, with special emphasis on its physical features, and an interminable reference by the geography master to 'Cape Finisterre' which I never succeeded in locating after a year's rigorous instruction. Dictation and handwriting were combined in one lesson. We had an exercise book which was specially ruled for this purpose. I knew my writing was bad. But if I wrote slowly, I would make a passable showing. But then the master in charge always dictated so fast that I invariably abandoned the handwriting part of the lesson and concentrated on the dictation. Bad writing meant illegible spelling; and when the master was in doubt as to whether a letter was a 'h' or a 'b', a 'l' or a 't', a 'g' or a 'y', his unchallengeable ruling had always been against me.

I was no good at all at drawing. Our master in this subject, the Rev. W. Eric Hodges, was a severe tutor. I was very good at logic which he also taught, and he never hesitated to extol me. But because I never could draw any object right, and because I could not draw a straight line without the aid of a ruler, he had felt impelled on one occasion to give me two shattering slaps. For this reason, in spite of our cordial association in the field of sports and in the realm of logic, I did not know whether to like or dislike him. I have since revised my opinion of him. He was a kind-hearted man, a just and uncompromising disciplinarian who rewarded every student according to his deserts in relation to a given assignment.

As time went on, however, I became somewhat unpopular with the African tutors. I continued to perform all the menial duties and manual labour assigned to me with unblemished efficiency. But beyond what I considered to be my obligation to the college as an institution, no one could make me do anything else, unless I wanted to. During the last term of 1927, several incidents happened which made the seniors with, I believed, the full backing of the tutors, determine to bring me to my knees. They did not succeed. Only three or four of such incidents will be mentioned.

Once it was arranged that girls at Kudeti Girls' School, Ibadan, should pay us a visit, on a Saturday afternoon. The arrangements were superb from the point of view of all the boys. There was to be tea for us and the girls. Tea and all its accompaniments were alien to the menu of the college. Before tea, we were to take the girls round our compound, with at least one girl to a boy. During tea each student would sit by one of the female guests. All this was to be done without the Principal or the tutors intruding themselves too much. They were to take charge of the female tutors from the girls' school. On the morning of the Saturday in question, each student put finishing touches to his attire in order to make the best possible impression. My college uniform was not only impeccable, but I went out on Saturday morning to buy a small jar of hair grease, a tin of face-powder, and a pair of handkerchiefs. One of them was really a lady's handkerchief (there was not too much nicety about such things in the college community), and

56

it was intended for the tiny breast pocket of my 'Agbada' (gown).

Someone in authority must have bungled. A few minutes before the arrival of the girls, the excitement which had pervaded the college atmosphere since the eve of that Saturday reached its peak. Every student was well attired. Each of us looked spick and span. Then as the guests arrived at the gate of the college compound, the monitor and his officers called upon the 'new boys' to lay the table for tea. My reaction was one of cool and unaffected defiance. I was determined to meet our female guests on an equal footing with my fellow-students no matter what their standing. If the orders for laying the table had been given in time for the work to be completed before the arrival of our guests, I would have performed my quota cheerfully. But now, it was not only too late but tended to strike at the root of my self-esteem in the presence of the fair sex. My name was shouted, but I paid no heed. I went through the afternoon's social function absolutely unperturbed. I was, however, ready for instant expulsion that night or the following day. I was 'gated' for several Saturdays instead. When I left the college in December 1927, I had about ten Saturdays 'gating' to do!

There were four terms in those days at the college. Besides, work in the college was divided into 'light', and 'hard'. The established custom was that a student should alternate between 'hard' and 'light', one week after another. During the last four weeks of the third quarter, I was put on hard duties in unbroken succession. I was a cook for two weeks, fetching firewood at the same time, and water drawer for two weeks. At the beginning of the last quarter, I was again put on hard duties for three weeks in succession. During the third of these weeks, I was to be a water drawer after having been a cook for two weeks. One's assignment usually started on a Saturday, to end on the night of the following Friday. I ignored the assignment. There were three of us on the job. The other two did their share—two old men on catechist course—but there was not enough water for use in the kitchen. The chief cook complained, and in due course I was summoned before the Vice-Principal, the Rev. Hodges. Obviously the monitor was fed up with me, or else he should have handled the complaint in the first instance. I stated my case before the Vice-Principal. He sent for the monitor who corroborated my story, but explained that there was that departure in my case because of my unbearable acts of insubordination and turbulence. The Vice-Principal did not appear to be impressed. He ordered me out of his presence. I did not know what he told the monitor. But I discovered that for that week and for some weeks in succession, I was placed on light duties only. My stock rose very high in the estimation of the 'new boys'. I had won the battle for fair play, and I felt truly triumphant.

One of the tutors once thought that I was impertinent. He called me. I heard. But because he anglicised the accents of my name, I did not answer. He called several times, I ignored him, and went my way. He must have been very furious. It was on a Saturday morning. He sent another 'new boy' to fetch me to his presence. When I appeared before him, he rebuked me, and demanded to know whether I heard him call me or not. I replied that I heard him calling 'Áwolòwò' but since my name was Áwolowo and not Áwolòwò I did not answer.* He grew more furious and in his anger ordered me to go and collect twenty-four stones and place them in front of his lodging. This I must do before he returned to the compound in the afternoon. He was ready to go out when he first called me.

Most dutifully, I collected twenty-four small stones each about an inch or so in size, and arranged them in a semi-circle at the entrance of his room. When he returned to find the huge joke I had made of his instruction, he must have felt unpardonably affronted by a rascally 'new boy'. He sent for me, and

* Áwolòwò means Cult uses, grinds or announces honour. Áwolowo means Cult deserves honour. (Yoruba **is** a highly tonal language, and hence accent plays a decisive role. One word may have three or more meanings all depending on the tone or accent in which it is pronounced. Hence Mú means drink; Mù means dive; Mũ means overwhelm; Mu means catch or arrest.)

58

wanted to know why I did not carry out his orders. I promptly replied that I had, and pointed to the stones arranged in front of his door.

'Say that again,' he shouted. 'Are these the things you call stones? These tiny pebbles?'

'Well, sir,' I remarked, 'you did not tell me what size, and so I used my common sense.'

'Your common sense must be very very poor and common indeed,' he declared. 'You ought to have known that when I said "stones" I meant stones of the size we use for the sides of our flower beds. Big stones!' He then pointed to the type of stones he had in mind.

'Sir, I am not a mind reader, and stones . . .' (What I wanted to say was: 'stones of this size cannot be found in the compound.') He did not let me finish the sentence before he declared that I was 'gated' for the rest of the term. When I told him that I was already gated for more than the rest of the term, he stared at me for a brief moment, and ordered me out of his presence 'instantaneously'.

Logic was introduced to the curriculum of Wesley College for the first and the last time in 1927. I must quite frankly confess to having contributed munificently to the causes that led to its short-lived existence. The Principal of the college—the Rev. E. G. Nightingale—could not see the utility of logic to students who were training to be teachers. But the views of Mr Hodges appeared to have prevailed, and so logic was introduced and was taught only to those 'new boys' who were doing teacher-training course as distinct from those doing sub-pastor or catechist course. The teaching of logic excited the envy of the senior boys. This envy was aggravated by the pedantic and arrogant use which some of us made of it, especially during college debates. Every speech of mine, or of my fellow-pedants, was introduced by the expression: 'Logically speaking' or 'Syllogistically speaking' or 'Hypothetically speaking'. We exhausted the forbearance of the final-year students by the use of these pompous phrases during one of the college

59

debates. Rightly or wrongly all the logicians clubbed together and remorselessly slashed the final-year speakers, one of whom was the mover of the proposition, with the sharp-edged knife of logic.

'Logically speaking, when the argument of the mover of this proposition is carefully examined, it will be found that it is full of fallacies. Two of these fallacies are: the fallacy of undistributed middle, and of non sequitur.' That was me, the logician speaking, and there were loud cheers from the 'new boy' bench. But in truth and in fact the argument of the mover had neither been carefully examined, nor was there a certainty on my part that the fallacies mentioned had been committed. But I was speaking with a view to putting the non-logicians in their proper place, and to evoke the applause of my fellow-logicians.

I was not the only offender. It was a night of 'fallacies', 'syllogisms', 'hypotheses', 'moods', 'categorical propositions' and suchlike. Even though none of the logicians could claim to understand one another's logic, we applauded ourselves all the same. And some of the lesser greats—the second and third years—joined. Then the final-year students decided to study logic. No text-book was prescribed. Mr Hodges only gave us notes, which we most jealously preserved. One of the 'new boys' who was a fag to one of the final-year students, who held the high office of food controller, was persuaded—contrary to our joint undertaking—to give his notes to his boss. The news reached us. Mr Oshuntoye and I organised a meeting to take place immediately after the close of the chapel service for the night. The seniors knew of our plan. Accordingly, the officer-in-charge of lamps (O/C Lamps as he was called) denied us the use of any of the college lamps. We held the meeting in the dark, and decided to punish the culprit. We ordered him to do extra manual labour. He obeyed. After he had been at work for about half-an-hour, he was ordered by the monitor to desist from carrying out our orders. We ate our humble pie. But it was the first time in the history of the college that 'new boys' dared to administer punishment to one of their number.

At the beginning of the last term in 1927, I decided not to return to the college in 1928. There was only one of two ways open to me. I could refuse to turn up at the beginning of term in 1928 without any previous notice to the Principal. In this case it would be up to the Wesleyan mission to make a search for me, if they thought it necessary, and if they found me to try and persuade me to teach for the equivalent period during which I had received free training from the mission at the college. I did not like this method. Apart from being cowardly, it would amount to an attempt on my part to break the bond into which I had entered to serve the mission in return for benefits received. I could also leave the college by expulsion for gross misconduct, or for very bad failure in the annual examination. In the former case one would be rejected for good by the mission; but in the latter one would be given the option of serving the mission or of being released from one's undertakings under the bond. Somehow, my activities in the college which had been unpleasant to the African tutors and seniors alike, had not proved sufficiently gross or grave to earn me an expulsion. Only one course was, therefore, open to me: to fail the annual examination in an inexcusable manner.

Two other classmates of mine also decided to leave at the end of 1927. They were the best boys in our class, always sharing the first and second places between them. In periodic tests and quarterly examinations, I always moved between fifth and seventh positions, reaching the third position only once. I led the whole class in mathematics. These two classmate friends and I had consultations together, and we decided to fail the annual examination. The first paper was Mental Arithmetic. Fifty questions were to be answered in sixty minutes. They were to me as simple as could be. But I did so badly in it that I only succeeded in getting ten per cent. My friends did likewise. We did much worse in the mathematics papers proper. The tutors always tried to mark as many of the papers as possible at the close of the day's work. The startling discovery was quickly made that the two best boys in the class and I, the best in mathematics, had failed woefully in this subject. Mr J. O. Ajibola who marked the papers had very strong suspicions. We were brought before the Principal the following morning. Mr Ajibola (who was then Senior Tutor and now a barrister-at-law and Customary Court Judge) suggested quite intuitively that our action was deliberate. He contended that we should each have got between 90 and 100 per cent in each of the papers thus far set. The Principal, who was familiar with our performances, wanted to know what the game was all about. His mien was grave, and his utterance was full of emotion. I told him at once that I wanted to leave the college and I thought the only honourable course open to me was to fail the examination in such a manner as to make my expulsion inevitable. My two friends made a similar confession. The Principal rose to the occasion. He wanted to know the reason, and on being told that we just wanted to leave, he gave us advice. He expatiated on the nobility of the teaching profession, and the advantages of going through, for four years, the physical, mental and spiritual discipline which Wesley College provided. He appealed to us to reconsider our decision which he thought was rash, unwise, and without foundation. He stressed that, in any case, it was far from being honourable for us to crown our career in the college with a disgraceful scholastic performance. He urged us to do our best in the annual examination, without prejudice to our freedom of action after we had pondered over his advice. Other papers were set for us in mathematics, and we passed with flying colours. We however stuck to our decision. I was expected to serve the mission for one year in discharge of my bond, but I actually served for two years as a teacher at Ogbe Wesleyan (now Methodist) School, Abeokuta.

In the last three months of 1926, I had had a smattering acquaintance with Shorthand. It was quite fascinating. But what was more fascinating were the legendary stories which were woven round that rare breed of men who were then known as 'shorthand typists'. They were said to be exceptionally fearless and could look any white man in the face. They were proficient in English—written and spoken—and were among the best-dressed persons in the country. In the matter of salaries, it was the shorthand typists, so the story-tellers said, who dictated what they wanted; and this might be as high as £25 per mensem—a truly royal sum of money in those days. I thought to myself that I could very easily develop the personality of a shorthand typist. I felt sure in my bones that the attribute of fearlessness was very much in me. I could be as well-dressed as any one else if I had the money. But I would have to master shorthand and typing and the English language if I was to become one of them.

During my sojourn at Wesley College, I pursued the study of shorthand in my spare time. I made sure that no one in the college knew that I was doing this. My ambition was all the more fired by the occasional advertisements which I used to see in the newspapers:

Wanted: A Shorthand Typist.
Apply to So-and-So stating speed, experience, and salary required.

I had no doubt in my mind that I could become a well-qualified shorthand typist after two years of hard work. After that I would be in a position to dictate to any prospective employer the salary I wanted! In my reflection, I compared this rosy prospect with what awaited me at the end of my teacher training course. After four years, I would be placed, as Certificated Teacher, on a salary of £3 6s 8d per mensem, with little prospect of a rise. Indeed, there was no guarantee, judging from the reports which from time to time reached the college, that this comparatively paltry salary would be paid regularly. Some teachers were in arrears of their salaries for three months. In any case, in contrast to shorthand typists, teachers appeared to me to be a race of meek and easy-going people, extremely obsequious in the presence of a white man.

Before leaving the college in 1927, I made up my mind that, after discharging my bond, I would embark on the career of a shorthand typist. As a matter of personal prestige, however, it was imperative that I should start on this career before my classmates, who stayed in the college to complete their course, came out.

63

In spite of my hectic time there I thoroughly enjoyed my short sojourn at Wesley College. I entered fully and with unabated zest into the life of the college. Most of the time, I regarded my interminable encounters with the seniors and tutors as exceeding fun. At times, I also regarded myself as a crusader. The tutors and seniors were undoubtedly flabbergasted by my apparent relish for troubles, and by my defiant and independent attitude unusual among 'new boys' in the annals of the college. During the second half of my last term in the college, I lived more or less on a basis of equality with the final-year students. After the incident before Mr Hodges, which I have previously related, it seemed that the seniors were chary of putting me on anything but light duties. The monitor, with whom I lived in the same room for the whole year, just left me severely alone.

Unknown to me at the time, the college and its authorities must have made deep and abiding impressions on me. The older I grow the greater my affection for the college as well as for the tutors and seniors in whose regime I served. Now looking back upon it, there are certain aspects of life in the college which are immensely admirable, and worthy of emulation not only by similar institutions but by all those who aspire to a position of leadership in any sphere of life.

I think it is an extremely useful experience that a young person should be made to do for himself certain menial and domestic jobs which, though distasteful, other people are nevertheless being called upon to do from time to time. It tends to instil in one a sense of understanding and sympathy which may come in useful in later life. At Wesley College the day-to-day activities imbue every student with a sense of humility, and inculcate in him a belief in the dignity of all forms of legitimate labour. Our uniforms consisted of 'Sokoto', 'Buba' and 'Agbada'. Most students did not like these then and, alas! they have now been changed to trousers, blazers and shirts! Contemporary Grammarians derided us for our 'clumsy' dress; but it is this same kind of attire that we now call 'national dress', and which is in popular vogue with most of the elite in

Nigeria. Our motto is the Yoruba translation of a portion of Luke XXII, 27: 'Bi Eniti Nse Iranse' (as he that serveth). This motto was also an object of ridicule among students from secondary schools whose mottos are invariably in Latin. But unlike most institutions we lived our motto. We did everything for ourselves. Even the seniors had their own share of duties. The officers were directly responsible to the Principal for the discharge of the duties entrusted to their charge. The dealings between the Principal and these officers were unknown to 'new boys'. But we could assess the gravity which the Principal attached to even the slightest dereliction on the part of these officers, from the seriousness and devotion with which they tackled their respective functions. Seniors who were not officers were always assigned to perform light duties in the morning and to join other students in doing manual labour in the afternoon. There were certain duties which were common to all students irrespective of their status. For instance, the new college chapel was built by the students themselves, and all ranks—officers and all—worked equally hard in the process of its erection.

The Principal of the college in my time, the Rev. E. H. Nightingale, B.D., suffered a good deal of unjustified criticism. Essentially, his view was that we should be proud of anything that was indigenous to us: our language, our culture and our style of dress. The official language in the classrooms and in the dining-room was English. But in the college compound you could speak any language you liked so long as you were understood. It was believed that Mr Nightingale fostered these policies in order to slow down our progress in the Western sense. I shared this view then, but I now think that he was a great pioneer. Practically all his critics are today doing precisely what he preached many years ago. He was an artist and a purist in the use of the English language. He had a quick wit, and a deep sense of justice and fair play. He was a great lover of music. He often took charge of the singing lesson himself, assisted most of the time by Mr Ajibola. He had a sensitive ear for the detection of a discordant note however slight; and sometimes he would rush from his office, when a singing practice was in progress, to complain that the alto or the bass, whichever it was, was flat or not the right pitch.

The third-year and final-year students constituted the most cohesive, impregnable and formidable hierarchy that I have ever known. This was all the more so, first because they were at the same time free from all taint of partial affections in their dealings with the juniors *inter se*, and secondly because whatever happened behind the scenes, it was the policy of the Principal and Tutors to back them in the open. It was absolutely impossible for a 'new boy' to get any member of the hierarchy to listen to any gossip about or criticism against any other, or to get any tutor, much less the Principal, to entertain any complaint against any of the seniors. If you offended one of them, you had offended all the others. When I came into my first series of clashes with some of the seniors, I had some feeling that I would get a powerful protection. The monitor, the water bailiff and the sanitary inspector who respectively are today the Rev. A. S. Solarin (Superintendent Olowogbowo Methodist Circuit and Acting Chairman of the Methodist Western District), the Rev. N. O. Salako (Superintendent Ibadan Methodist Circuit) and the Rev. E. F. Adubifa (Superintendent Owo Methodist Circuit), were all fellow-townsmen from Ikenne. Two of them, the Revs. Solarin and Salako, were schoolmates, though my seniors, at the Wesleyan School, Ikenne. I also had a cousin among the final-year students. He was Mr Simon Awolowo, now deceased. I thought they would do me the favour of affording me gratuitous support and collaboration. I was grossly mistaken. But when I noticed that they were not going to exhibit any interest in my tribulations, I trod on their toes too. I regarded them and their colleagues as an unnecessarily strict and ruthless cabal. I now know better. It must be said to their credit that they took an early step, at a meeting with me one night, to warn me of the unorthodox and insufferable nature of my behaviour and the consequences that would be attendant upon it. I was unimpressed and bluntly told them to mind their own business.

During holidays and away from college, the seniors could be the friendliest and pleasantest of mortals. They then mixed freely and treated all students alike. But once inside the college, their attitude changed. They became the rigid disciplinarians that they really were, and they drew the line quite sharply between juniors and seniors, regardless of any other forms of relationship. Notwithstanding my intractable attitude to them, the seniors once did me a very good turn. I travelled in their company on foot from Ibadan to Ijebu Remo. About six miles from Ibadan, I fell seriously ill and could not walk. Some of the seniors including the monitor had to carry me on their backs in turn all the way to Ode Remo, that is for some 30 miles or so. Back in college after this incident, I was too busy with pursuing my own independent lines of action to requite this great favour. But today the Revs. Solarin, Salako, Adubifa, and many other seniors of the time and myself are the best of friends. Occasionally we enjoy recalling some of the episodes of those days when they and I were at Wesley College together.

CHAPTER 6

YEARS OF PREPARATION

In January 1928, I started work as a teacher at the Wesleyan (now Methodist) School, Ogbe, Abeokuta. Because I had done one year's course in a Teacher Training College, I was officially classified as a 'Provisional Teacher', and *ipso facto* my salary was fixed at the handsome figure of £2 per mensem. This was increased to £2. 5. od in January 1929. It was my unbounded pleasure to note that, monetarily, I was not very much below my college-mates who completed their course and left the college at the same time as I. I got somewhat elated, and drifted with precipitate rapidity into the company of gay young men. We wanted to be as well-dressed as Beau Brummel, with a view to achieving a position of consequence in the town's social circles. At first I saw nothing wrong in our aims and objects. But in due course, I was disillusioned. Sure enough, £2 a month enabled me to present a clean and pleasant appearance, but there were clothing materials of a quality which that income could not procure. And it was this type of expensive materials which those with whom our precocious group wanted to compete were in the habit of using. In addition, our superior competitors were more accommodating in their generosity to girls and other persons, simply because their incomes were much higher than ours. They also rode the best available bicycles, which we did not possess. Above all, I discovered (a most salutary discovery indeed) that Abeokuta society, like all sophisticated societies, was neatly stratified. If you tried to venture beyond your certified or obvious stratum, you were certain to get a rebuff which was both cold and biting. I got my share of well-deserved rebuffs. After nine good months of running after what was plainly a will-o'-the-wisp, I applied the brake.

I did not regard the nine months as by any means wasted. I learnt valuable lessons which have not departed from me. Ever since that time, I have never aspired to any position or level of society unless I feel sure that I have the capacity to work for it, and that I have the means and qualifications both to command and deserve it as well as maintain it. Any position, status or preferment that comes only by mere patronage or favouritism has never since interested me.

My political foundation was also well and truly laid at that time. Our gay team consisted of some of the most radical elements that could be found in the country at that time. We were regular and voracious readers of the *Lagos Daily News* as well as conscientious believers in the opinions expressed in that paper. Back in 1922 and when I was peregrinating from one school to another, my young mind had been saturated with the belief that the late Herbert Macauley was 'The Champion And Defender Of Native Rights And Liberty'. This belief must have been engendered by almanacs and calendars which carried Herbert Macauley's photographs together with eulogistic captions on the man's political exploits, and by adulatory remarks made to my hearing about him by knowledgeable elders. The *Lagos Daily News*, of which Herbert Macauley was proprietor and editor at the time, was an inflammatory sheet: ultra-radical, intensely nationalistic, virulently and implacably anti-white. Africans who were friendly with white men, or who went to the length of dining and wining with them, were denounced as imperialist agents, and branded as having sold Nigeria for their personal gains and advancement. With all these and other views expressed in the paper, our team readily concurred. It was one of our aims and objects to demonstrate our contempt for and equality with the white man whenever an opportunity offered itself. Such opportunity was however rare, and when it did occur we seized it firmly by the forelock. It was forbidden in our circle to say 'Sir' to, or take off our hats in the presence of a white man, as was the general practice. We resolved that on no account would we fraternise and dine with white people, who were the symbol of our political enslavement. Now looking back upon it, our resolve was really uncalled for; first of all because we were beneath the notice of the white men in Abeokuta in any case, and secondly because we were too far below the level of the handful of Africans in Abeokuta who were eligible for invitation to meals or socials with them. I must however confess that, ineffective though it was when it was made, the resolution had made a much deeper impression upon my mind than I realised at the time. It was not until 1953, a year after I had been in office as Minister of Local Government and Leader of Government Business in the Western Region of Nigeria, that I sincerely felt free to fraternise and eat with white officials. It is on record that before 1952, all the invitations to social parties that were sent to me by the Chief Commissioner, Western Region, and the Governor of Nigeria, were spurned by me out of hand. In spite of myself, I did not even show the courtesy of acknowledging them. The spell and the impact which the personality and the views of Herbert Macauley cast and made on me must have been enchanting and profound. It was some twenty years later that I was able to wade out of the slough of prejudices with which I had been indoctrinated against certain Nigerian leaders, and to make my own independent appraisal of the part they had played in our national struggles.

Furthermore, during this nine months I read as widely as possible. This was imperative, because our circle, apart from being 'gay' and 'political', also wanted to appear literary and well-informed; and the habit of reading good books which I then cultivated has not deserted me. My literary acquaintances then were fairly large and varied: Shakespeare, Dickens, R. L. Stevenson, Emerson, Lord Avebury, Sir Walter Scott, Hazlitt, Elbert Hubbard and several others. Shakespeare is my favourite. I have read all his plays, and have re-read some of them—like *Julius Caesar, Hamlet, The Tempest, Antony and Cleopatra* and *Henry V*—more than three times. Some of the mighty lines of Shakespeare must have influenced my outlook on life. But there were two books which helped me to evolve a philosophy of life to which, with some modifications which my own experiences dictate, I still cling. The first book was *The Human Machine*, which was a free gift to anyone who took a correspondence course with Bennett College, Sheffield. The book was a collection of terse, powerful articles, loaded with the practical and well-tested doctrines of applied psychology. These articles had been previously published under the serial title of 'The Human Machine' in the well-known weekly journal, *John Bull*. The second book was written, if I remember rightly, by an American author, and its title was *It's Up To You*. The philosophy of the latter book is very simple but also very true and fundamental. I will state it in a nutshell; and here I am speaking from memory as I no longer have the book. Take a jar; put in it small beans as well as big beans, making sure that each of the big beans is heavier in weight than each of the small beans; put the big beans at the bottom of the jar and the small beans at the top; shake the jar and, behold! the small beans rattle to the bottom and the big beans shake to the top. Repeat the process as often as you wish, and the result will be the same. Now the world is like a mighty jar, and all of us in it, in our different theatres of operation, are like beans with varying sizes and weights. In normal circumstances, each of us is where he is because of his size and weight. By means of favouritism and nepotism, or of some other deliberate and iniquitous tinkering with the contents of the jar, some beans which are small in size and weight may get to the top and stay there for a time, but they are sure to rattle to the bottom sooner or later. Said the author in words which I vividly remember: 'Nobody can fool the jar of life.' The *sine qua non* for anyone who wants to get to the top, therefore, is to increase his size and weight in his particular calling—that is mentally, professionally, morally, and spiritually. Getting to the top is one thing and remaining there is another. To maintain your place at the top you must make sure that you do not at any time shrink in size or lose in weight. But evaporation as well as wear and tear takes place all the time; and unless these are constantly replaced, the man who gets to the top by dint of his own specific size and weight is also sure to rattle. I am a firm believer in this philosophy.

71

It only remains for me to add that I also believe that the essence of this philosophy is applicable to political or economic organisation as it is to an individual.

Above all, I threw myself wholeheartedly into the physical and games activities of Ogbe School. As a result, I was appointed the Games' Master of the school, and the captain of its football team—there were many big boys and big girls, some as old as myself, in the school. This was of course the common pattern in all schools at that time. In my capacity as physical instructor, I received the special commendation of one Colonel Laming who visited Nigeria in 1928 or 1929 as Inspector in Physical Training, for my enthusiasm and proficiency. The headmaster of the school, now Oba A. O. Okupe, the Alaperu of Iperu, highly valued my services. Though I could appear carefree and all that outside the school, I was a stern disciplinarian among pupils, and the headmaster knew it. I took a keen interest in the pupils, particularly those in my class; but I did not permit any kind of undue familiarity between them and me. The headmaster trusted in my sense of discipline and responsibility so much that on two occasions he left me in charge of the entire school, over the heads of certificated teachers, when he was away for a few hours on some outside engagements. When I left the school, the headmaster gave me a testimonial recounting my services to the school in superlative terms.

Towards the end of 1928, I concentrated my attention mainly on the pursuit of my ambition. I took correspondence courses in English, Commercial Knowledge, Book-keeping, Business Methods, and Shorthand. I saved as hard as I could. During the June holidays in 1929, I went to Lagos, and learnt touch-typing which was not very common in those days. In order to continue my typing practice, I persuaded Mr Mould to buy a typewriter. He bought a second-hand one. I took charge of it. I was now able to draft, unaided by him, all the letters, applications for work and petitions which he handled in the course of his trade, and type them for him as well. He was very pleased with me. He offered me tips which I refused. But I accepted his offer to have free meals with him whenever I wanted. By the end of 1929, I had become a fully-fledged shorthand typist: shorthand speed—100 to 120 words a minute: typing speed: 40 words a minute.

When I arrived in Lagos on 31 December 1929, in search of a job, I was full of high hopes for the future. Early in March 1930, I was appointed a shorthand typist by the German firm of J. W. Jaeckel & Company. There were about thirty applicants from among whom I was chosen. My salary was £6. 10. od per mensem. This was much less than what I had expected, but at the same time much more than I ever received as a teacher and about double what my classmates would receive in 1931 after they had completed their course. For a while I felt that I was on the high road to realising my hopes. But in August 1930, I lost my job with J. W. Jaeckel. My immediate boss, a Mr Ruppel, tall and handsome, was a nice and jovial man. He and I got on very well together, almost as pals. The General Manager, a Mr Vogt, short and obese, was very stiff and aloof, and in any case I had no dealings with him at all in the course of my duties. He spoke very little English. All his letters to the head office in Hamburg were written in German, and he dictated them to Mr Ruppel who was himself a first-rate shorthand typist. One morning, on my arrival at the office I noticed that Mr Ruppel looked somewhat morose and uncommunicative. As I was about to settle down to work he asked me to see the cashier. There I was paid off. Before I returned from the cashier to collect my coat and hat, my successor was already rattling away at the typewriter. He was one of the applicants who were rejected when I was appointed by Mr Ruppel. His brother was, however, an important personality in Lagos, and he was obviously a friend of the General Manager whom he visited from time to time. For nineteen months thereafter I was unemployed. For some months I was able to live, with economy, fairly comfortably on my accumulated resources which consisted of my savings and a month's salary in lieu of notice. The trade depression of that period was having its adverse effects on Nigeria's economy, and both government and mercantile houses were retrenching staff. Nevertheless, I was hoping

73

against hope that I might get another job. So I never tired of writing applications. But the result was the same: no vacancy.

The choice was always open, and indeed offers were repeatedly made to me to return to teaching. But I was resolved not to enter any employment in which I would find myself in a position of inferiority to my former classmates at Wesley College. I was prepared to do any other legitimate work or starve instead. It was also open to me to take the Senior Clerical Examination, and if I passed (and I had no doubt I would), seek appointment in a government department. But I had a strong aversion for the Civil Service because it was dominated by white officials, and by African 'yes-men' who would run when called by a white man, who would put their hands behind their backs in his presence, who would not dare to see anything wrong in anything the white man said or did, and who would punctuate every sentence they uttered before him with innumerable 'Sir's'. Whilst in the employ of Jaeckel I had taken and passed the Interpreter's Examination, but I had refrained from following it up. With my attitude of mind, I felt sure that I was not the type to make any progress as a civil servant.

When the monstrous reptile of starvation was creeping close, I struck on an idea, which I quickly put into operation. I organised evening classes for those preparing for the Preliminary Cambridge and Junior Preceptor's examinations. What I made from this source was very meagre, but, with occasional help from friends to whom I had done some good turns, I eked out some sort of existence. The nineteen months were among the most trying periods of my life. My most cherished hopes had been dashed. My span of life up to then, though short, had seen some ups and downs, with more downs than ups. I had many moments of anxious reflection.

During this period, I made the best possible use of my time. I polished up my mathematics, started the study of Latin, and read as many books as I could afford to buy or borrow. In the course of my incursion into the wide realm of literature, I came across a big tome of a book which was a collection of the essays and lectures of Robert G. Ingersoll. I started to read it, and I

74

found that the more I read it the more fascinated I became. It was said of him that Ingersoll was a smashing orator and a forceful personality. From his essays and lectures which I read most avidly, I saw him as a matchless moralist and humanitarian, as well as a literary giant with a style which was at once lucid and in the best classical traditions. His language was so choice, his sentences so balanced and pithy, and his arguments so cogent, incisive, irresistible, and so replete with scientific and classical illustrations, that I found myself racing breathlessly along with this amazing man, as he delivered deft, precise, and shattering blows at all that is taught in the Holy Bible from Genesis to Revelation.

The story of Adam and Eve, and of Cain taking refuge with human beings and marrying one of them in a world in which Adam and Eve were said to be the first creatures; the story of the Flood and of Noah's Ark; the immaculate conception; the miracles performed by Christ; all these and others came under the blazing fire of this bellicose rationalist. There was no scientific evidence in support of the Flood, he contended. As for Noah's Ark, its capacity was physically inadequate for its stated contents, and much more so for the immeasurable quantity and variety of food which all the animals, reptiles and birds which had taken refuge in the Ark, would require for the duration of the Flood. How did Noah succeed in preventing the lions, the tigers and their ilk from devouring their normal prey? If the story of the Flood was true, then it would follow that some slow-moving creatures like the tortoise and snail, which had their natural habitats at places several thousands of miles away, must have received a warning about the imminence of the Flood and must have started on their journeys to the Ark several thousands of years before the very earth itself, according to Genesis, was created, and hence before those creatures themselves were brought into being by a heavenly decree. He was particularly hard on God for hardening the heart of Pharaoh. If God was Almighty and All-merciful, he argued, and I am recalling what I read from memory, he should have set the children of Israel free without bringing so much suffering and sorrow on the Egyptians in the process, and without goading the Pharaoh and his army to perdition in the Red Sea. He was fierce and furious too in his castigation of God for aiding Moses, Joshua and other Israelite leaders after them in their ruthless and inhuman massacres of their foes. These acts, he argued, are revolting to civilised conscience, and in diametric opposition to the ethical standards generally accepted by man. Either there was no God at all; or if there was one, He was either not good, or not the father of us all. For no good father would take partisan sides with only one group of his children in their brutal decimation of the others, as God was stated to have done for the Israelites as against the Canaanites, the Amorites, and the Jebusites among many others.

At the end of my literary and mental excursion with Ingersoll, I had become a hearty admirer of agnosticism. I made further progress in this new field. I read other books including T. H. Huxley's *Evolution of the Species*, Thomas Paine's *Age of Reason*, and another book whose author I don't now remember, entitled, *Bible On Hell*. I became a regular reader of the *Rationalist Review*. From the time of my mental acquaintance and communion with Ingersoll, I attended church only occasionally, when there was a wedding ceremony, memorial service, or when my wife successfully insisted on my keeping her company. I found it hard to disbelieve in or to doubt the existence of God. But I vehemently disavowed the legends and fictions which the Israelites and their successors in dogma have woven round Him. I positively held the view that, down the ages, different groups of men have at different times created their own God in their own warped image, and that so long as these dogmatic erring fanatics continued to project their own self-created God instead of the true God, so long would there be room for rational men with the courage of their conviction to feel impelled to repudiate the man-made God.

During my stay in the United Kingdom from 1944 to 1946, I did not cross the portals of a church except for sight-seeing to Westminster Abbey and St Paul's Cathedral. Instead, I attended some of the Sunday meetings of the South Place

Ethical Society at Conway Hall. Each meeting followed the pattern of a church service, with some minor variations. There were no prayers, but we sang songs to the accompaniment of a piano, using popular church tunes. Our hymns were chosen from a hymn book entitled *Hymns Of Modern Thought*. As in the church, the lesson for the day was read. This was usually chosen from the writings of great scientists, or of agnostics and atheists of undisputed erudition. Darwin, Huxley and Wells were among the favourites. Then there was an address in place of a sermon. For some Sundays running, Professor Keeton of London University did a series on 'The Laws of Moses and of Hammurabi'. Each time I attended the meeting, I always came away with the question in my mind: 'Why this imperfect and irrational imitation of the Christian mode of worship?' It dawned upon me, more than ever before, that human beings naturally love rituals and ceremonies. Whether they believe in God or not, they always like to worship and venerate something: a flag or a shrine; the tomb or effigy of a dead hero or the person and presence of a living one; and so on and so forth. I sincerely thought that something was missing at the Conway Hall meetings of the South Place Ethical Society, and a process of re-evaluation of Christian ideals and practices as compared with agnostic, rationalist or atheistic concepts was generated within me. Eventually I returned to the Holy Bible and to the Christian fold. Throughout the period of my oscillation between agnosticism and Christianity, my wife stood immoveably for the latter. Her constant admonitions and steadfastness did more than anything else to restrain me from going beyond the point of no return.

Early in April 1932, I was informed by telegram by my cousin Simon Awolowo that the post of 'College Clerk' was vacant. It was newly created; there was no such post in the college up to the end of 1931. I went to Ibadan immediately to apply in person. We were three applicants in all, and a day was fixed for us to do a test. I won. As College Clerk, I combined the work of a shorthand typist with that of a book-keeper. I was thorough, discreet and efficient in my work. Of my own voli-

77

tion, I worked in and out of office hours, all depending on the volume of work on hand at a given time. It was part of my duties to type and cyclostyle examination papers for divinity students, sub-pastors and teachers in training, among all of whom I had many friends. In all matters appertaining to my duties, the Principal and the College Authority trusted me absolutely. A tribute to this effect was paid to me in the testimonial given to me when I left Wesley College as its Clerk. I am still proud of it, and it reads:

Wesley College,
Ibadan, Nigeria.
31st August, 1934.

Mr Obafemi Awolowo has been employed as clerk at this College since 20th April 1932. His work has been chiefly correspondence and copying. He can take down letters etc. to dictation at a reasonably quick rate and is a rapid and accurate copyist. He is thoroughly conversant with the cutting of stencils for duplicating work.

In the course of his duties a considerable amount of confidential matter has passed through his hands and his honesty and discretion have never been in question.

He is resigning on his own initiative in order to secure a better salary and I have pleasure in recommending him to anyone requiring an efficient office assistant.

(Sgd) Edward G. Nightingale
Principal.

For the two-and-half years odd that I spent at Wesley College as its Clerk, I took myself extremely seriously. I exercised spartan control and discipline over myself, and went about my business independent and unafraid. I enjoyed the respect of all those with whom I came into contact. In certain respects, however, I must have been a puzzle to the Principal and his staff. I did not enter the college chapel once, and I don't remember ever sharing a joke with the Principal or with anyone else other than my intimate friends. For some months, I was not on speaking terms with the Vice-Principal—Mr Hodges. During the absence of the Principal on leave, I went to him to collect certain drafts for typing. He handed them to me, and I turned away. He then called me back and asked if I knew what the custom in England was when something was handed by someone to another as he had just done. I had not been to England, and I told him so. He then explained that an Englishman on receiving the papers would have said 'Thank you.' So I told him that customs differed, and that among the Yoruba people, you only say 'Thank you' when you are the recipient of a gift; and that in any case since I was not an Englishman I did not see why I should be expected to know and observe this particular English custom. He was annoyed more by the way I addressed him than by what I said. He fined me a sum of money which he deducted from my salary at the end of the month. Since then and until the Principal intervened, we both had regular business intercourse, but it consisted only in my going to his office to collect drafts from him or from his desk, and turning away without saying as much as 'good morning' or 'good day'.

Only once the Principal asked to know why I did not attend the chapel services. I replied that the only thing that I enjoyed in a church service was the melody of the songs. It happened, I explained, that my room was near enough to the chapel for me to be fully entranced with the sweet voices of the college choir. It was a mark of exemplary tolerance on the part of the Rev. E. G. Nightingale that he did not remove me from my post in the college on account of my general disposition, and my attitude towards the church. I on my part made no attempt to interfere with the religious views and practices of my friends, or of the staff and students in the college. But if anyone tried to preach church-going and the teachings of the Bible to me, as was occasionally the case, I very quickly worsted him. It is my candid view then and now that the vast majority of Christians, including the clergy, are too ill-equipped dialectically to combat with success the aggressive detractors and traducers of our great religion.

CHAPTER 7

FRATERNITY OF THE PEN

I ENTERED the employ of the *Nigerian Daily Times* in September 1934 as a reporter-in-training. During my period as College Clerk, I took correspondence courses for the London Matriculation Examination and in journalism. I took the London Matriculation Examination in January 1934 and failed. I was commended by my tutors in journalism. I decided not to repeat the London Matriculation Examination until later. I had wanted to pass the examination not with a view to becoming a teacher or civil servant, but so that if at any future time I had the money to do Law I would have no difficulty in securing admission into one of the Inns of Court. I wanted to do journalism mainly as a means of raising money for my legal studies, and partly because I was interested in the profession. Having failed the examination, I thought it was better that I made the money first before I had another try at the examination.

But journalism was an unprofitable, frustrating and soul-depressing career at that time in Nigeria.

There was a general but inarticulate contempt for newspapermen, particularly the reporters. They were regarded as the flotsam and jetsam of the growing community of Nigerian intelligentsia: people who took to journalism because they were no good in anything else. Journalism was not as well-paid then as a good job in the civil service or in a mercantile house. Only editors and their immediate assistants could afford to own a bicycle. Even Mr Ernest Ikoli, the most brilliant and most formidable journalist of the time did not own one: he could not afford it. The Editor of the *Nigerian Daily Times*, the only prosperous newspaper, used a bicycle for a long time. Then he owned a car which was nothing more or less than a ramshackle box on four wheels. I thought it miraculous that the Editor— short, fat, with a protruding belly—could get into it at all and that after being in, the strange mechanical contrivance did move! We of the fraternity of the pen were feared rather than respected. We were accorded recognition at social functions; but this was done on purpose. Those concerned wanted to see their names in print in the best possible light. In this connection, certain hackneyed expressions must be used in the report. It would not do to say 'Mr & Mrs So-and-So, etc., etc.' It must be 'Mr So-and-So, a worthy scion of So-and-So and his amiable consort Mrs So-and-So (*née* So-and-So), etc., etc.' For the report to be any good in the estimation of those concerned, the 'wife' must be 'consort' and she must be 'amiable'. The words in brackets '*née* So-and-So' must be added in order to show that the 'consort' was doubly blue-blooded, through marriage and by birth. If after a few days the host or chief guest or celebrant, as the case might be, did not see anything about his function in the paper, he called upon you at the office, or accosted you in the streets, to find out why he had been so maltreated and humiliated. If you belonged to the drinking and gluttonous species of *homo sapiens*, and if, during the function, you had helped yourself to several quarts of beer or shots of whisky, and to a good quantity of food, the displeased individual might even venture to question your propriety for failing to perform your own side of an implied 'socio-journalistic' contract. I never experienced this form of affront myself because I never drank, and was then and still am too shy to eat in public. To the extent that my income for the time being permitted, I had indulged myself, from my days as provisional teacher, in cigarette-smoking; but I abjured the habit on 6 March 1934 as one of my birthday resolutions. Besides, I always tried to be tidy and clean in my appearance, and to maintain at the very least a façade of supreme self-confidence. I was, therefore, a reporter with a difference in a society which was riddled with

81

vanity, snobbery, pseudo-Victorian aristocracy, and 'England ladies'.*

The newspapers circulating at the time were not commodities of which, from the points of view of literary art and technical craftsmanship, any self-respecting person connected with them could feel justifiably proud. The *Nigerian Daily Times* was technically the best paper then in circulation; but it was, on a strictly professional assessment, an unpardonably dull journalistic and literary product: a veritable stagnant pool of stale, colourless news; and a musty reservoir of articles which lacked animation, pungency and nationalist flavour. In contents and style the *Nigerian Daily Telegraph* under the editorship of Mr Ernest Ikoli and the *Lagos Daily News* were the very antithesis of the *Nigerian Daily Times*, and therefore much better. But most of the time, the *Telegraph* was printed in types so battered that only a long-suffering person could bear the ordeal of reading more than the short, bracing and thunderous editorial. The *Lagos Daily News* had ceased in 1934 to answer to the name of a daily paper. It published only when Herbert Macauley alias 'The Moghul' alias 'H.M.', alias 'The Wizard of Kirston Hall' could afford to buy newsprint and ink and persuade his irregularly paid and half-starved compositors to work. Whenever this paper made its appearance it sold like hot cakes.

When I left Wesley College to join the *Nigerian Daily Times*, I did so with my eyes open, and after mature consideration. For the whole of my time as Clerk of the College, I was on a salary of £3 per mensem only, the same as my former classmates at the college were earning as certificated teachers. Two attempts to get the Principal to give me a rise in salary were of no avail. I found myself in a cul-de-sac, and I decided to leave, giving the Principal five months' notice. I felt certain, and I

* 'England ladies' is a phrase which was common in Lagos in those days, and it was used to distinguish 'ladies' who had been to England or any part of the United Kingdom for further studies from those who had not. They were in a class by themselves, and they looked down upon other ladies and all gentlemen who had not been to U.K. as inferior beings. But some of us who had not been to U.K. regarded them as contemptible. For one thing, all they studied in U.K. was domestic science or music. For another, the life they lived, morally, was far from edifying.

was proved right in this, that whatever happened I would make more than £3 a month as a reporter. I also thought, and here I was proved flatly wrong, that overseas newspapers would accept my articles for publication and pay me well for them. At the time when I was doing a correspondence course in journalism, I wrote some articles, of interest to West African readers, for the *West African Review* but they were neither published nor returned. The topics were mainly political. Six years later, in 1940 I believe, two of them were published, and I was paid a few guineas for them. The editor was presumably short of manuscripts and had no alternative but to look through his old files and, on discovering my articles, used them. When I was in the *Nigerian Daily Times*, I sent many articles to other overseas newspapers through an agency, but they came back to me with the same solemn regularity as I had despatched them. My literary agent was a most sympathetic gentleman; he never failed to write to pat me on the back each time he returned my manuscripts. They were good, he would say, but the subject matter (they were invariably diatribes against British rule) would not appeal to English readers. I tried my hand at short stories, but their fate was the same, save that, in this case, my agent made it clear that my technique was not quite up to the required standard.

I spent about eight months altogether with the *Nigerian Daily Times*: three months in Lagos as a trainee without pay, and five months as the resident correspondent in Ibadan. My fellow-trainees and colleagues were Mr Olatunji Idewu (then Hamzat Ishola) and Mr R. A. B. Jose. They were respectively posted to Ijebu Ode and Oshogbo, also as resident correspondents. For our services, each of us was paid £2 per mensem as retainer fee, and 2d per inch per column for every report that was published. It was in the matter of publication of news, on which our real living remuneration depended, that all sorts of influence came into play. In its precarious journey from the sub-editor's table to the head printer's desk, anything could happen to your report. It could suffer either total extinction or violent diminution. Even when your reports had been published, you

83

must go at the end of the month, armed with your own ruler, to make sure that you did not lose several inches through the deliberate miscalculation of the clerk in charge.

Our Editor was Chief C. A. A. Titcombe, the Ligegere of Ake, Abeokuta. He was every inch an aristocrat, always riding his high horse: distant and not easily accessible to people at our level. He was nevertheless kind-hearted and humorous. The news that mattered to him most was, in order of importance, that relating to the late Sir Adeyemo Alakija and his family, the Roman Catholic Church, and Egba affairs. Any criticism of the first two and of Egba Native Authority was taboo. In addition, unless definite instructions came from the very top, nothing critical must be written about the Nigerian government or expatriate officials. And things were happening which aroused the just resentment and indignation of young Nigerians. As there was no effective vehicle for the vigorous ventilation of suppressed grievances, a journalistic vacuum was thus created which Dr Azikiwe very cleverly exploited and usefully filled when he returned to the country in 1937 to establish the *West African Pilot* which, whatever its literary defects, was a fire-eating and aggressive nationalist paper of the highest order, ranking in this regard with the *Nigerian Daily Telegraph* under Ikoli, and the *Lagos Daily News*, but much better produced. It was naturally very popular, the very thing the youth of the country had been waiting for. Newspapermen in the employ of the *West African Pilot* were better paid and they assumed a new status in society. Civil servants, teachers and mercantile employees resigned good and pensionable posts to lend a hand in the new journalistic awakening. Some of these enthusiasts were eventually disappointed and disillusioned on other grounds, but the fact of a journalistic revival and revolution was widely recognised and acknowledged. The *Nigerian Daily Times* was very swiftly reorganised, in order to meet the challenge of the *West African Pilot*. A substantial amount of foreign capital was injected into it, and the dead wood in the editorial section was cut out to yield place to younger and more imaginative elements. R. B. Paul, Esq., head of the 'West African Newspapers' came to Nigeria himself and, for a while, personally directed the initial operations. An expatriate Editor, Mr H. C. E. M. Bates, was appointed. He and Dr Azikiwe soon fell foul of each other, and there was a fierce press war. As a result, there was plenty of hot and scintillating stuff to read in the *Pilot* and *Times*; but my sympathy and that of all Nigerian nationalists was with Dr Azikiwe.

In spite of his bias and predilection for certain personages and institutions, and the dullness of his paper, which I have mentioned, Chief Titcombe did not by any means lack the news instinct of a good journalist. One afternoon one of the other two and I sat down in the office, chatting. Chief Titcombe then emerged from his sanctum sanctorum. We pulled ourselves up under the glare of his big eyes and over-awing personality.

'What are you folks doing there?' he inquired, and as he did so something of a smile lightened his face.

'Just chatting!' we replied.

'You should be out collecting news,' he said.

'Well, sir, it is all dry in town. No news,' I explained.

'Then let one of you go and jump into the lagoon to oblige the other!' he remarked with a big smile, and both of us and Mr Ayo Lijadu roared with laughter.

The only person who did not appear to see anything to laugh about in this joke and who was as sphinx-like as ever was Mr A. B. Laotan, the Assistant Editor. He was a fastidious and rather over-serious character, a very industrious and devoted worker, and a journalist with greater flair for a weekly magazine than for a daily paper. His chief task was to edit special articles for publication. Somehow I had very poor luck with him. Mr Jose's luck with him was no better than mine. Both of us were in the habit of indulging in controversial matters. As for Mr Idewu he had a breezy, inoffensive style, and his subjects were equally breezy and non-controversial. I did several articles, but they were left untouched on Mr Laotan's over-laden table. I decided to migrate from the controversial field to the non-controversial and so I did one article on Shakespeare's *Julius Caesar*. It suffered the same fate. I got to the office very early one morning, dug it out of the pile of manuscripts on his table, and brought it to his notice on his arrival. He had read it, he said, but apart from the article not being topical, he thought it was too big for my name. Since I was the author, I did not quite understand what he meant. I later sent it to the late Duse Mohammed Ali Effendi who published it in his *Weekly Comet*, and wrote me a glowingly commendatory letter into the bargain.

The triumvirate in the editorial section of the *Nigerian Daily Times* in my time consisted of Chief Titcombe, Mr Laotan, and the late Mr Ayo Lijadu. Mr Lijadu was the brightest and best of them all. He was a literary stylist; and withal a taciturn individual who wielded a mighty pen. He was the sub-editor, and in that capacity he did all in his power to encourage the three of us both during the time of our training, and when we were out in the field. I had boundless admiration for the man. I disagreed with him only on one issue—which I then considered to be very vital—and that was his assessment of the literary and political merits of Dr Nmamdi (then plain Mr or Professor) Azikiwe. Dr Azikiwe did a series of articles on the liberty of the press for the *Nigerian Daily Times*. Mr Lijadu thought they were not worth publishing. They were learned stuff all right, thought Mr Lijadu, but they were neither original nor were they written in a language suitable for a newspaper. Chief Titcombe thought differently and he published the articles. I myself agreed that there were too many long and ponderous words in them, and that many a reader would have to have a dictionary by his side in order to understand what Dr Azikiwe was talking about. But the point remained, I argued, that Dr Azikiwe did not direct this kind of articles to the average reader. They were meant for those who were sufficiently educated to understand and appreciate them. I had not met or even seen Dr Azikiwe then.

Because of my admiration for the man, I was given an assignment to cover the three lectures which Dr Azikiwe delivered on his arrival in Lagos towards the end of 1934. The first lecture was at the Methodist Boys' High School, and the subject was: 'There is Joy in Scholarship.' The audience was very small, but the fame of the brilliance of that lecture reached all corners of Lagos and the mainland in no time. The other two lectures were delivered at Faji School and Ansar-Ud-Deen School, Alakoro. The crowd at Faji School was a big one— so big that I found it too stuffy and inconvenient to stay inside. I went out and stood on the ground beneath the windows behind Dr Azikiwe. There, with the light through the windows, I made my notes. The organiser of this lecture was my friend, now Senator Olujide Somolu. The crowd at Alakoro was much bigger and indeed so tumultuous that the lecture had to be given in the open air. The highlights of these last two lectures were the expositions by Dr Azikiwe of his economic and political philosophy for a New Africa. This philosophy was elaborated under four main headings: (1) political risorgimento; (2) economic determinism; (3) social resurgence; and (4) spiritual balance.

In a manner which was both charming and disarming, he subtly and implicitly laid claims to fields of learning which were truly catholic and almost limitless. 'Now let us run through the pages of history,' he proclaimed at Faji School; and there was thunderous applause which lasted some two minutes. It was the first time in Nigeria, so we his hearers believed, that any Nigerian was academically competent and self-confident enough not only to enter just a few of the pages of British history, British Empire history, or European history, but to run through the pages of *all* history, as we were made to understand. Dr Azikiwe's reputation had preceded him to Nigeria through his book *Liberia In World Politics*, and there was a general belief that he was the most outstanding Nigerian scholar in the academic history of the country. Now this declaration by him proved it. Whether he actually succeeded in running through the pages of history, whether he was accurate in the route he chose in the race, or whether the milestones and landmarks to which he pointed were genuine and true to fact, no one cared to inquire. The genius of New Africa had spoken, and there was an end of the matter.

87

Then at Alakoro he said, among others, the following, at carefully chosen intervals:

I am not a very good student of the Hebrew language, but Professor So-and-So of the University of So-and-So in a very scholarly exposition, discourse, treatise, thesis, or dissertation, written in Hebrew (the English translation is not available) said so-and-so.

I am not a very good student of the German language, but etc., etc.

I am not a very good student of the French language, but etc., etc.

The uproar of applause which greeted each expression in identical terms is better imagined than described. The impression was definitely created in the minds of Dr Azikiwe's hearers that he was a linguist who understood and spoke several languages including those he mentioned in the course of the lecture. But Mr Ayo Lijadu was unimpressed. The only other person who did not think much of Dr Azikiwe's political philosophy and scholastic claims at the time was Mr Ernest Ikoli.

Mr Idewu stuck the *Nigerian Daily Times* longer than Mr Jose and I did. He was more fortunate in his posting. He had scarcely arrived in Ijebu Ode when one of Nigeria's famous trials, known as the Ijebu Ode Conspiracy Case, started. The trial of a number of chiefs and leading men in Ijebu Ode, charged with conspiring to kill Oba Daniel Adesanya, the Awujale of Ijebu Ode, lasted several days. And the *Nigerian Daily Times* carried pages of the report of the proceedings in the case every day. It was a fortuitous windfall for Mr Idewu. It was hard going in Ibadan, but worse still in Oshogbo. As between Mr Jose and me, I do not now remember who left the *Nigerian Daily Times* before whom. In my case, it was clear that I would never succeed in raising enough money to become a lawyer from the reporting business.

My interest in journalism and association with newspapers did not cease with the severance of my connection with the *Nigerian Daily Times*. There is something in the saying: 'Once a journalist always a journalist.' In the midst of my dissatisfaction with the *Nigerian Daily Times*, I entertained the ambition that when I came into my own, I would establish a newspaper which would be livelier and better run than that paper. In the meantime I made up my mind to be a free-lance, which in the then Nigerian context simply meant writing for the love of the art and for no pay. I wrote a number of articles for the *Nigerian Daily Telegraph*, and *not* for the *Nigerian Daily Times*. At a later stage I contributed unnumbered articles under various pen-names including 'Afric' and my own initials 'O.A.' to the *Daily Service*. I was in fact the unofficial volunteer Legislative Council reporter of that paper for some three-and-a-half years. My articles were mainly political and always highly controversial. I must have antagonised the powers-that-be in the process, but I couldn't have cared less. I was gratified that I had the approval of the majority of my people for the views which I expressed. There was one which I wrote which evoked the most controversy of them all. It was entitled 'Hints to the Clergy'. The theme of it was that God did not answer prayer, and did not need to. I quoted Paul in support of my contention. Says he in his Epistle to the Galatians, VI, 7: 'Be not deceived; God is not mocked: for whatsoever a man soweth, that shall he also reap.' What was paramount therefore was the seed we sowed. If we sowed good or bad seed, neither the want of prayer nor its profusion would detract from or alter for the better the quality and the nature of the seed already sown. The Christian churches felt outraged, and I remember that churches of the Anglican confession devoted one Sunday to controverting my heresy, and, I believe, to praying for the redemption of my soul as well. There were many rejoinders in the papers too.

Though we were all members of the Nigerian Youth Movement, it was the *Daily Service*, as the official organ of the Movement, fighting for survival against the onslaught of Dr Azikiwe, that brought Mr Ernest Ikoli, Chief H. O. Davies, Chief S. L. Akintola (Premier of the Western Region of Nigeria), and me constantly together. Mr Ikoli and Chief H. O. Davies practically slaved for the paper on salaries of £15 and £12. 10. od respectively. And they were paid these paltry sums only when there was enough money in the paper's coffers. Chief S. L. Akintola and I earned nothing for our part-time literary labours on the paper. The motto of the Movement was 'Selfless Service', and we sincerely rejoiced in rendering such a service.

It was the practice in those days for people who wanted their photographs to appear in the newspapers to pay for the blocks. As a matter of principle, I declined to pay either for my photograph or for its block. I held the view that if I had to pay for these things, then I had not grown big enough for my photograph to appear in the papers. Therefore, rather than pay for it to appear, I should increase my size and stature, until newspapers would themselves beg for my photographs. In the absence of an accompanying photograph, and in view of my unobtrusiveness, there were many people who attributed articles written by me under my initials 'O.A.' to Mr O. A. Alakija, who was much better known than I. The first time that my photograph appeared in a newspaper was when I wrote a lengthy open letter to Sir Arthur Richards (now Lord Milverton) on the proposed Richards Constitution in 1945— eleven years after I had been connected with newspapers. Chief S. L. Akintola was the Editor of the *Daily Service* at the time. I learnt later that he secured the photograph free from a mutual friend and he made the paper pay for the block.

When I was a law student in the United Kingdom I continued my free-lancing. My first published article after my arrival in the United Kingdom was on the White Paper, Cmd 6554 of September 1944, on the marketing of cocoa. I sent it to *West Africa*. By return of post, I received a letter from the Editor, Mr Albert Cartwright, expressing delight at receiving my article as well as an earnest desire to meet me. We met, and we became very good friends afterwards. He was old enough to be my grandfather when I met him, but he treated me with deference and affection. Mr Cartwright was in a class by himself. Though he had spent many of his long years in South Africa, yet he possessed not even one iota of the evil traits which distinguish the average South African whites from the rest of humanity. There was no trace of colour-bar or racial superiority in him. He was a versatile and almost omniscient journalist, a great authority on African affairs, and a genuine believer in and fighter for accelerated political advancement for the Africans. Mr Cartwright set great stock on me, and did all in his power to help me. He published in his papers (*West Africa* and *West African Review*) everything I cared to write, and paid me for it. Through his unsolicited recommendation, I was appointed by the British Council to do a fortnightly bulletin of not more than 1,000 words for which I was paid £5. 5. od. He taught me a lesson in humility when he appealed to me to allow him to decline the offer to write a Foreword to my book *Path To Nigerian Freedom*, on the ground that there was someone else worthier than himself to undertake the task. He suggested Miss Margery Perham whom I had not then met, but some of whose books I had read. After I had been called to the Bar, Mr Cartwright asked to know from me whether I would be willing to consider an offer to become the Editor of the *Nigerian Daily Times*. I respectfully told him, I would not.

CHAPTER 8

MY BUSINESS ADVENTURES

WITH £60 in my hands and with an additional sum of £30 from a friend who came into partnership with me, I ventured into the money-lending business. I specialised in small loans ranging from £2 to £10. My main clients were civil servants who never seemed able to live within their means. For a short while, I did good business; but I didn't like its seamy side, and so I abandoned it. To be honest, the money-lending business in Nigeria, outside the banking and other reputable financial institutions, is a usurious undertaking. The borrowers pay exorbitant interests far in excess of the rates laid down by statute, but on the face of the agreement everything is legally in order.

Along with money-lending, I engaged in public letter-writing under the Illiterates' Protection Ordinance. I did make some money from this, and I sometimes wondered why I didn't think of it when I was unemployed for nineteen months in Lagos. But having abandoned money-lending, I was satisfied that I could never save enough from my earnings as a public letter-writer to enable me to proceed to the United Kingdom to do law. Some new ideas occurred to me: produce buying and the motor transport business. If I was able to organise these ventures successfully, I would make enough money to fulfil my legal aspiration. But I did not have enough capital for the two ventures. I could tackle each separately, but it would be in a small way, and I was getting rather impatient. I contacted some of my friends and acquaintances, and invited them to come into a form of partnership with me. In this way I succeeded in raising about £650 over a period of twelve months. With the first instalments from my partners to which I added my own share, I got cracking. I operated two taxis and a lorry, but this line came to grief. The competition among motor transporters was cut-throat; both the drivers and the conductors were far from being honest; and the traffic police were, to put it very mildly, a perfect nuisance. Whenever I had accompanied the lorry myself, the situation had been worse: for some inexplicable reason, the engine might give trouble, and the traffic police became more hostile than ever before. I nevertheless persevered in this venture in the hope that it would sooner or later turn out right. The produce-buying side went well for a time. I dealt in cocoa, palm kernels and cotton. There were grave hazards in dealing in these commodities. The mercantile houses to which we sold were in the habit of manipulating prices, so that there were several artificial falls or rises in price in one day. Tonnages declared for £X per ton when there were cuts in price might still not have been fully purchased by the time the price had risen to £X+3. The same firm gave different prices to different customers; and different competing firms gave competing prices to their respective customers. When the firms competed among themselves, the African buyers reaped some advantage. But in 1937, the firms entered into an agreement to offer identical prices to all their customers at the same time. The agreement was known locally as the 'Cocoa Pool', and it evoked acrimonious reaction in Ghana and Nigeria, leading to the appointment in February 1938 of the Nowell Commission on the Marketing of West African Cocoa. During the 1935/36 season and in the midst of the worst possible price fluctuations by manipulation, I made profits, and my business associates had their due shares of profits either paid to them or ploughed back into the business to swell their capital, as they directed. The 1936/37 season witnessed the best cocoa boom for many years. There was a continuous rise in price. Business was brisk all round, and it was all too easy to make money. As a matter of fact, I made enough profit during this season to pay my associates their capital and shares of profit in full, and to enable me, with strict economy, to proceed to the United Kingdom to study law. But there were rosy forecasts for the 1937/38 season. Besides, I was already engaged to a beautiful damsel whom I planned to marry by the end of 1937. I, therefore, decided to continue in business until the 1937/38 cocoa season after which I would go to the United Kingdom accompanied by my wife. Many produce buyers including myself speculated heavily and in very high spirits in preparation for the 1937/38 season. The forecasts for the season proved all wrong; there was a big slump, and I not only lost everything but also became indebted to the firms for whom I bought produce. When I was getting married on 26 December 1937, I knew that I was on the brink of a business collapse, but I was still hoping, like many others, that what was already lost could be redeemed during the months of January and February.

This was not to be. Instead, I spent the next five years—1938 to 1942—striving with might and main to pay to the firms the debts I owed. I bought produce when I could and also traded in merchandise on a cash-and-carry basis. The handicaps under which I had to labour, however, were many and tantalising, as my credit with the firms had been impaired. Indeed one of the firms to whom I owed a lesser sum of money complicated the situation for me by distraining and selling my house at Ikenne, my personal property, and my trading equipment wherever it was. My house at Ikenne, which was then uncompleted, was sold for £40 in 1940. I recovered it from the buyer for £47. 10. od two years later. My Chevrolet saloon car was sold for £25 to a friend of the bailiff, who resold it for a big profit. When my personal effects were sold on 8 May 1939, I was personally present together with three friends of mine. The bailiff had left me with only one suit, and I needed a few more to make a presentable appearance in public. I also wanted to make sure that these personal effects were not sold at a give-away price like my car. My three friends were to take part in the bids. They bought some wearing apparel with their own money which I reimbursed to them after some time.

Many people were obviously astounded to see me at the

94

sales. Some friends and acquaintances who had bought a few things before they were aware of my presence there, surrendered them to me, and assured me that in any case it was their intention to preserve what they had bought for me. Their behaviour, and the remarks they made in my hearing at the commencement of the sales did not bear out their protestation. I, however, accepted it, and later reimbursed them for the articles they had surrendered to me. Two business rivals who were well known to me and who, I understood later, had come to the sales with a view to buying some of my furniture, disappeared very swiftly on hearing that I was in the crowd. The astonishment and mild sensation which my presence created among those who witnessed the sales was expressed by one of the Nigeria police constables present. He approached me where I was standing and asked:

'Are you Mr Awolowo?'

'Yes,' I answered.

'And you can come here to witness these sales?' he inquired with undisguised amazement.

'Yes! Why not?' I rejoined.

'Sir, you are a man!'

After making a momentary and an uneasy survey of me as I stood there unperturbed, the policeman shook his head, and walked away.

In the midst of my business troubles I felt pained and disappointed when some of my friends and business associates wrote to me demanding their capital contributions as well as profits, and calling me names. Two of them instructed two of the leading solicitors in the country (late Eric O. Moore Esq. and the firm of Messrs Alakija and Alakija) to write to me to the same effect. One of the letters dated 8 July 1940 emanating from Messrs Alakija and Alakija and signed by the late Sir Adeyemo Alakija, contained the following passage:

From the facts in our possession we cannot accept your repudiation that you are not liable, and we warn you that should you compel us to resort to legal proceedings the result may be unpleasant to you.

I was not sure of my legal position.

Up to the end of 1940 it was my determination that if I paid off all the debts owed to the firms and had enough money left, I would reimburse my fellow-adventurers their full capital contributions. I felt keenly and profoundly the financial inconveniences which they were already experiencing. Certain passages from a letter which I addressed to them in 1939 are relevant:

The utter failure of the Progressive Economic Corporation is a foregone reality.

Believe it or not, my heart aches and bleeds when I think of the whole position of things. I think of the members severally, and I am sore distressed at the resulting reflection. In every case the contribution invested had been extracted from meagre, hard-earned salaries; salaries which are so poor that a saving is only possible by subjecting oneself to extreme discipline of mind and body. The contribution was both a joyless and joyful task. Joyless because of the sufferings attendant upon it; joyful because of the happy thought that one was providing for a rainy day. Now the rainy day is come, and the supposed shelter, on which so much labour has been expended, is found to have been utterly blasted by an unforeseen economic gale. . . .

Now, that is just one side of the sombre picture. On the other side of the picture is myself solitary and alone, struggling uncheered and unappreciated; without the slightest gesture of sympathy from a great majority of the members, but with every venomous rebuke and noxious imputation from some members.

There is another belief among almost all members which is bad, and which I must take this opportunity to explode once and for all. From their talks and letters to me, I find that they look upon me as their ungrateful and unwilling debtor, while they are the benevolent, all-too-patient creditors.

This is grossly erroneous. I am no debtor to you, Sir, and you are no creditor to me either. We are only mere members of a Corporation of which I happen to be, fortunately or unfortunately, the accredited Agent with Full Powers. The business of the Corporation has failed through no avoidable act of mine.

I approached a solicitor who got a guinea out of me in order to hear an outline of my story. When I had finished, he demanded ten guineas to be paid down before he could study all the papers connected with the venture and give me a considered opinion. So it was as easy as that to make money in the legal profession! My ambition for the profession was all the more enkindled; but I must first of all get out of the financial woods in which I was. I couldn't afford to pay ten guineas, so I decided to do some research myself. There were thirty of us in the venture, and I discovered for the first time that we constituted neither a partnership in law nor a company incorporated under the Company Ordinance. Though I was appointed as its Accredited Agent, the name of the venture was neither registered under the Business Names Ordinance, nor was it used in the course of my business transactions. My confusion was worse confounded. In sheer desperation, therefore, and in answer to and defiance of my detractors, I wrote to all the members, in 1941, inter alia, as follows:

As I have told you repeatedly the business of the Progressive Economic Corporation of which you are a member had failed.

Ever since its failure, I had done all in my power to bring the Corporation to its feet again, but I was not successful.

In the course of the operation of the business of the Corporation, I have incurred a good deal of liabilities which amount in cash to hundreds of pounds. The firms with whom I did business on behalf of the Corporation have refused to grant me any more credit until the previous liabilities are made good. The War has made them more adamant than ever in this respect.

This being so, with credit facilities gone, and with heavy liabilities to meet, all prospects of ever bringing the Corporation back to its feet again are automatically gone.

In the circumstances, therefore, I cannot continue to be the Agent of a Corporation which is practically *non est*, and whose business there is no prospect of reviving.

I am therefore hereby relinquishing the post of the Agent of the Progressive Economic Corporation to which I was appointed by you and other members, and hereby repudiate all responsibility for reimbursing you for your investment which has been lost as a result of the failure of the Corporation.

As a partner with me in business, I know it is your responsibility to share with me, in proportion to your investment, the liabilities incurred in the course of the business of the Corporation. All the same, this is an important question which I do not want to decide alone until I receive expert advice on the matter. This will cost some money; and when I have the means of doing so, I shall accordingly write you again, and furnish you with all the details of the liabilities, indicating the share to be borne by each member.

And in this respect I may add that if any member feels that he is entitled to receive anything from me as Agent of the Progressive Economic Corporation, there is nothing to prevent him from seeking his remedy in Law. But in such event, there shall be nothing to prevent me from claiming in return from him forthwith his share of the liabilities of the Corporation even before I have gone through the process mentioned above.

After this, I was no longer bothered with insinuating or importunate letters from members or their solicitors; nor were the threats in the latter's previous letters put to the test. An understanding of the situation on the part of the members seemed to have crystallised, and, as time went on, my erstwhile friendship with the great majority of them (some twenty-six out of thirty) reasserted itself with a much firmer tone. That friendship continues till today. I must admit that there was something in my character which made those who were not close to me doubt that I was genuinely in business trouble. In the midst of the 'fearful odds' with which I was confronted, I remained calm and unperturbed. I even started to study afresh for the London Matriculation Examination. I took this step in order to shorten the period that would be required for passing all the examinations on which I had set my mind, if at a subsequent time I succeeded in raising money to study law. Apart from my studies, I also engaged in political, trade union, literary and social activities, as I never did before. I was Secretary of the Nigerian Youth Movement, Ibadan Branch, Executive Member of the Yaba Club, Assistant General Secretary of the Nigerian Motor Transport Union and the Secretary of its Ibadan Branch, Secretary of the Ibadan Branch of the Nigerian Produce Traders' Association, and Literary Secretary of the Wesley Guild. In Ibadan, I was the ace organiser of public lectures, debates, cinema shows, dances and soirees—all of which were designed to raise money chiefly for the Nigerian Youth Movement and sometimes for other organisations. Judging from my multifarious activities, it was impossible for anyone

to imagine that I was in serious business and financial difficulties, and that I had only recently lost all that I had previously accumulated in the form of property and possessions
under the bailiff's hammer.

Then one day in July 1959, eighteen years after I had written
the letter, extracts from which were quoted immediately above,
I came across the papers and accounts connected with this
venture. At the sight of them, I was seized with an overpowering urge to pay to each of the members—friends and non-
friends alike—what he had contributed to the business. There
was neither legal obligation nor moral compulsion upon me to
do so, but I yielded to the impulse. Accordingly I directed that
money orders be sent to each with an accompanying compli-
mentary slip in the following terms:

With the compliments of

CHIEF THE HONOURABLE OBAFEMI AWOLOWO

P.O. BOX 136,

IBADAN.

WHEN THE LORD TURNED AGAIN THE CAPTIVITY OF
ZION, WE WERE LIKE THEM THAT DREAM—PSALM 126:1

The following extracts from five of the letters written to me
are indicative and representative of the reaction of the members
of the defunct corporation to my gesture. As will be seen from
the extracts from two of the five quoted letters some members
declined to accept payment, and I had, personally or through
another friend, to persuade them to.

No. 1: . . . The Corporation died a natural death due to no fault
of your own.
    Whatever you may become today, through your own
hard work, it is most unfair to ask you to bear all the loss of
the Corporation, especially when one considers all the
sufferings you went through alone. . . .
    I must say that your willingness to bear all the loss of the

99

Corporation alone is proof of your honesty of purpose and integrity.

In conclusion I am grateful for the money you sent to me as I have forgotten everything about it. . . .

No. 2 :   I have to acknowledge receipt of the sum of £80 sent to me by you. . . . Words fail me to express my profound gratitude. It is just surprising and stupendous.

It portrays your godly mind, your clear conscience and your honesty of purpose. Ah! What a devout, honest, religious and godly man you prove to be. May the Lord help you, guide you and guard your steps in life (Amen).

No. 3 :   I received by registered post a letter addressed to me. On opening the envelope, all I found inside is a Nigerian Money Order gummed to another piece of paper. . . .

I was thrown into a big puzzle. . . . Upon deep reflection, however, it occurred to me and the suggestion was later confirmed from other directions that it is an attempt to make a refund of what was my due in the Progressive Economic Corporation of 1936–38. If this guess is correct, then it is noble, most gracious and highly creditable; and that is the measure of my thanks to you.

No. 4 :   Your memorandum with a Money Order was received, and surely, it was like a dream.

I do not expect it as I have forgotten all about it. When I discussed with my friend Mr. . . . that I wish to return it he informed me that you will not take it back.

I therefore sincerely thank you.

No. 5 :   I am fully aware of the reasons for the failure of this venture and I have never held the view that you were personally responsible for it.

In the circumstance, therefore, I find it extremely difficult to justify my conscience for accepting this money which I am convinced is from you personally as Chief Awolowo and not from any source connected with the said venture.

Normally, I would gladly accept any gift in cash or kind from any man in your exalted position, but as a matter of principle I respectfully decline, and I return herewith the sum of £22.

Throughout the years of my business struggles, there was a motto by which I was unfalteringly guided. I formulated it on

my thirtieth birthday anniversary and recorded it in my
private journal on 7 March 1939. It reads:

> After rain comes sunshine;
> after darkness comes the glorious dawn.
> There is no sorrow without its alloy of
> joy, there is no joy without its admixture
> of sorrow. Behind the ugly terrible mask
> of Misfortune lies the beautiful soothing
> countenance of Prosperity. So, tear the mask!

But I had to work patiently and dauntlessly for eight good years
before I was able to behold 'The beautiful soothing counte-
nance' behind the mask.

CHAPTER 9

IT IS A GOAL

By the end of 1942 I was completely free from the shackles with which my business debts had enthralled and cramped me. Thus financially liberated, I resolved to make a last and powerful bid for the attainment of my ambition. I set a time limit for myself. If by the time I was forty years old, I had not acquired the requisite funds to proceed to the United Kingdom to study law, I would settle permanently to a business career. That was my grand strategy, and the tactics I adopted was to launch a five-year plan for myself beginning with 6 March 1943, my thirty-fourth birthday. Only two persons knew of my plan: my wife and my great friend Mr Ernest Ikoli. Mr Ikoli really knew of the plan when it had run for some eight months. In a letter to him dated 21 November 1943, I told him that I had decided to hibernate (that is from politics) for the next four years to carry out my private plan. In that time I was going 'to make myself formidable intellectually', 'morally invulnerable', 'to make all the money that is possible for a man with my brains and brawn to make in Nigeria', and 'to acquire a profession'. 'After getting this profession,' I added, and as it turned out, prophetically, 'I should like to make more money. That may take another five years. Then I shall start a new offensive.' I accomplished my first five-year plan one year ahead of schedule, for I was called to the Bar in November 1946. My next five-year plan was fulfilled exactly within schedule. In 1951, I launched 'a new offensive' by the public inauguration of the Action Group.

As I said before, I decided on my first five-year plan on my thirty-fourth birthday anniversary. I calculated that it would cost me about £1,400 to study for three years in the United

Kingdom. I had no doubt that if all went well I could make this amount of money before the end of the first quinquennial period. But it occurred to me that I might shorten the period of waiting by raising a loan, and so I wrote the letter reproduced below to a wealthy Nigerian who is even wealthier now than he was then. He and I are today good friends but both of us have been discreet enough not to refer to the episode of this letter in any of our countless conversations and chats. He fights shy of it, I believe, and it is not my intention to embarrass him. I am reproducing the letter in full, first because it is to me of historic importance, second because it is a candid portrayal of certain aspects of my innate character, and third because it contains information which has so far not been given, but which I believe would interest those who read this book.

Dear Mr . . .
    I think it will be an exceeding saving of time and more business-like if I avoid all sweet preliminaries and go straight into the object of this letter, and say that I am writing to ask you to be good enough to lend me a sum of £1,400 (One thousand and four hundred pounds) free of interest for 12 years.
    It is a staggering figure! More staggering indeed does it become, when it is realised that I, who am asking for this loan, have nothing in all the world to give as a security for this money, excepting my good faith and my brains which again are of value only so long as I continue to breathe the breath of life!
    Nevertheless, I here proceed to outline in brief why I want this big loan from you. And I hope you will be kind enough to sacrifice some time to go through what I have to say, even though in the end you might find yourself unable to do me this grand favour.
    One great ambition of mine since my boyhood days is to be a lawyer, a politician, and a journalist, rolled into one. I cherish politics and journalism as a career; and I desire advocacy as a means of livelihood. For, you will agree with me that a politician or journalist who has no money with which to support himself and family comfortably, is like a blade which has no razor.
    Now, at one time, I was on the verge of making enough money with which I could proceed to England in order to pursue the objects of my ambition; but I suffered a twist in my fortune, and I crashed. Ever since, I have tried without success to recover lost

grounds, financially. But spiritually and intellectually, I have made appreciable advance in spite of towering difficulties, all of which have now been surmounted.

As you are aware, I have just passed the Intermediate Bachelor of Commerce Examination. Next year I am taking the Final B.Com. Examination, and I hope to pass it.

But passing the B.Com. Degree is not my goal. I hate to be a government or mercantile employee. Otherwise, there are opportunities for me here and there to get a suitable and well-paid job under government or one of the mercantile houses. As you know, however, once I become an employee of government or of a mercantile establishment, that is the end to my career as a politician and journalist. I have therefore resolved that under no circumstances will I take up such employment.

That is just by the way. I am now 34 years of age. After careful thought, I have come to the conclusion that if I could raise a loan free of interest sufficient to cover my expenses, I should go to England, this year, and within three years I should qualify as a Barrister-at-Law, and also obtain with Honours the LL.B. degree of London University in addition to the B.Com. degree. The two additional degrees apart from giving me good backing as a solicitor and advocate will help me immensely as a politician and journalist.

But where on earth could I get the money? Who in Nigeria today could give £1,400 free of interest to help his fellow men? J. Henry Doherty, Esq., of illustrious memory who did the like to many successful Nigerians is no more. But after meticulous searching, sifting and weighing, I hit upon you.

I have no doubt whatsoever in my mind that out of the bounty with which Providence blesses your grit and efforts as a business man, you can well easily afford to advance such a sum of money. I have no doubt too that as a young and progressive man you will be quite happy to give me the money for the pursuit of the project for which I desire it.

But then, could you take the risk?

That is the question. As I have said before, I have no security whatsoever for this loan. Moreover, I want it free of interest. So that you stand to gain absolutely NOTHING in the whole transaction, except *the satisfaction that by helping me to achieve my ambition you are indirectly or even directly helping Nigeria or even Africa.*

The risk becomes greater when it is borne in mind that I might die in the course of my studies or immediately after, so that, since I have no security or surety, you stand the chance of losing not only the money but also the satisfaction which you may cherish that you are contributing to the uplift of Africa. It is indeed a great risk, the greatest any man ever embarks upon.

But, this is a big BUT. BUT, if I live, as I have no doubt I will do, you will not only get your money back in full, but you will, to the end of your days, have cause to rejoice that you have done one of the most outstanding and most philanthropic acts any human being ever does.

Among other things, I shall make excellent use of the money while in England by breaking records in my examinations. On my return to Nigeria, I shall strive to be one of the foremost advocates, politicians, and writers in West Africa, and while I do all these I shall make it a point not only to pay your money back in full, but also to repay your kindness and generosity towards me in every way I can.

All the same it is a big risk! So, Sir, I like you to think seriously about it, and see if you cannot take it in the interest of a young man who has brains, industry, and determination to back his ambition, but lacks the money.

I know we have never been close friends, but I have a shrewd idea that you may take the risk and help me.

On this assumption, therefore, I proceed to the next and last stage of this letter.

I shall not require the whole £1,400 in a lump sum. To start with you will help me to pay a sum of £208. 13. 3d to the Inner Temple. I have already received an application form from this Inn of Court; and from the details forwarded, I gather that this sum of £208. 13. 3d will cover all the cost of training as a Barrister, examination fees excluded.

When I am ready to sail, you will advance me a sum of £100 to cover passage, provision for my family, and any other incidental expenses. (NOTE: If I got torpedoed on the way, you would certainly lose this £100 but you will recover the £208. 13. 3d).

At the same time you will remit to a London bank the sum of £491. 6. 9d. It is out of this amount that I shall pay the university fees for LL.B. course, and for special courses in political science and journalism, when I land in England. That is to say, the initial advance will total £800.

At the end of the first year, provided I make satisfactory progress in my studies, you will remit to the same bank a sum of £300. At the end of the second year, you will remit another £300 to the same bank. Out of this £300 per annum, I shall meet all expenses of living, buy books, pay examination fees, get books for practice when I return, and pay my return passage.

The money will remain your property in this London bank, but you will give instruction to the bank to honour all cheques from me drawn on this account.

There will be an agreement to be signed by me and yourself embodying these conditions. The same agreement will embody the manner of payment of this money by me on my return.

On my return, I shall require TWO years within which to establish a solid practice and build a good reputation. After these two years, I should commence to pay at least £200 per annum either in monthly, quarterly or annual payments. So that in SEVEN years after the first two years, I should pay back the whole sum of £1,400. That will be NINE years after my return from England. And that will be TWELVE YEARS from the time you help me to pay the first sum of £208. 13. 3d. Supposing you help me pay this in April or so this year, then I should be due to pay the whole of £1,400 by April, 1955.

Now, as you yourself will see, this is the farthest limit within which I can pay the money. It may be possible for me to pay the money within THREE to FIVE years of my return. As a matter of fact, the sooner I pay it off, the better. But it is much better to be on the safe side in a matter like this. It is no use making promises now which will be difficult of fulfilment in future. On the contrary it is better to mention a period of twelve years and pay within SIX or EIGHT years than mention FIVE YEARS and fail to pay within TEN years.

Personally, I prefer that I should fail to get the loan under these unattractive but sure conditions, rather than succeed in getting it under attractive but precarious conditions.

Now, this is all I have to say. You have my request before you, and the reasons why I make the request. It is left to you to decide whether it is worth your while to take the risk of helping me in the manner outlined above or not.

If you do me the great favour, not only myself and all that are mine, but also God and Africa will be grateful to you for ever and ever. If you do not do me the favour, I shall have no cause whatsoever to grumble or to blame you, FOR THE RISK IS GREAT.

Since this is a very selfish request, I enclose herewith a stamped addressed envelope for a reply to be sent to me under registered cover.

With very kind regards,

Yours sincerely,

(Sgd) OBAFEMI AWOLOWO.

When after about six weeks I did not receive a reply, I followed the letter up in person. The result was negative. From that moment, I resolved to fight for the next five years, if need be unaided, the long-drawn battle for raising funds to acquire a profession. I had a number of intimate friends who could help me with small sums, but what they could assemble at that time would even fall short of what was required for paying my enrolment fees to the Inner Temple.

I got another idea, and strove hard for its realisation. My efforts were soon rewarded. I was awarded a contract, towards the end of 1943, to supply the army units based in Lagos, Ibadan, Abeokuta and Kaduna with yams and yam flour. It was a profitable business, but when I judged that what I had made from this source, together with what my close friends were in a position to lend me, was sufficient to sustain me in the United Kingdom for two years as well as pay all the necessary fees for tuition and examinations, I withdrew from the contract. I was not going to take the risk of losing what I already had, in the process of trying to make more. I at once took steps to obtain passport, exit permit and passage for the United Kingdom. At that time, it would normally take a private student at least six months or even a year to get passport and all. In my case it was not so, and in any event I was not in the mood to wait for more than a month to get all the formalities through. On 8 August 1944, I went to Lagos primarily to pursue as vigorously as ever I could the steps for obtaining passport etc., and secondarily to attend a meeting of the Trade Union Congress of which I was an officer. The next day after my arrival in Lagos a friend appraised me that there was a boat sailing on 14 August 1944 for which the passage was only £24. That was much cheaper than the £98 or so which I had estimated for this purpose. This was a great saving, and I made up my mind to travel by this boat instead of by another one which was to sail some weeks later. I had only four days to make my final arrangements and to get through all the tedious formalities. I had just filled a form for an exit permit, but it was not the habit of the Nigerian Secretariat to move fast in such matters.

Nonetheless, I went into action right away. Mr Ernest Ikoli who was then a member of the Legislative Council was a bosom friend of the late Mr J. R. P. McEwen. The latter was the officer-in-charge of exit permits, and Mr Ikoli got him to take action even on a sick-bed. Mr Ikoli also accompanied me to the immigration and Elder Dempster's offices and exerted all his influence on my behalf. And it was a tremendous influence in those days, to be a Legislative Council Member, and, in the case of Mr Ikoli, to be a distinguished journalist as well. Within three hours, it was all over. I did not actually obtain my exit permit, which at that time had to be authorised by the Colonial Office, until I arrived in Liverpool. There it was handed to me on board ship before I disembarked. The great kindness which Mr McEwen had done me consisted in his giving instructions to the officers concerned to let me leave Nigeria, whilst at the same time he saw to it that steps were taken to ensure that an exit permit to enable me to land in Britain was ready for me on arrival there.

I had already taken the B.Com.(Lond.) examination in June 1944. I was confident of success, and in fact, when the result was known in February 1945, I did pass with Second Class Honours (Lower Division). When I sailed for the United Kingdom on 14 August 1944, though I had not then started the study of Law, yet I was determined to do all the LL.B. and Bar Examinations before the end of 1946. I had to make sure that I did not run out of funds before finishing my finals. My wife, who was expecting a child, assured me that with the small capital in her hands she would keep the home front contented and happy by trading.

It is I think pertinent that I should, at this juncture, say a word or two about my wife and what she has meant to me. Throughout all the changing fortunes of my life since I married her on 26 December, 1937, my wife Hannah Idowu DideOlu Awolowo (née Adelana) has been to me a jewel of inestimable value. She is an ideal wife; and I am sure she too regards me as an ideal husband. The outpouring of her love and devotion to me and to our family is exceeding and beyond words. She is a resourceful business woman; and in this regard she is a worthy upholder of the traditions of her mother (Madam Elizabeth Oyesile) and grandmother (Chief Adebowale Oyegunle) both of whom are successful women traders. The grandmother at the age of over 100 is still carrying on her business, though now on a token scale. She opens her shop regularly every day from dawn till dusk. My mother-in-law at 77 would wish to be as active as ever in business, but my wife and I have succeeded in persuading her to slow down considerably.

With my wife on my side, it has been possible for us to weather all financial storms. Because of her charm, humility, generosity and ever-ready sympathy and helpfulness for others in distress, she is beloved and respected by all our friends and acquaintances. She has courage of a rare kind—I have that too. But I am no match for her at all in her exercise of infinite patience and forbearance under all manner of circumstances. She absorbs without a word of complaint all my occasional acts of irritability. By her unique virtues, she has been of immeasurable assistance to me in the duties attached to my career as a public man. She has taken more interviews and listened to far more representations from the members of the public, than I have time, or sometimes patience, for. I do not hesitate to confess that I owe my success in life to three factors: the Grace of God, a spartan self-discipline, and a good wife. Our home is to all of us (us and our children) a true haven: a place of happiness, and of imperturbable seclusion from the buffettings of life. It is on record to my wife's credit that she never made a financial demand on me throughout my stay in the United Kingdom. Besides, she always sent me good news every week about herself and the children; but when I returned home, I learnt that she had passed through many anxious times with four children the oldest of whom was only five when I left home, and the youngest of whom arrived four months after my departure.

It is a matter for joy and profound gratitude to Almighty God that our mutual love and devotion has been richly blessed. We have five children—two boys and three girls—(1) Olusegun (son—21) now a Law student at Cambridge University; (2) Omotola (daughter—19) now studying at Alexandra College, Dublin, with a view to entering a Medical School; (3) Oluwole (son—17) now a student at Leighton Park School, Reading; (4) Ayodele (daughter—15) and (5) Tokunboh (daughter—12) both of whom are now students at St Anne's School, Ibadan.

By a special dispensation, I was allowed to enrol for the Intermediate and Final LL.B. at the same time, since there would not be sufficient time for me to enrol for the latter after passing the former. I had only nine months to work for the LL.B. Finals. I merely had a pass, contrary to my expectation. But I made up for this deficiency by passing the Bar Finals with Second Class Honours, and by beating fellow-Nigerians like Chief H. O. Davies, Q.C., and Dr T. O. Elias. Mr Justice G. B. A. Coker, also in the Second Class, was the only Nigerian who came before me in order of merit.

I began the study of law on 1 October 1944, and sat for my Bar Finals as from 3 October 1946. In the two years, I worked much harder than I ever did before. In addition to working for the two examinations already mentioned, I wrote several articles for the *Daily Service* and *West Africa* and some for the *West African Review*. For a while, I did a Fortnightly Bulletin of interest to African students, for the British Council. I also wrote *Path to Nigerian Freedom*, a book published by Faber and Faber and exceedingly favourably received by both the press and the public.

Whenever I look back on the years 1944/45 to 1946, I can never help feeling that they were my most productive years from the point of view of sheer exertions and output, matched only by my eight years of office as the Leader of Government Business and Premier in the Government of the Western Region of Nigeria.

When I was called to the Bar on 18 November 1946 as a member of the Honourable Society of the Inner Temple, I felt triumphant. At long last, the golden objective for which I had laboured without ceasing and with unflagging perseverance for upwards of twelve years had been achieved. It was a goal, scored by me in a grand style; but only after a protracted epic play against the resistant and disconcerting forces of Fate.

At the Bar, I had a lucrative practice. My average annual net income for the period of 1947 to 1951 both years inclusive was £4,300. In my five years of legal practice it was my good fortune to be numbered among the leading advocates in Nigeria. I handled, with honour to my name and praise for my professional accomplishment, a good number of complicated and, in a local sense, celebrated cases. My clients trusted me absolutely and I gave them the best possible services for their fees. I worked very hard, and among other things I developed a special technique in cross-examination. Sir James Pyke-Knott, a brilliant and quick-witted Administrative Officer in Oyo Province, Western Nigeria, and later Lieutenant-Governor of the Eastern Region of Nigeria, once paid me the tribute of describing me as 'a terrible cross-examiner'. I kept him in the box under cross-examination for two days in the famous case of Memudu Lagunju v. Olubadan-in-Council and Another. He was a very acute witness with a special skill for verbal fencing; and his evidence was of paramount importance to my case. I won the case in the Supreme Court but finally lost it in the Privy Council. No costs were awarded against my clients by their lordships. It was a great pleasure and a matter of satisfaction for me to cross swords at the Bar, from time to time, with undoubted legal luminaries like Chief the Hon. F. R. A. Williams, Q.C., Mr Justice J. I. C. Taylor, and Chief H. O. Davies, Q.C. and others. It was also my unbounded pleasure to have Chief the Hon. F. R. A. Williams in my cabinet from 1 October 1954 until 12 December 1959. When the revised Macpherson Constitution was to be introduced in October 1954, I decided to strengthen my Cabinet. I accordingly invited Chief Williams to accept the portfolios of Justice and Local Government, which offices he occupied with great distinction and to my unalloyed satisfaction. Chief Williams is a man of physically giant stature, who is worth much more than his weight in gold. He has wit, and a sense of humour which is so expansive that it leaves no room in him at all for bad temper. He has a massive capacity for hard work, and his intellectual magnitude makes him a star both at the Bar and in government.

To tell the truth, until some four years ago, I used to have a nostalgic longing for the Bar. To engage, without bitterness or animosity, in the fiercest contention; to cultivate the habit of always examining both sides of a problem, and to present the side you espouse with forensic forcefulness and assuredness; to identify yourself with your client and to enter into his feelings as if you were the plaintiff or defendant or the prisoner at the Bar; to propound and urge points of law which are sometimes difficult, sometimes not all too tenable, or sometimes so fine and abstruse that it is not at all easy to distinguish one point from another; to be utterly fearless and unsparing in combat; to acquire an independence of outlook in all things and to enjoy immunity in all you say and do at the Bar so long as it is legitimate and within the bounds of professional etiquette; to take part in fostering the cause of justice and equity in their total impartiality before the very bulwark of the citizens' liberty and individual freedom—all these and more are the inherent and distinctive attributes of a noble profession which I very much love and will for ever cherish.

CHAPTER 10

NIGERIAN YOUTH MOVEMENT

THE Nigerian Youth Movement was the first nationalist organisation ever to make real efforts to bring within its fold all the nationalists and politically conscious elements in Nigeria. The imperishable impact which this Movement made on political thought in Nigeria has never been fully appreciated. Since 1945, when the Richards Constitution was introduced, the speed with which Nigeria has sallied forth to its political destination is so fast that the older politicians of the days of the Movement tend to forget, whilst the younger breeds have been so immersed in the problems of the present and of the immediate future that they have had no time to inquire into and find out the truth about, the political happenings of the past. The result is that there is a good deal of confusion of thought on the part of most students of Nigerian politics, as well as inevitable misinterpretation of the conduct of some Nigerian political leaders. An objective study of the rise and fall of the Nigerian Youth Movement is, in my view, a pre-requisite to the proper appreciation and interpretation of the evolution and development of political ideas and parties in Nigeria since 1944. Having regard to the space at my disposal, I am doing no more here than to give an outline of this historic landmark in our political history, and to stimulate further research and study.

Before the advent of the Nigerian Youth Movement, the only well-known militant political party was the Nigerian National Democratic Party. This was founded by Herbert Macaulay in 1923. In content, the aims and objects of the Democratic Party were 'Nigerian National'; but territorially and in its membership, the party was in no way 'Nigerian' or 'National'.

Its activities were confined to the island of Lagos and its mainland, and the best of its time was consumed in fighting for the enhancement of the status of the Oba of Lagos, then known as the Head of the House of Docemo and Ado. The party was founded, run and controlled by Herbert Macaulay, who remained its General Secretary from its inception to the time of his death in 1946. 'H.M.' was, in his time, a political colossus; and all those who assembled under the shadow of his giant stature obeyed his words without question. Anything short of this was unthinkable and unacceptable to the 'Moghul'. As I have already pointed out, he was not only an uncompromising critic of colonialism and white rule, he was also a ruthless denigrator of any African who associated and was friendly with white officials. To the masses of the people in Lagos and in the southern parts of Nigeria the 'Wizard of Kirsten Hall' symbolised the irrepressible resistance of the Africans against foreign rule. To them he was a legendary figure and something of a superman. But to most of the elite and intellectuals in Lagos, who knew him intimately, he was not quite IT. 'H.M.' was by profession a civil engineer, at one time employed by the government of Nigeria. It was after he had resigned his post with the government and was practising as a licensed surveyor that he entered politics. He was later imprisoned for misappropriation of trust funds. This incident had two opposite effects: it boosted his popularity among the masses (inside and outside Lagos) who were led to believe that the charge had been trumped up in order to destroy him as a political force; but it widened the gap between him and his opponents, among whom were Sir Kitoyi Ajasa, Sir Adeyemo Alakija and Henry Carr, all of them men of undoubted integrity. These patriotic but misunderstood Nigerians could not brook Herbert Macaulay's autocracy and methods; and they saw much in his character which repelled rather than attracted them. Many a wealthy Lagosian had been led to utter financial ruin by being implicitly faithful to the causes which Herbert Macaulay championed. They were from time to time called upon to make substantial financial contributions to one cause or another. In the view of 'H.M.'s' opponents these contributions were uncalled for, and he was bluntly accused of trading on the gullibility of his unsophisticated but well-to-do adherents.

As time went on, and for the reasons just mentioned, more and more of the intelligentsia in Lagos drifted away from him. The admiration for the doughty fighter was there all right, but they denied him their political association and collaboration. Consequently when the incident which I shall relate presently occurred, the Lagos Youth Movement was inaugurated, in preference to and as distinct from the Democratic Party, as the rallying platform for mass protest. The incident was of national significance.

In 1934, the Nigerian Government inaugurated the Yaba Higher College. This institution, which was not affiliated to any British university, was to award its own Nigerian diplomas in a number of faculties, including medicine, arts, agriculture, economics and engineering. This institution was assailed by Nigerian nationalists. In the first place, it was inferior in status to a British university; and under no circumstance would an institution of higher learning which bore the stamp of inferiority be tolerated by Nigerians. In the second place, the diplomas to be awarded by the institution were also inferior, since the holders of these diplomas were only expected, in various government departments and institutions, to occupy posts which were permanently subordinate to those filled by the holders of British university degrees (mostly expatriates) in the same faculties and professions. Africanisation of the civil service had been in the air for some time, and it was believed that the Yaba Higher College was an infernal device by British imperialism to foil this legitimate aspiration. This view was further strengthened by the fact that, only five years previously, the Nigerian government had planned to introduce a Nigerian School Certificate in place and to the exclusion of the then Cambridge and Oxford School Certificates. The plan was dropped as a result of the undivided opposition to it by all the political leaders in Lagos, irrespective of their party leanings, Mr P. J. C. Thomas, Mr Eric Moore, Dr Akinola Maja, Sir

Adeyemo Alakija, Henry Carr, 'H.M.' himself and other stalwarts in the public life of Lagos, spearheaded the agitation. In the third place, the diplomas to be awarded by the college would only enjoy an inferior recognition in Nigeria and would not command any respect, much less recognition, outside the country. In the fourth place, though the diplomas were in all respects to be inferior to university degrees, the time required to do a course was longer than was the case for a university degree in the same subject. There was, therefore, widespread resentment in political circles in Lagos, and in some circles in Southern Nigeria. It was in order to canalise this resentment, and to present a united front to the Nigerian government in representing the feelings of the people, that the Lagos Youth Movement was founded by Dr J. C. Vaughan, Mr Ernest Ikoli, Oba Samuel Akisanya, and others. I remember the memorandum submitted by the Lagos Youth Movement, the Movement's rejoinder to the government's reply, and Oba Samuel Akisanya's open letter to Duse Mohammed Ali Effendi, who in his paper *Comet* had criticised the leaders of the Movement and had described them as 'half-baked critics'. All these remonstrances were analytical, constructive, scathing and crushing. In them, the Movement elaborated its reasons for opposing the establishment of the college as it was then constituted, and made suggestions for its improvement. The Nigerian government, however, persisted in going on with its scheme as originally conceived. The Lagos Youth Movement, on the other hand, continued in existence to initiate and conduct agitations against other unjust manifestations of British rule in Nigeria. In 1936, as a result of clamour from different parts of the country, the name 'Lagos Youth Movement' was changed to 'Nigerian Youth Movement'.

It must be pointed out that though the Movement was originally 'Lagos' in name, the matters which it handled were Nigerian in scope. In this connection, it must be borne in mind that up to 1936, Lagos and Calabar were the only towns in Nigeria where any group of people could presume to form, and be members of, political parties. The only organisations which were common in the hinterland were tribal or clan unions and literary societies. These were inherently non-political; but there were occasions when they addressed petitions to the powers that be on purely local political issues, or when in the guise of literary debates they criticised government actions. Lagosians and those resident in Lagos had greater freedom of expression than those in the Protectorate. Lagos was a British colony; it was then the home of the vast majority of Nigerian intelligentsia; those born there were British subjects and they, together with those who were resident there, were not amenable to native customary laws and usage. To a large extent, the British way of life was imitated and emulated. This was not the case in the Protectorate. The system of administration was indirect rule, which operated harshly to curb the articulateness of progressive Nigerians. Native laws and customs which could be fluid and arbitrary in the extreme, all depending on the whims of those who interpreted them, were the operative laws and usage.

Consequently, individual freedom was severely limited in the Protectorate. Two instances may be mentioned. When Herbert Macaulay visited Iroko in Oyo Province in 1923 in the course of his professional duties, he was given less than twelve hours on 20th February of that year within which to leave the province. The order banishing him from Oyo Province, purported to have been made by the Alafin was not revoked until 'H.M.'s' death. The ostensible reason for this order was that he had come to Oyo to do the survey of a disputed piece of land without informing the Alafin of Oyo or the Bale of Ibadan. But the real reason was because he was a political agitator. The following extracts from I. B. Thomas's *Life of Herbert Macaulay* on this episode are of interest. The scene was the interview between 'H.M.' and Captain W. A. Ross who was then Senior Resident, Oyo Province.

Mr Ross: Good afternoon Mr Macaulay; I am surprised that you should have come up to this Division to make a survey of a 'divisional boundary' without informing the Alafin of Oyo or the Bale of Ibadan. They are both very angry about this. . . .

Mr Macaulay: I am indeed sorry. But I have not come up here to survey the 'divisional boundary' between Ibadan and Oyo but to make a survey of the territorial area of Iroko Land with reference to a dispute between the Oniware and the Oniroko, the Fiditi boundary and Ijaiye boundary with Iroko. Had I been told it was the 'Divisional Boundary' of Ibadan Province, which it is not, I should not have come up as that would be the work of the Official Surveyor.

Mr Ross: But you see, Mr Macaulay, you have a bad reputation, indeed an unsavoury reputation as *an agitator*, and we are a peaceful and prosperous people here. We have been here 20 years and there has been no trouble. Where we have had trouble, and even blood-shed, the cause had been traced down to Lagos; and the Isehin trouble was also traced to Lagos, you see.

Mr Macaulay: Having such a reputation is most unfortunate, sir. But I do not think the causes you have traced down to Lagos as you say, sir, were traced to me?

Mr Ross: No, not to you, Mr. Macaulay, but you have been saying and publishing a good many things when you were in England.

Mr Macaulay: Certainly not about Ibadan, sir? And I do not think you can recall one single article, . . . ever written by me about Ibadan.

Mr Ross: Well the Alafin of Oyo has decided you should leave his territory.

Mr Macaulay then withdrew, and he left Ibadan with his men, tent, and things before midnight, arriving in Egba Territory at Adio at 2.45 a.m. on Wednesday the 21st February, where he joined the Lagos train at 8.50 a.m. to Lagos.

For writing an article commenting adversely on the Ibadan Library, I was, one fine morning late in 1935, summoned before the Ibadan Inner Council of Chiefs. The new library was the creature of the Senior Resident, Oyo Province, Mr H. L. Ward-Price who succeeded Captain Ross.

Mr Ward-Price was very proud of the library, and all Ibadan chiefs and dignitaries had been brought there to witness the opening ceremony. For a number of reasons which I gave in my article in the *Nigerian Daily Telegraph*, I thought that the public library, if it was worthy of that name at all, was un-becoming a city of the size and importance of Ibadan. Mr J. G. Kelly, who was acting for Mr Ward-Price when the article was written, closed down the library after the publication of my article. In due course, however, the precincts of the library building were overgrown with weeds and elephant grass, and the signboard on which the words 'Ibadan Library' were written just managed to exceed the grass in height. I then wrote another article in which I pointed out that visitors to Ibadan, on seeing a signboard marked 'Ibadan Library' in the midst of weeds and elephant grass, and in front of a small abandoned building, would be compelled not only to doubt our literary taste, but our sanity as well. Mr Ward-Price had returned to Ibadan when this second article was published. He himself was present at the Inner Council Meeting. He told the chiefs (all of them old and illiterate people) that I had insulted them by making impudent comments on their library, and that it was left to them to deal with me as they pleased. The chiefs were indignant (or at least they feigned to be), and I was asked to appear before them the following morning at 10 o'clock. I knew what that meant. If I went, I would for a certainty be pilloried in the presence of the large crowd which usually fore-gathered at Mapo Hall when the chiefs were in attendance there, and might be sent to gaol summarily for contempt of the Ibadan Native Authority into the bargain. I, therefore, took certain steps to forestall them, or at best to make sure that those who mattered in the enlightened politics of the country knew what had happened and was going to happen to me. Immediately on my return from the Inner Council, I wrote the full story of the incident, sent a copy to the Resident himself, and sent copies to the editors of all the Nigerian newspapers, to legislators in Lagos, to Sir William Geary, Bart., a popular British lawyer who was a strong critic of British rule in Nigeria, and to Oba Samuel Akisanya, then General Secretary of the Lagos Youth Movement. I telegraphed a summary of the story to the newspapers and to the same people, and urged them to view the matter with grave and urgent concern as it involved the fundamental issue of freedom of expression by an individual, and indirectly of the liberty of the press as well. After I had des-patched a copy of my story, I learnt that Mr Ikoli, Editor of the *Nigerian Daily Telegraph* and Executive Member of the Lagos Youth Movement, was in town. I went to see him and told him all about it. He was to have an interview with the Resident shortly after. He seized the opportunity to tell the Resident his mind about the steps that I had taken, and what action he proposed to recommend to his colleagues on the matter. As a result the Resident contacted the present Olubadan of Ibadan, Oba I. B. Akinyele; Archdeacon Latunde, and Chief Akibiyi, and requested them to intervene and dissuade me from pursuing the action which, he understood, I had already initiated. I was prepared to do so provided the decision of the Inner Council that I should appear before them the following day was revoked. After a meeting in the afternoon of the same day at the old Ibadan Grammar School premises with the important personages mentioned, I wired to those I had contacted to inform them that the matter had been amicably settled.

Notwithstanding the restraints on individual freedom, however, many people in the West and in the East, were courageous enough to move to the periphery of the political arena loudly to cheer the gallant fighters, and, as time went on, to take part in the fight themselves. The North was indifferent to what was going on. It was only the Southerners resident there that cared to give support for what was being done in Lagos.

When the Lagos Youth Movement became the Nigerian Youth Movement, branches were founded in urban areas in different parts of the country—East, West, and North—save that membership of the Movement in the North was confined to Southerners. The first and perhaps the only Northerner ever to enrol as a member of the Movement was one Mallam Jumare. He was a teacher in a Middle School in the North; but he lost his job for his political courage. He later became in 1942 the Under-Secretary of the Movement at the Lagos Headquarters.

The 'Nigerian Youth Charter' which embodies 'The Official Programme of the Nigerian Youth Movement' is a political document of far-reaching historical importance. Even though it was published in 1938, the charter can hold its own side by side with the policies and programmes of the major political parties in Nigeria published in recent times. The best way, in my humble opinion, to do justice to it and to clinch the points I want to make later, is to reproduce some extracts from the Charter:

THE PRINCIPAL AIM—The principal aim of the Nigerian Youth Movement is the development of a united nation out of the conglomeration of peoples who inhabit Nigeria. It shall be our endeavour to encourage the fullest play of all such forces as will serve to promote complete understanding and a sense of common nationalism among the different elements in the country. We will combat vigorously all such tendencies as would jeopardise the unifying process. While pursuing this great principle with consistency as its chief aim, the Movement declares itself, in its short-range policy, as a constructive critic of the Government as at present constituted. That criticism it offers in a spirit of constitutional opposition. It shall also work for the removal of inequality of economic opportunities as well as for the correction of those abuses which militate against the cultural progress of our people in Nigeria. The Youth Charter will therefore be divided into three sections, namely, the Political Charter, the Economic Charter and the Cultural and Social Charter.

THE POLITICAL CHARTER—The goal of our political activities is a complete autonomy within the British Empire. We are striving towards a position of equal partnership with other member States of the British Commonwealth of Nations. . . .

The Movement aims at the abolition of property or income qualification for the exercise of the franchise and the substitution of universal suffrage. We believe that every person within the community has the inalienable right to representation and should be given a vote. We will therefore press forward for a vote for every person in Nigeria who is above the age of 21. . . .

For better and more satisfactory administration of justice, the Nigerian Youth Movement believes that a complete separation of the judiciary from the executive is absolutely necessary. For this end the Movement pledges to work. The Movement will also advocate and press for more use to be made of Nigerian barristers for judicial and legal appointments. . . .

THE ECONOMIC CHARTER—We pledge ourselves to demand for our people economic opportunities equal to those enjoyed by foreigners. We will therefore strive for the economic progress of our people and oppose all forms of privileges. In fact, we will urge on the Government to protect our people against unequal competition, if necessary, by legislation. This aim of ours is co-terminous with the avowed principle of trusteeship that where our interests clash with those of foreigners in this country, it is the duty of the Government to see that ours prevail. . . .

We pledge ourselves to encourage and to support all forms of local industries. It shall be our duty to protect all Africans in industry and to resist every attempt by foreigners to oust them out of the field. . . .

The economic and physical welfare of the African workman in the employment of industrial firms is our concern. We will work consistently for the steady amelioration of such welfare. We shall demand for him better wages and better conditions of service. It is our duty to champion the good cause of the labourers employed under the railways, at the docks and workshops of the Government, at the colliery at Enugu, at the tin mines of the Bauchi plateau and on the gold fields.

The Movement therefore stands for a reasonable standard of living among the labouring classes in this country as it firmly believes that under-nourishment is a direct effect of the extremely low wages now being paid.

We will strive for the better regulation of the conditions of work for the mining labourers so that they may obtain better wages and better compensation in case of accidents and better relief in case of illness due to their work. . . .

We stand for

(1) better pay for Africans in the civil service—particularly in the clerical and less subordinate branches;
(2) more higher executive appointments for Africans within the service;
(3) more use being made of Africans in forming the personnel of the administrative branch of the service.

We are opposed to all discriminative emoluments within the service as between Nigerians and Europeans. We believe that salaries should be attached to the work done and not to individuals and that the criterion of selection should be nothing more than ability to hold the job down. . . .

We will advocate a careful compilation of the cost of living and the equation of the minimum pay of Junior Clerks to that cost plus a margin. Such margin will encourage thrift and efficiency. . . .

CULTURAL AND SOCIAL CHARTER—We believe that mass education ought to be the true pivot of the educational policy of our Government. We will therefore urge on the Government to make elementary education progressively free and compulsory. . . .

GENERAL—The Movement in general will interest itself in all affairs which make for the political, economic and cultural progress of Nigeria. It will co-operate with all bodies whose aims and aspirations are similar to its own. It aims at establishing branches throughout Nigeria and integrating both the branches and the affiliated bodies into a central executive in Lagos.

The Movement has never been more convinced of the justice of a cause than it is of its aims and objects. It has the highest hopes of success and looks forward to co-operation from all sections of the community.

Up to 1943, the Nigerian Youth Movement pursued the policy and programme adumbrated in its charter with unabated vigour and consistency. Wherever and whenever national duty called, it was there to respond. There was no iota of tribal taint in its programme, nor was there any in its mechanics for effectuating it. It fought unremittingly for the Africanisation of the civil service, and for the abolition of discriminative practices against Africans which were then rampant in the governmental and commercial life of the country. There were in government certain posts generally known as 'European posts' which were rigidly closed to Africans, no matter what their academic or experimental qualifications. Banking and commercial houses were prepared to give credit and preferential treatment to the most infamous non-African alien, which were denied to Nigerians. The Movement combated the Cocoa Buying Agreement, otherwise known as the 'cocoa pool' with all its might. Mr Ernest Ikoli and Oba Samuel Akisanya did a comprehensive tour of the cocoa-producing areas in order (1) to rouse the producers to the danger of the situation, namely a combine on the part of European cocoa-purchasers deliberately to depress the price of this commodity; (2) to persuade them to adopt the policy of a 'hold-up' of their produce as was done in Ghana; and (3) to secure their support for the abolition of the 'pool'. It stimulated the organisation of trade unions, and as far back as 1940, it demanded a national minimum wage of 2/6d per diem for daily paid workers. It is on record that the Nigerian Railway Union and a number of other unions not only received advice from the leaders of the Movement as and when they liked, but also owed the drafting of their constitutions and rules to the Movement's Executive Committee. When the rumour gained wide currency in political circles in Nigeria in 1938 that Neville Chamberlain was planning to transfer Nigeria to Hitler as part of Britain's appeasement policy, the Movement quickly organised a mass meeting at the race course in Lagos to make a protest and to demand a categorical and unequivocal denial of the rumour. The rumour was promptly denied by the Colonial Secretary; though it was authoritatively stated in some circles that Chamberlain did in fact attempt to transfer Nigeria to Hitler as a sop to the Nazi Cerberus.

Also when Colonel Oliver Stanley visited Nigeria in September 1943, the Movement was the only organisation which submitted to him a memorandum of a comprehensive nature and national importance. This memorial was prepared by a committee of the Movement consisting of Mr Ikoli (as Chairman), Chief H. O. Davies, Chief S. L. Akintola and myself (as Secretary). In it, the Movement demanded, among many other things, (1) 'that definite pronouncement should be made as regards the rights of the Colonial peoples to be brought within Clauses 3, 4, 5 and 6 of the Atlantic Charter'; (2) that government should 'guarantee for the African workers a reasonable standard of living'; (3) that 'the government ought to find money for free education'; (4) that government should 'create 200 annual scholarships for the brightest students in Nigeria to study abroad . . . in all branches of studies, e.g. agriculture, industry, commerce, science and arts'; (5) that government should 'introduce measures to enable the peasant population to derive maximum benefit from the land'; (6) that government should 'formulate and carry out plans for ensuring that within five years, free medical facilities will be made available to all men and women throughout the country'; and (7) that 'as a first step in training for self-government, and as proof of sincerity on the part of (British) government', African ministers 'who will be directly concerned with the formulation of government policies, should be appointed by the Governor from among the members of the Legislative Council as Heads of these Departments: Agriculture, Public Works, Education, Health, Information, Rail and Road Transport, Commerce and Industry, and Labour.'

Furthermore, the Movement always gave full and unreserved backing to any agitation which aimed at fostering the political advancement of the people or the enhancement of their economic and social status. In respect to the one, its members were to be found in the vanguard of political and administrative reforms all over the country. The 'indirect rule' system was under fire here and there, and the autocracy and tyranny of the Administrative Officers did not escape caustic censure. The Ibadan branch of the Movement fought successfully in 1940 for the wider representation of the people on the Outer as well as the Inner Council of the city. I was the Secretary and the chief spokesman of the Ibadan branch throughout the agitation for this reform. In regard to the other, there are two important agitations with which I was connected. They were fully backed by the movement. The first was against what was called 'double licence fee' and the second against the 'palm kernel ban' of 1940. Strangely enough, certain aspects of the first are topical even today.

In the early thirties, the Nigerian railways were being run at a loss. The government laid the blame for the regular deficits of the railways at the door of motor transporters who were accused of unfair competition, and it decided that such competition should be discouraged. Accordingly, the traffic regulations were amended so that any lorry plying between areas from which the railways normally procured its traffic would pay double the licence fee imposed on other lorries. This 'double licence fee', which was intended to act as a check on road-rail competition, was applicable to specified routes throughout the country. When I became a motor transporter in 1936, I inspired the Nigerian Motor Transport Union to intensify its agitation against the iniquitous system. Oba Samuel Akisanya, who was then an employee of Messrs Joe Allen & Co. Ltd., but closely associated with the Motor Union, gave us constant guidance. At a meeting of the Ibadan Branch of the Nigerian Motor Transport Union held on Sunday, 3 January 1937, I successfully urged that we should refuse to obtain licences for that year, and that we should go on strike in order to impress upon the government that we were in earnest in our agitation, and that we were not going to allow our business to be sacrificed on the altar of a grossly mismanaged railway system. The day of the strike was fixed for 7 January 1937, provided I succeeded in persuading the other branches concerned to agree. On 4th and 5th January, I headed a mission to Ile Ife, Ilesha, Oshogbo, Ijebu Ode, Abeokuta and Lagos. At this stage four entries in my diary are relevant:

January 4, 1937: *Monday:* I went to Ile Ife, Ilesha and Oshogbo on the mission of the STRIKE. I was successful there too after storming some drastic opposition. M. J. Sumola accompanied me throughout.

January 5, 1937: *Tuesday:* I go to Lagos today via Ijebu on the mission. I hope I shall succeed again.

On my return from Abeokuta I made a record as follows:

I met Lagos representatives there [that is, at Ijebu Ode] at T. Odutola's. The opposition by Ijebu Ode was fierce against Ibadan, but I succeeded in storming and breaking it. . . .

January 6, 1937: *Wednesday:* Arrangements were made for the strike which is to commence the following day. I spent many hours at Union's office at Bere [in Ibadan].

January 7, 1937: *Thursday:* THE GENERAL STRIKE [so we called it]. It has been dead at one time [that is to say it had been proposed at one time and dropped; that was before I became a motor transporter and member of the Union.] but I revived it.

126

If it is successful, I shall regard it as the most glorious achievement in my life—so far.

The strike lasted six days only. But it had scarcely started when several attempts were made to break it by mercantile houses which were badly hit by it, and by some blacklegs who were aliens and who were in the transport business in Nigeria. It became necessary for us to mobilise all available forces to our side. We approached Herbert Macaulay, Dr the Hon. C. C. Adeniyi-Jones and Sir Adeyemo Alakija for help. We were thoroughly let down by Herbert Macaulay. At first he gave us support; but when he learnt that we had also enlisted the assistance of Sir Adeyemo Alakija, he was enraged, drove us from his house, and threatened to break the strike. He then wrote an article in his paper calling upon the government to enact a law making strikes illegal. There had not then been any law in Nigeria regulating the establishment, or the affairs and the working of trade unions. The first Trades Union Ordinance was enacted in 1938; but before then there had been two strikes: the one now under discussion, and a one-day strike by the railway workers.

The following entries in my diary speak for themselves:

January 8, 1937: *Friday:* We went to Lagos and discussed several aspects of the strike. We left for Lagos 6.10 a.m. and returned to Ibadan at 9 p.m.—about. All our men were firm and resolute. Offer was made by X [a European firm] to increase freight to £1 a ton each way—Lagos Road.

January 9, 1937: *Saturday:* This day was successful. Agbaje [Chief Salami Agbaje] informed us of the same offer of increased freight to and fro Lagos. Y [another European firm] broke our rule and ran their lorries under police escort.

I phoned Akisanya and received report of Alakija's and Jones's interview with the Chief Secretary. I also wired Times [that is, the *Nigerian Daily Times*] to cable their London representative to publish news our strike in the English press.

We organised patrols for the affected roads in order to do picketing and to prevent any attempt by blacklegs to make the strike fail. I was in charge of the Ibadan-Lagos Road and

Ogunpa motor park. In the course of my assignment I came into clashes with high-ranking police officers. Of the Commissioner of Police I recorded on 7 January 1937, as follows:

The Commissioner of Police was hostile in the morning but calmed during the afternoon. Commissioner interviewed. I phone Akisanya.

When lorries belonging to European and other alien firms began to ply the affected routes under police escort, there was dismay amongst our people. My own attitude was that this business of police escort could not continue indefinitely, and that if we persevered we would win. But it became clear that the strike could no longer be sustained and we had to call it off. I was very much grieved by the failure of the strike, and I did so record as follows in my diary:

January 13, 1937: *Wednesday:* THE END OF THE STRIKE: It is simply ignominious, shameful, and most humiliating. If I could find tears I would weep. But I must confess my ineffable grief.

When I penned the above remarks, I little realised that the strike had been a success, though then unknown to us. The 'double licence fee' was operative only for the year 1937. It was abolished as from January 1938, and the railways were still in a bad way financially.

In 1940, the Nigerian Government imposed a ban on the export of palm kernels from the western provinces of Nigeria. The ban was imposed, we were told, because Britain had no need for the palm kernels exported from Nigeria. The ban was, however, limited to the Western Provinces only because the people of the West had other export commodities to fall back on, whilst the same was not the case with the Eastern Provinces which depended almost wholly on oil palm produce. This government measure was contrary to a categorical statement made by Sir Bernard Bourdillon on 3 September 1939, giving assurance to producers of palm produce that there was an unfailing market for their products. The relevant portion of the statement reads:

The British Government at home will want all the produce it can get from this country—such as palm produce, groundnuts, cotton, etc.—and the prices of these are likely to rise. Every farmer will find that it will pay him to grow more and more of them, and however much he grows he may be certain of a market and feel that he is doing what he can to help win the war.

Furthermore, the points were made and quite cogently (1) that considerable sections of the western provinces (Ijebu, Benin, Warri (now Delta) and part of Ondo and Abeokuta provinces which relied almost wholly on palm produce) would be hard hit by the ban, and (2) that even in cocoa-producing areas there were hundreds of thousands of people who relied only on palm produce as their cash crop, and who would be gravely distressed by the ban. Mass protest meetings were organised by me in Abadan, under the auspices of the Ibadan Branch of the Nigerian Produce Traders' Association of which I was Secretary. The *Daily Service* conducted a vigorous campaign against the ban. The Nigerian Produce Traders' Association wrote to the Chief Commissioner, Sir Gerald Whiteley, asking for an interview. He decided to meet the peasants themselves at Mapo Hall, instead of meeting the representatives of the union in his office. He was obviously under the impression that the mass of the peasantry in Ibadan did not feel much concern about the ban. The gossip in official circles was that the whole agitation was being artificially engineered by produce buyers, aided and abetted by the leaders of the Youth Movement. I suggested to the union that we should reduce our representations into writing and get leading farmers to sign the document. This was agreed. We were to meet the Chief Commissioner at 10 a.m. at Mapo Hall on Thursday, 22 August 1940, and I was requested on the 20th of the same month to prepare the farmers' case for submission to him. I worked on it all night and this is what I recorded in my diary on 21st August: 'Sleep at 2 a.m. this morning when I finish writing the Giant Petition against the ban on kernels.'

Over 10,000 farmers attended the Mapo Hall meeting convened by the Chief Commissioner. When the petition was read in English and interpreted into Yoruba, there was dead silence. But no sooner did the Chief Commissioner open his mouth to reply than there was pandemonium. He was rather garrulous and self-righteous in the way he spoke. If we had been under German rule, he said, they (the Germans) would have refused to buy any of our farm products; and even if they bought any they would have refused to pay for them. Besides, he had made a slip when the petition was being read. He declared that the statement to which I have referred, and which was also quoted verbatim in the earlier portion of the petition, was untrue. He challenged the petitioners to produce an authentic copy of the statement. There was a tense period when I left the hall to fetch the printed copy of Sir Bernard Bourdillon's speech in which it was contained. I returned in due course and handed the relevant publication to the Chief Commissioner with the portion in question duly underlined. When he admitted the correctness of the disputed statement, there was an uproarious applause for me; and the mass of farmers no longer wanted to believe anything the Chief Commissioner said. On Sunday, 25th August, at his invitation, I met the Chief Commissioner in his office. He accused me in very provocative terms of having written an inflammatory petition for people who were mostly illiterate. He reminded me in a solemn tone that it was a serious offence to write in that manner, particularly in wartime. I was truculent in my reply and I told him that the petition had been submitted by the farmers themselves, and he had no right to go behind the signatures to identify the writer. He piped down; and we then had a cordial discussion which lasted fifty minutes.

A delegation of the Nigerian Youth Movement consisting of Mr Ernest Ikoli, Chief H. O. Davies, Oba Samuel Akisanya and myself later met His Excellency the Governor, Sir Bernard Bourdillon, on the same subject. With the Governor were the members of his Executive Council. The Chief Secretary to the government was very unreceptive. 'You had better forget about your palm produce; it has no future,' he declared. All the same, not long after this interview the ban was lifted.

The irony of this ban was that about six months after it had been lifted, a gargantuan campaign was launched throughout the country for the maximum production of palm kernels. They were urgently needed, we were again told, for the quick dispatch of Hitler and his army. There were numerous posters published by the government showing how a bunch of palm fruits fell upon and killed Hitler. Indeed, that man was right who had said that foresight is not one of the national attributes of the British people!

Before I end this chapter, I would like to make certain observations which I consider to be pertinent. The Nigerian Youth Movement was, to all intents and purposes, a vigilant, dynamic and selfless nationalist organisation. It lived up to and worked for its declared objectives and ideals, and spared no pains in fighting to uphold them. By its intrepid and enlightened leadership, it emboldened agitators in the country, regardless of where they lived, to speak their minds and damn the consequences. It provided a unique platform for the unification of all the diverse ethnic groups that constitute Nigeria, and a forum whereon all conscientious and right-thinking Nigerian patriots and nationalists could unfold their ideas and display their talents for the common good. The credit for the genesis of political awakening throughout the country, and of fostering this awareness without the slightest appeal to tribal or ethnic sentiments, belongs alone to the Nigerian Youth Movement. When Dr Azikiwe returned to Nigeria in 1937 he merely strengthened the leadership of the newly emerging Nigeria. Dr J. C. Vaughan, Mr Ernest Ikoli, Oba Samuel Akisanya, and Chief H. O. Davies had already lighted the flame of the new era of nationalism. They took Nigeria for granted, and so did those of us that faithfully followed them. All organisations with which the Nigerian Youth Movement or its supporters were connected, no matter where founded and no matter what the composition of its membership, bore the nationalist stamp 'Nigerian'. With his *West African Pilot*, better produced and better run, and enjoying much wider circulation than its forerunners the *Nigerian Daily Telegraph* and *Lagos*

Daily News—the anti-imperialist campaign which Herbert Macaulay had begun years before, and the new nationalism which the Nigerian Youth Movement had initiated in 1934, were conveyed in cold print to all the literate sections of the public throughout the country.

The fact that in the leadership of the Nigerian Youth Movement there were more Yorubas than those belonging to other ethnic groups was an accident; and it was in fact not noticed as a strange or undesirable phenomenon until 1941. Under the constitution of the Nigerian Youth Movement, supreme authority was vested in the Lagos Branch which was the Parent Body. Officers and executive members elected by the Lagos Branch alone, therefore, constituted the Central Executive of the Nigerian Youth Movement. It was only to be expected that in the pre-war Lagos community, where there were very few non-Yorubas who cared to take part in politics, and that those Yoruba professionals and merchants with an almost obsessional urge for politics should predominate in the ruling hierarchy of the Nigerian Youth Movement.

CHAPTER 11

TWILIGHT OF THE GODS

WHEN Dr Azikiwe returned to Nigeria in 1937 with his ideas about new nationalism and New Africa, one of three choices was open to him for the concrete realisation of those ideas: to join the Nigerian National Democratic Party (NNDP) and expand the territorial influence and activities of that party to other parts of Nigeria outside Lagos; to enrol as a member of the Nigerian Youth Movement (NYM); or to start a new political party or nationalist movement of his own. He chose the second, and became a member of the Nigerian Youth Movement. He was at once elected into the Central Executive Committee of the Movement. For a while—a very short while indeed—he proved to be an asset to the Nigerian Youth Movement. He was one of the famous, volcanic nationalist quartet: Mr Ikoli, Oba Samuel Akisanya, Chief H. O. Davies and Dr Azikiwe. Whenever these four were billed to speak at any public meeting in Lagos—and it was always in Lagos—there was a tumultuous stampede to get a seat or a vantage place. The Nigerian Youth Movement was already popular with the masses before Dr Azikiwe's return. But he brought with him a propaganda technique which was new in politics and journalism in Nigeria, and which further boosted the popularity of the Nigerian Youth Movement and disarrayed its opponents. Little wonder, therefore, that in opposition to the veteran NNDP the NYM won in 1938, and in a resounding manner, all the three Lagos seats in the Legislative Council, and all but one of the elective seats in the Lagos Town Council. But apart from the role which he played in these two electoral battles, it was Dr Azikiwe who delivered a succession of blows—now subtle, then hard and heavy, but always accurate and harmful —which, aggravated by a series of bungling and mismanagement on the part of some of its leaders, brought about the fall and the ruin of the NYM.

Dr Azikiwe caused many ears to prick up at the discordant note which he sounded when the campaign for the Lagos Town Council election in 1938 was at its peak. Oba Samuel Akisanya was one of the NYM candidates and the only one who lost among them. Most of the Ijebu Remo people resident in Lagos were opposed to his candidature, because the Odemo had sided with Ijebu Ode when the people of Ijebu Remo had demanded separation from the latter. The Remo opponents of Oba Akisanya used the *Nigerian Daily Times* as their medium of attack. Two or three letters to the editor had been published in the paper. Then one morning the paper carried an item of news that a flood of letters had poured into the Editor's office opposing the candidature of Oba Samuel Akisanya. On the afternoon of the same day, Chief H. O. Davies paid the Editor, Mr Bates, with whom Dr Azikiwe was in a state of journalistic war, a surprise visit. He demanded to see the 'flood of letters'. Mr Bates was embarrassed, and was only able to show him some three letters in his tray which were awaiting publication. Whereupon Chief H. O. Davies told him that it was neither accurate nor honest to describe three letters as a flood. Mr Bates who, because of his conflict with Dr Azikiwe, was an object of detestation in Nigerian circles, tried to exploit Chief H. O. Davies's visit in his own favour. He carried a news item the day after Davies's visit simply mentioning the fact but omitting the purpose of the visit. Chief H. O. Davies promptly explained the purpose in a statement published in the *West African Pilot*. Nevertheless, Dr Azikiwe wrote an editorial in his paper in which he referred, with disapprobation, to this visit, and described Chief H. O. Davies as a simpleton. To me, this open abuse and rebuke of a worthy colleague and compeer cut very much against the grain. It was quite out of tune with the spirit of comradeship and mutual respect which was expected to dominate the leadership as well as the followership of the NYM. At another time, he created more than a tremor throughout the rank and file of the movement when he wrote editorials in the *Pilot* calling upon the Government not to appoint Sir Adetokunbo (then Mr) Ademola a magistrate, as was then strongly rumoured. His ground for this action was that Sir Adetokunbo had not then had the statutory post-call experience. When the appointment was in fact made, he criticised it on the same ground. This act of his was in diametric opposition to the movement's policy of Africanisation of the civil service and the judiciary.

By the end of August 1940, I was certain in my own mind that Dr Azikiwe was not a conscientious member of the Nigerian Youth Movement, and that, for some reasons best known to himself, he was bent on destroying this nationalist organisation. At the same time, it seemed clear to me that his policy was to corrode the self-respect of the Yoruba people as a group; to build up the Ibos as a master race; to magnify his own vaunted contributions to the nationalist struggles; to dwarf and misrepresent the achievements of his contemporaries; and to discount and nullify the humble but sterling quota which older politicians had made to the country's progress. Other incidents which happened thereafter merely went to strengthen my beliefs.

After the 1938 elections, the NYM and some of its leaders were projected in the *Pilot* in an unfavourable light. Statements, articles and reports inimical to the interests of the NYM, and derogatory of its leaders were accommodated on the pages of the *Pilot*. There were three instances of this which I considered to be disloyal. During the currency of the rumour that Neville Chamberlain was negotiating to transfer Nigeria to Hitler, Mr O. A. Alakija wrote an article in the *Pilot*. In it he said that Nigerians had accepted Britain not as a conqueror but as a protector. If she was no longer capable of performing that role, she should quit and Nigerians would then either protect themselves or invite some other nation to protect them until they were able to stand on their feet. The Nigerian government thought that this article was offensive and inflammatory. The

Chief Secretary, therefore, invited Sir Kofo Abayomi and Mr Alakija, at different times, in order to tell them so. Sir Kofo Abayomi was said to have made certain remarks when he spoke to the Chief Secretary at which the other leaders of the Movement, including Mr Ikoli, Oba Samuel Akisanya, Chief H. O. Davies, Dr Azikiwe and Mr O. A. Alakija took umbrage. A meeting was held at the house of Sir Kofo Abayomi to thrash out the matter. True enough it was a stormy meeting, but it was all done in secret. Only very few members of the Movement knew about it. Then to the horror of everybody there was a front page banner headline in the *Pilot*—'YOUTH MOVEMENT TOTTERS.' A garbled story of this behind-closed-doors affair was then told. Another instance. There was a bye-election in 1940 to fill a vacant seat in the Lagos Town Council. It was a straight fight, as before, between the NYM and the NNDP. Oba Samuel Akisanya was the candidate of the NYM; but Dr Azikiwe launched an all-out attack against him on the pages of the *West African Pilot*. The things that were written about Oba Akisanya are too crude for reproduction here. Yet another instance. When the NYM was founded, it published a quarterly journal which was its official organ, entitled *Service*. It had been hoped that in due course this journal might be published monthly or weekly. With the advent of Dr Azikiwe, *Service* was abandoned, and the NYM placed complete reliance on the *Pilot* for the propagation of its ideals and for the defence of its cause. Most of the leaders of the Movement soon discovered, however, that if the ideals of the Movement were to be widely disseminated and unflinchingly defended, some medium other than the *Pilot* must be invented. It was, therefore, decided to convert *Service* into a daily paper to be known as the *Daily Service*. Dr Azikiwe was still a member of the Central Executive Committee of the NYM when this decision was taken. But he lost no time in criticising it openly. Chief H. O. Davies, who was appointed by the Movement to tour the country in order to solicit shares from members and supporters of the Movement, also became the victim of scurrilous and damaging attacks in the *Pilot*.

We were used to 'H.M.'s' calling certain people imperialist agents. These people were re-christened by Dr Azikiwe 'imperialist stooges', 'Uncle Toms', and 'Auntie Jemimas'. So far so good; but as time went on, he added on to this list of 'Uncle Toms', etc., the names of people whose patriotism and nationalism had never been in doubt. You only had to disagree with him on any issue, however minor, and you at once qualified to go on the black-list. At the same time, he skilfully lauded himself to the very skies. Almost every day there were letters to the Editor, published in the *Pilot*, eulogising Zik for doing this, that and the other new and hitherto unknown and unheard-of good things for Nigeria, 'nay, Mother Africa'. Some of the writers acclaimed him as the 'Gandhi of Africa', whilst others declared that certain things that he had said, written, or done, had 'elec-zik-ified' them. These epistolary panegyrics were apparently written by persons who were dying to see their names in print. They got the desired publicity, and in due course more and more of them competed with each other in the game of 'Gandhisation' of Zik and 'elec-zik-ification' of themselves. Whatever any one may say about Dr Azikiwe, it will be readily conceded to him that he was the first consummate propagandist that Nigeria produced. He observed neither modesty nor reck in inflating his own ego or in deflating that of his opponent. In this connection he is in the direct line of succession to Herbert Macaulay, whom Dr Azikiwe has claimed to be his journalistic and political father. But like all sons who are worthy of their parentage, he is greater than his 'father' in this particular respect.

When the agitation against the 'cocoa pool' was raging, though the *Pilot* carried one or two articles and reports on the subject, Dr Azikiwe himself showed no interest whatsoever. Also when the ban on palm kernels was imposed, the *Pilot* supported it. Said the *Pilot*:

. . . the measure by the Government is fair. Instead of reducing the whole country into poverty, only the Western Provinces will be affected and they can switch over to other avenues to make body and soul live.

As a result of his indifference to these two economic crises, which threatened the livelihood of the people of the Western Region as well as the economy of the country as a whole, some of us began to wonder what Dr Azikiwe's 'economic determinism' really meant in practice. In other circumstances, Dr Azikiwe would have dipped his pen in gall, as was his wont, and on the pages of the *Pilot* under his own name or in the editorial column, would have denounced the 'cocoa pool' as an 'imperialist device or stratagem whose aim, object or purpose was to oppress, repress, depress and distress Nigerian cocoa producers and dealers economically'. In the same manner, he would have vehemently declaimed the ban on palm kernels in the Western Provinces as 'a gross betrayal of trust; an indelible stain, blemish and stigma on British imperialism; a vain attempt, a complete misfire and a palpable boner in the realm of divide et impera.' (The words in quotation marks were not exactly Dr Azikiwe's, but they are typical of his early style.) If the man could not go out and campaign against those unwelcome government measures, he could at least write in his paper in support of the agitators. He did not.

An article written by Zik himself, published on the front page of the *Pilot*, and entitled: 'Football Iliad, 1940 Edition', shocked many people. It was a big step forward in an insidious campaign which had gone on for more than two years on the pages of the *Pilot*. A football team composed of students of the Christ the King's College, Onitsha, came to Lagos to play a 'Win the War' football match against St Gregory's College. The CKC team from Onitsha defeated St Gregory's team by 5 goals to 4. To the ordinary man in the street, let alone the highly sophisticated elements, there was nothing extraordinary or unusual in one school or college defeating another in a game of soccer. But not so with Dr Azikiwe. He saw in the sporting exploits and triumph of the team from Onitsha the inherent superiority of the easterners over their opponents, and he went to very great pains to establish this fact, by means of careful choice of words and emphasis. These extracts from the article are relevant:

And then to think of the great combination of the Spartan heroes who crossed the lordly Niger, journeyed through the good earth of Benin, hurried across the domains of the Oshemawe of Ondo, of the Atanla of Owo, of the Owa of Ilesha, of the Oni of Ife, of the Alake of Abeokuta in their invasion of these islands!

Who, but heroes of mighty brawn and exceptionally developed brain would have dared to make this invasion and to succeed in carrying to their River Niger home, the Golden Fleece of Inter-Collegiate Soccer Championship of the Eastern and Western Provinces?

Yet they came to Lagos, they saw the irresistible defence put up by their opponents, and they conquered impressively, convincingly, and were graceful even in victory!

Could their achievement be paralleled?

Would it not be better for me to leave the answer to the laps of the gods?

On 24 August 1940, however, the same CKC team played in Ibadan against the Olubadan XI in another 'Win the War' match. The CKC were beaten 3–2 by the Olubadan XI which were an undiluted Yoruba team. Apart from sending the news to the *Daily Service* myself, I also saw to it that it was wired to the *Pilot*. It was after there had been clamours in the *Daily Service*, in form of letters to the editor, that the news of this Ibadan match was published some two weeks later in the *Pilot*. Even then, it was a small item on the back page, and it was explained in it that the CKC team were already tired and that some of them were in fact limping, before they went into the field against Olubadan XI. This was of course untrue.

I said before that the CKC episode was a big step forward in an insidious campaign which had gone on for more than two years on the pages of the *Pilot*. One or two more instances will be given. By the time the *Pilot* had published for a year, an important feature of the paper had become manifest. The Ibos in particular were given inordinate publicity on the pages of the paper. Perhaps this was as it should be. The Ibo had never had a share in newspaper publicity before the advent of the *Pilot*. But equally so, no Yoruba man of the class of the Ibos publicised in the *Pilot* ever had a share of publicity in any paper either. In those days one had to be an outstanding politician, a big shot in society, or a well-connected person, for one's name to appear in the *Nigerian Daily Times, Nigerian Daily Telegraph* and *Lagos Daily News*. Of course if you had a friend working in the news or composing section of a paper, no matter who you were, you might be slipped in. Names of people like myself appeared in the papers simply because we were agitators or free-lance journalists. All the same, it was generally agreed that the Ibos needed all the boosting they could get.

But Dr Azikiwe went about it in a manner which disgusted those of us who were used to describing citizens of Nigeria as Nigerians or Africans, and regarding their achievements as reflecting credit on Nigeria, indeed Africa, as a whole. The following are typical of the titles of front page news items and of editorial articles in the *Pilot*.

1. 'Ibo Young Man to Sail to U.K.' is the heading of a front-page story and picture on September 23, 1938. The young man is Mr Jaja Wachuku, now Speaker of Nigeria's House of Representatives.
2. '14th West African Student, 10th Nigerian, 8th Ibo in U.S.A.' Another front-page story on January 28, 1939. The 8th Ibo is Mr Nwafor Orizu, now Senator in Nigeria's Upper House.
3. 'Ibo Medical Student Passes Exam In First Class Honours.' Yet another front page story, on June 26, 1940, of the brilliant success of Dr S. O. Egwuatu.
4. Editorials:
   (i) 'A Model Union' (August 8, 1938) in praise of the Ibibio State Union.
   (ii) 'One Year Ago' (August 18, 1938) celebrating the first anniversary of the call to the Bar of the first Ibo lawyer, in the person of Mr Justice Louis Mbanefo, now Chief Justice of the Eastern Region High Court.
   (iii) 'The Ibo Are Coming' (December 31, 1938)—The very title is sufficiently indicative of the contents.

These are but a few examples of the publicity given to Ibos as a group. But as against these, the achievements of Yorubas and, in particular, the academic laurels of their scholars received, if at all, inconspicuous notice in the *Pilot*. When an

Ibo did or was about to do something praiseworthy, he was invariably given a two-column headline and report in the *Pilot*, and was always described by his ethnic origin in the headlines. But when the Ph.D. degree of London University, indeed of any university for that matter, was conferred on the first Nigerian ever, the historic news was given a small single-column space in the *Pilot*, and the headline read: 'Nigerian Economist Passes Ph.D. London.' The scholar concerned was Dr Fadipe, a Yoruba. As late as 1945, two Nigerian law students of Cambridge University, one Yoruba and one Ibo, passed the Law Tripos Examination. The Yoruba passed with second class honours (upper division), and the Ibo also passed with second class honours but in the lower division. The latter got front page publicity in the *Pilot*, but the former got a small space given to him on the back page a few days after the report of his Ibo colleague had appeared. As for outstanding Yoruba public men, they were all of them daubed as 'imperialist stooges' and 'Uncle Toms'.

Apart from failing to give publicity to the achievements of the Yoruba, and holding their public men to obloquy, the *Pilot* always made sure that all their misdoings received due publicity. As many of the unsavoury aspects of Yoruba life as its news-gatherers could muster received banner headlines in the *Pilot*. In contrast to this, care was taken to ensure that any misdoing of the Ibo was kept out of the newspaper. Whenever a non-Yoruba name was mentioned in the *Pilot* in connection with a trial or conviction for a crime, meticulous care was taken to indicate the tribe of the accused or convicted person. Not many people then and now could differentiate an Ibo name from an Edo name or Ijaw name for instance. So, in order to make assurance doubly sure that the reading public were not misled into thinking that an Ibo man had been mixed up in any reported ugly business, a non-Yoruba name was invariably correctly identified by its tribal origin.

The examples given in this chapter are only a small fraction of suchlike numerous acts perpetrated by Dr Azikiwe. A stage was reached when even his apologists felt very strongly that, for over two years past, Dr Azikiwe had been consistently conducting himself in a manner which was not only antiparty and contrary to the noble ideals of the Movement, but also unnationalist, tribalistic and egocentric. Accordingly, at a meeting of the Central Executive Committee held in September 1940, a decision was taken that a letter should be addressed to Dr Azikiwe inviting him to appear before the next meeting of the Central Executive Committee fixed for Monday, 7 October 1940, to show why his membership of the Movement should not be determined. Three of us were co-opted from the branches to attend this meeting: Senator Chief T. A. Odutola (the Ogbeni Oja of Ijebu Ode) who was Chairman of the Ijebu Ode Branch of the Movement; Chief J. O. Kashimawo, Secretary, Abeokuta Branch; and myself from Ibadan Branch. The meeting commenced at about seven in the evening and continued till well after midnight. It was one of the best attended meetings of the Central Executive. All the powerful batteries of the Movement in Lagos were there: Dr Akinola Maja, well-known nationalist and philanthropist, and Chairman of the Board of Directors of the National Bank of Nigeria Limited; Mr Ernest Ikoli; the Hon. H. S. A. Thomas, then First Lagos Member in the Legislative Council; H. A. Subair, Esq., Manager of the National Bank of Nigeria; Alhaji Jibril Martin, a lawyer of fortune and one of the pioneers of Muslim education in Nigeria; Ogugua Arah, Esq., a fire-eating nationalist from the east; Oba Samuel Akisanya; Chief H. O. Davies; Olympus Luther, Esq., an orator with Oxford accent; J. A. Ojo, Esq., a master at King's College, solid in physique, slow of speech but agile in wits; and so on and so forth. But because of the prevailing circumstances they all proved that night to be batteries with dry cells.

When the decision was taken to invite Dr Azikiwe to the meeting, three persons (Akisanya, Ojo and Luther) were charged with the duty of assembling all the facts which supported the indictment against Dr Azikiwe of disloyalty to the cause and ideals of the Movement. These three persons were also to lead the case against Dr Azikiwe at the meeting. After the September meeting and before October 7, the Hon. Olayimika Alakija, Third Lagos Member in the Legislative Council, elected in 1938 on the platform of the Movement, died; and the date for a bye-election to fill his place had been fixed. All those who aspired to be candidates as well as many of those who thought that Dr. Azikiwe's co-operation was indispensable to the Movement's victory at the bye-election, developed cold feet at the meeting. Mr. Ikoli, who presided, started by assuring Dr Azikiwe that he had not been brought before the Executive Committee as an accused person. Leaders of the Movement were puzzled about a number of things about which they required explanation from him. They had no doubt that he (Dr Azikiwe), as a loyal member of the Movement, had good reasons for everything that he had done.

'What!' I did not know when this exclamation escaped my lips; and of course all the pacifists were startled. As for Dr Azikiwe, he cast a deadly glance at me. I then whispered to my comrades from the Provinces (I sat between Senator Odutola and Chief Kashimawo). 'So, this is the way this awful business is going to be handled. Amazing—they are already satisfied that the man is a loyal member of the Movement. Then why this mockery?' Dr Azikiwe sat close by the three of us, and his ears no doubt caught some of my words, but at that stage he showed no reaction. Dr Maja and one or two others spoke in support of Mr Ikoli. Then Dr Azikiwe begged to be allowed to say a few words; but he actually spoke for about two hours! He had nothing against the Movement as such or its ideals which were indeed noble, and which were being sincerely 'practicalised'. But he had been offended by some leaders of the Movement personally, particularly by Chief H. O. Davies and Oba Samuel Akisanya. I interrupted and heckled him a number of times in the course of his long statement. Once he asked the Chairman to warn 'the comrade from Ibadan' to desist from interrupting him. This request evoked a warning in these words: 'Comrade Awolowo, please!' I kept quiet, and spent some time in scanning the faces of our leaders at the meeting; and their reaction was unmistakably one of sympathy, or

143

pretended sympathy, for Dr Azikiwe. I was compelled to ejaculate 'Incredible! What is now happening? An accused turned prosecutor!! The simple truth is that the man is disloyal to the cause and he should be told so.' Dr Azikiwe quickly rejoined that I was one of the victims of H. O. Davies's propaganda against him, that I had slandered him by describing him as a disloyal person (the word I used that night was much stronger than 'disloyal'), and that unless I withdrew my remarks, he might be compelled to take legal action against me. 'Legal action, my foot!' I retorted. 'He speaks as if he is going to be both plaintiff and judge. Besides, I most vehemently resent the suggestion that I am one of the victims of H. O. Davies's propaganda. I am 31, and I am old enough to make up my own mind on any issues of the day.' Mr Ikoli then said that he really must appeal to me to stop all these interruptions. They would do nobody any good. I remained silent for the rest of Dr Azikiwe's speech. But I must confess that all that he said was a palpable affliction to me. He wound up his speech by saying that in view of the incompatibility between him as a person and the persons he had mentioned, he had no alternative but to tender, there and then, his resignation from the Movement. As soon as Dr Azikiwe resumed his seat, there were volleys of appeal to him from different sides of the meeting, begging him to withdraw his resignation.

I spoke, and recounted some of the doings of Dr Azikiwe which amounted to a breach of faith on his part with the Movement, and a deliberate subversion of its ideals. It appeared to me most strange and utterly indefensible that a person with Zik's education and professed political beliefs should seek, by subtle devices, to destroy the only nationalist organisation in the country, simply because, as he had just said, of personal differences between him and some members of the Movement. I felt sure, I added, that the man had some ulterior motives for his conduct. I urged that he should be expelled that night. If we continued to harbour him in the Movement, he would eventually destroy it.

'That is not the temper of this meeting, Comrade Awolowo',

144

said a number of voices. And in reply I said: 'What then is the temper of the meeting? Condoning indiscipline and disloyalty? I strongly press for the expulsion of this man before he grows too monstrous for us to cope with.'

Chief Kashimawo spoke, criticising the past conduct of Dr Azikiwe, but was silent as to whether he should be expelled or not. Senator Odutola also spoke. He opined that all the confusion and tribal hates that were then rearing their heads in the country were the products of Dr Azikiwe's 'New Africa'. 'During the days of our "Old Africa",' Chief Odutola remarked 'the Ibos and Yorubas lived together as Nigerians. It seems to me, therefore, that the remedy for the present troubles is this. Azikiwe has brought his "New Africa" from America. He should return it there either by post, or by taking it back there personally. If need be, his passage to and fro should be paid by the Movement. But mark this,' he concluded, 'unless this Azikiwe's brand of "New Africa" is done away with there will be no harmony in this country.'

Further appeals were made to Dr. Azikiwe by the Lagos leaders, and he withdrew his resignation. Thereupon, it was agreed that some leaders of the Movement should meet with Dr Azikiwe at the Bar Beach, Lagos, in order to ensure a complete rapprochement, and work out a concerted plan for an electioneering campaign for the approaching bye-election. I was not invited to the Bar Beach meeting, which I understood was held over tea-cups 'in an atmosphere of the utmost comradeship and cordiality'.

Alhaji Jibril Martin was selected as the Movement's candidate for the bye-election. He was preferred by the Movement's selection meeting with 90 votes to Maja's 87, Davies's 86, Ikoli's 80, Akisanya's 68 and Azikiwe's 33. Before this time, and for five years afterwards, Dr Azikiwe had always protested that he did not wish to seek election into any colonial legislature, but would rather content himself with being a 'king-maker', until Nigeria was free from foreign rule. It would appear from his subsequent conduct, however, that he did not like his defeat at this selection. For in spite of the settlement of the night of October 7, and of the cordial tea-party at the Bar Beach, he allowed Dr C. C. Adeniyi-Jones to make use of the pages of the *Pilot* to open very devastating broadsides against the Movement and its candidate. All the same, Alhaji Jibril Martin won the bye-election.

Early in 1941, the seat held by Sir Kofo Abayomi as Second Lagos Member in the Legislative Council was declared vacant, because of his long absence from Nigeria. He had gone to the United Kingdom at the time to do a specialist course in ophthalmology. A general meeting of the Lagos Parent Body was convened to select a candidate. I attended the meeting; but being a provincial branch member I could speak, but had no voting right. At the commencement of proceedings, Mr Ikoli who had only just been elected President of the Movement for the year, declared his desire to contest the bye-election. That declaration, in my view, settled the matter, and there were many who shared this view. In 1938, the Parent Body took a decision of policy that where the President expressed his intention to contest any election, he should automatically be selected. The result of this policy was that though there had been three seats to be contested in 1938, only two were open to members of the Movement for nomination, since the President Sir Kofo Abayomi had expressed his wish to stand as a candidate. I cited this precedent in my speech at the meeting, and argued that it would be unfair and inconsistent to depart from it. There was a long and heated debate on this point, and eventually it was defeated by a narrow margin. The meeting then proceeded to the selection which resulted in 108 votes for Oba Samuel Akisanya, 60 for Mr Ikoli and 37 for Dr Maja. After they were known, the meeting decided that the results should, as on previous occasions, be referred to the Central Executive Committee which, in its discretion, would decide whether to affirm or vary them. The following extracts from a report and an editorial in the *Pilot* of 11 and 12 October 1940 respectively, concerning the nominations for the 1940 bye-election very neatly set out the established and accepted procedure:

OCTOBER 11 : The Executive Committee of the Movement will consider these nominations and report to the general meeting its decision on the choice of actual candidate to contest the bye-election.

OCTOBER 12 : It is understood that the Executive Committee of the Nigerian Youth Movement will be held, tonight, when the final selection will be made from the six names nominated by the general meeting.

The Executive Committee met in due course and varied the decision in favour of Mr Ikoli. Oba Samuel Akisanya, who had also just been elected Vice-President of the Movement, was present at the meeting of the Executive. He congratulated Mr Ikoli on his selection, and assured him of his support. The Odemo's friends, however, were not satisfied with the decision of the Executive Committee. When a general meeting was convened to announce Ikoli's candidature to the members, therefore, these friends, mostly Ijebus, turned up in large numbers. I was there too—'all the way from Ibadan.' The announcement of Ikoli's candidature was not well received. But the Odemo himself got up and spoke congratulating his friend and colleague and promising his fullest support in the ensuing campaign. He was cheered. When the meeting adjourned, all the leaders of the NYM were happy that an eve-of-election crisis had been averted. But we were all mistaken. For when nomination for the bye-election closed, it was discovered that Oba Samuel Akisanya was standing as a candidate against Mr Ikoli. On 20 February 1941, the *Pilot* carried the sensational news of this fact, and also the equally sensational news that Dr Azikiwe had resigned from the Movement. The following extracts from the front-page story in the *Pilot* are of interest and importance. They set out Dr Azikiwe's reasons for deserting the first truly nationalist organisation in Nigeria:

The political cauldron which had been seething since the Vice President of the Nigerian Youth Movement opposed the candidature of the President of the N.Y.M. for the March bye-election assumed another aspect yesterday.

Mr Nanmdi Azikiwe has tendered his resignation from the Movement. It will be recalled that on the eve of the last bye-

147

election to fill the seat of the Third Lagos Member, 'Zik' offered to resign from the Movement, in view of disagreement of views and methods between him and two officers of the Movement, but he was advised by an overwhelming majority of the members of the Executive Committee to withdraw his resignation, which he did.

On that occasion 'Zik' explained how he had lost materially and otherwise, as a result of the election campaign of 1938, for the political support which his business gave the Movement, only to be told in the end that its aid, if any, was inconsequential.

He asked that his letter should be accepted as his resignation from the Movement and he hoped that 'Our Movement (may) live long and make worthwhile contributions towards the crystallization of a new Africa'.

Several efforts were made to get Oba Akisanya to step down, but they were abortive. There was a general meeting which broke up in disorder, and there was a special 'peace meeting' presided over by the Rev. I. O. Ransome-Kuti. It lasted for twelve and half hours, from 5 p.m. to 5.30 a.m.; there was no break for dinner. This too did not avail.

The stand taken by the pro-Akisanya group was that Oba Samuel Akisanya had laboured much for the NYM and was overdue for rich reward, and none could be more appropriate and befitting than his election to the Legislative Council. Reference was made to two previous incidents. Before the 1938 General Election, he was on the verge of being nominated when a non-member of the NYM, the late Olayimika Alakija, had been brought in by his influential friends in the NYM to supersede Oba Samuel Akisanya. In the Lagos Town Council general election of the same year, he was deliberately assigned to the most difficult ward where his colleagues knew he would fail. The pro-Ikoli elements, of whom I was one (and I was dubbed a 'firebrand' for the uncompromising stand which I took), made a telling reply. No one had laboured more than Ikoli in the cause of the NYM in particular or of the Nigerian nation in general. He had had a promising career before him at King's College, but he abandoned it in order to devote his full time to the service of his country. He was more than overdue for rich reward and, therefore, more qualified than Oba

Akisanya for nomination to contest the bye-election. With regard to the 1938 General Election, both Ikoli and Oba Akisanya were in the running for nomination, and it was anybody's guess who of the two would have been nominated if Mr Olayimika Alakija had not been pitchforked into the fray at the last moment. It was untrue to suggest that Oba Akisanya was deliberately assigned to a hopeless ward during the LTC General Election.

At this juncture, I would like to say something about the character of Oba Akisanya. He is one of the most courageous men on earth, with a touch, in those days, of the reckless. He is self-confident to a fault, and because of this he is sometimes accused of being conceited. He was a crowd-puller and a tub-thumping orator, with a sense of the dramatic. Whenever he was going to address a mass meeting, he would carry tomes and tomes of books in his armpits, and might even hire young persons to help him to carry those he was unable to carry himself. The impression he sought to create was that he was going to make citations from all these books in the course of his address. More often than not, he never even made a single reference to the books. But on his entry into the hall with all these documentary impediments, he automatically evoked thunderous and prolonged applause, with shouts of 'Saki!' 'General Saki!'

He it was, confident of his popularity, and of his ability to fight and win in any ward in Lagos, who volunteered to pitch his tent against the formidable Dr C. C. Adeniyi-Jones. He did so in order to ensure that the NYM did not lose a single seat. How could it be said, therefore, that he had been made cannon-fodder in the 1938 LTC election? Above all, Ikoli was the President, and as such he had expressed the wish to contest the election. Furthermore, in accordance with established and indubitable practice he had been selected by the Executive Committee in preference to Oba Akisanya.

When all efforts at settlement failed, the battle was joined in earnest. The bye-election was fought by both sides in a fiendish manner. I moved almost permanently to Lagos during the period of electioneering. I was one of the speakers at the first campaign meeting of the Movement at Campos Square. For my speech at this campaign meeting, I was called names in the *Pilot*. 'All The Way From Ibadan' was the title of an editorial article in the *Pilot* devoted to me alone. In a number of articles which I wrote for the *Daily Service* on the election, I made a fitting retaliation. Chief S. L. Akintola, Chief H. O. Davies, Mr Ikoli and others also made very sharp thrusts and counter-thrusts. At first the *Pilot* made it appear that 'if either contestant plays the game according to the rules of the game, this news-paper will *not* take the initiative, so far as acts of aggression are concerned.' But it added a rider in this vein: 'But if there is reasonable ground to believe that one of the contestants had descended to play a "dirty" game, indeed, this newspaper will go to the rescue of the victimized politician and will reserve to itself liberty of action, as it sees fit . . .' (Editorial: 21 February 1941). This was of course a mere cloak for the vicious campaign which Dr Azikiwe and the *Pilot* later conducted in support of Oba Akisanya. What was heart-rending to many of us was the element of tribalism which was introduced into the campaign with a view to swaying the minds of the people in sympathy for Oba Akisanya and embittering them against the Movement. The candidature of Oba Samuel Akisanya had been rejected because he was an Ijebu, declared the *Pilot*. And the Ijebus naturally felt outraged, and went all out to fight in defence of the good name and prestige of their tribe. I knew it was not true that Oba Samuel Akisanya had been rejected because he was Ijebu. The view that eventually prevailed at the meeting of the Central Executive was that since Ikoli was the President of the Movement, and he had expressed a wish to contest the only seat at the bye-election, it was improper that any other officer or member of the Movement should come into the run-ning at all. If Ikoli was good enough to be number one man in the Movement, he was also good enough to represent that organisation in the Legislative Council. I strove hard to per-suade the Ijebus that they were being deceived, but in vein. I stood firmly by Mr Ikoli to the end, and he won.

On polling day, March 5, I was extremely depressed and

agonised by the unabashed demonstrations of tribalism which I witnessed. All the Easterners, particularly the Ibos, and all the Ijebus in Lagos, teamed up with Dr Azikiwe and Oba Samuel Akisanya; and all those who dared to disagree with them were openly abused, jeered at, and condemned as traitors. For the first time in my life I was called a traitor and 'Uncle Tom', all because, on principles which appeared to me sound and just, I supported an Easterner against my own tribesman. But of course Ikoli is an Easterner with a difference—he has never stooped to worship at the shrine of Dr Azikiwe. When the polls closed, I was in front of the Glover Memorial Hall. There I was surrounded by a large number of Ibos and Ijebus who were abusing me, and were raining curses and imprecations upon me. At first I replied to them in kind one after another, but I was soon overwhelmed. Some of them threatened to assault me. It occurred to me that discretion lay in my extricating myself from the hostile crowd. At the same time, I did not want to give the impression that I was running away; so I stood my ground, come what may. Then, like a *deus ex machina*, Senator Somolu, at that time a member of the editorial staff of the *Pilot* and a very good friend of mine, appeared. He was greeted with broad smiles by all my maledictors. He approached me and we engaged in conversation. The crowd were nonplussed, and for the nonce left me alone. I then took him along with me until I got clear of the crowd. I said goodbye to him and went my way. Before we parted, Senator Somolu left me in no doubt that Oba Samuel Akisanya, alias 'General Saki', was winning. As I wended my way to Apongbon Street, the headquarters of the Movement and of the *Daily Service*, I felt a sense of wrong and grief. 'So, this is New Africa!' I mused to myself. When I reached the front of the African Church Cathedral, Broad Street, Lagos, I stopped, closed my eyes, and made a resolution. It was the eve of my thirty-second birthday, and I said within me: 'If the Movement lost this election, I would never again fight in the cause of truth, principle or right. But if we win, I solemnly vow to the God of my Heart that wherever the fight

151

is thickest and fiercest in the cause of truth, principle, justice and right, there I will always be. So Mote It Be.' I then opened my eyes and proceeded to Apongbon Street. I was over-joyed when I heard that Mr Ikoli had won. But it was the last electoral battle and the last electoral victory of the Nigerian Youth Movement.

With the exit of Dr Azikiwe and Oba Samuel Akisanya from the Movement, all the Easterners excepting a handful of non-Ibo intellectuals, and most of the Ijebus, left the organisation. It was futile to preach the Movement and its ideals to the Ibos or Ijebus after this incident. The Movement was a Lagos affair, they would argue, and its leaders who were mostly Lagosians had contempt and hatred for the people from the hinterland. They would therefore have nothing further to do with them. This campaign of Lagosians versus the rest spread like wildfire. The branches of the Movement in the Provinces died out as a result, the only survivors being Ibadan and Abeokuta. Loyal members, mostly Lagosians, in different parts of the country tried, in their individual capacities, to keep the flag of the Movement flying, but they did not succeed in keep-ing branches as such alive. The campaign against Lagos and Lagosians was so effective that, for a long time afterwards, any organisation which originated in Lagos was suspect, and shunned by people in the Provinces. 'I will have nothing to do with those Lagos people,' many a person would say. 'They are too proud and self-seeking.'

Nevertheless, the Ibadan Branch of the Movement launched a revival crusade. Apart from regular branch meetings, we organised public lectures, debates, cinema shows and dances, and soirées. At one time, we invited Herbert Macaulay to give a lecture under the auspices of our branch. I went to see him personally. He was willing but unable to come to Ibadan because, as he maintained, the order banishing him from Oyo Province was still in force. At another time, we invited even Dr Azikiwe to deliver a lecture. He wrote a nice letter, declining the invitation on the ground that he was very busy. But during the same week as we wanted him to give a lecture on our platform, he visited Ibadan on what he described as a 'good-will tour' and delivered a public lecture under his own auspices. In the bid to revive Ibadan Branch, we succeeded immensely; thanks to the active support of a number of nationalist intellectuals of western and eastern origin who were then resident in Ibadan. Most of them are now holding key posts in the governments of the Federation, and I will, therefore, not mention their names. But the name of the Hon. Okoi Arikpo can be mentioned. He was as active as any of us. We were all determined to nip in the bud any attempt by anyone to introduce tribalism into our national life. After the 1941 election, the Ibadan Branch emerged as the most virile unit of the Movement, so much so that in relation to the Parent Body in Lagos we were described as the tail that wagged the dog.

We did not content ourselves with merely running a successful branch. We also wanted the revival which had taken place in Ibadan to spread to other parts of the country. We were strongly of the opinion that the first step in this direction was for Lagos to cease to be the so-called Parent Body, and to convert to an ordinary branch. The second step was to create Regional Executive Committees and devolve authority to them. If this were done, the members of the Central Executive Committee would no longer be selected from among those resident in Lagos only, but would be drawn from different parts of the country. Furthermore people in the hinterland would have the assurance that the Movement was also theirs, and the organisation of the Movement would be all the more efficient. To this end, we suggested that the Representative Council of the Movement should be convened to make the requisite amendments to the constitution, to elect the new Central Executive Committee, and to stimulate the emergence of regional bodies. We were cognizant of the fact that the Representative Council would not be truly representative of all the diverse peoples that inhabit Nigeria, but steps would have been taken to the knowledge of all (1) that supreme authority in the NYM was no longer the monopoly of Lagos, and (2) that members in each of the Regions could exercise final authority over their internal affairs. I spearheaded this agitation for the reform of the NYM; but in vain. There were some people in Lagos who believed that Lagos was the alpha and omega of political sagacity and wisdom, and that only those who lived within its confines should essay to lead the country. Chief H. O. Davies was one of them. He stoutly opposed our proposals for reform. He was even much slower than the other members of his school of thought in realising that Lagos was not Nigeria. As late as January 1950, he wrote an article in the *Daily Times* in which the following passage occurred:

Realities of the existing situation demand a frank recognition of the fact that leaders of opinion—politicians, professionals, labour leaders, teachers etc.—are today strongly concentrated in Lagos and that this position might well remain for many a long day. Lagos, therefore must be represented strongly in the Central Legislature. So that she may lead the rest of the country, not only in domestic affairs, but also international relations. I, myself, believe that it will be a pity if the genius of the country is stultified by narrow representation of Lagos in the Western Region.

I believe that he wrote another article in similar vein, in a rejoinder to which Chief Rotimi Williams criticised him for thinking that one Davies was equal to more than one Balewa.

When efforts to bring about a reform in the constitution of the Movement seemed abortive, the Ibadan Branch inaugurated a Western Region Conference of the Movement in 1942. The purpose was to use the conference, partly as a platform for rallying the remnants of the members of the Movement in the Western Provinces; partly as a suitable medium for stimulating revival in areas represented at the conference; and partly as a forum for the ventilation of views on some matters of national interest. This 1942 Regional Conference, of which I was organiser and Secretary, was a huge success. It was well attended, it lasted for two days (28 and 29 November), and the subject-matters of the resolutions passed thereat include the following:

(1) Abolition of Sole Native Authority Institutions;
(2) Democratisation of Native Authority Councils;

154

(3) Native court reform;
(4) Appointment of Nigerians as Administrative Officers;
(5) Introduction of free primary education in Divisional Head-
    quarters throughout Nigeria; and
(6) Health of school-children.

After the 1941 bye-election, the Parent Body lost heart,
became listless, and its leaders failed to grasp the nettle as they
should. Even when we in Ibadan took the initiative and made
proposals for reform we were given the cold shoulder. As if
the departure of Oba Akisanya with his followers from the
Movement was not a serious enough loss, Chief H. O. Davies
also left the management of the *Daily Service* and the General
Secretaryship of the NYM, to become a civil servant as an
Assistant Marketing Officer. We of the Ibadan Branch were
shocked. When the news that he was going to accept a government appointment first reached us, I dismissed it as fabrica-
tion by the enemies of the Movement. It was too much for me
to believe that the Davies I knew could be lured into the civil
service at that juncture in our nationalist struggles and in the
life of our great Movement. He was a remarkable man with
many distinguished accomplishments: a brilliant scholar and
writer; a fearless and resourceful nationalist; the sole author
and genius of the 'Youth Charter'; a dazzling theoretician who
propounded one new idea after another with such rapidity that
he was later written off by most of his colleagues as an unstable
visionary. I went to see him in Lagos, and I was acutely distressed when he confirmed the news.

Two events then followed which rocked the Ibadan Branch
violently. First, without any consultation with the surviving
branches, the Central Executive Committee declared amnesty
for all members of the Movement who were expelled because
of their support for Oba Akisanya during the 1941 bye-
election. The reason given for this action was that the amnesty
was designed to bring back within the fold of the Movement
those who had left with Dr Azikiwe and Oba Akisanya. I was
so upset by this decision that I felt in honour bound to tender
my resignation from the Movement at once. All the other

officers (excepting the Chairman) and members of the Ibadan Branch Executive followed my example. Our resignations were not accepted, and we were persuaded to withdraw them, on the definite understanding that an early step would be taken to look into our grievances as a branch. On 29 August 1943, representatives of the Lagos Branch including Dr Maja, Mr Ikoli, and Chief Akintola met us in Ibadan. In a meeting which lasted nine hours we stated our case to which Lagos spokesmen replied. In the end, it was agreed that the amnesty should be withdrawn forthwith, and that our proposals for reform should be put into effect without delay. Chief H. O. Davies remained the genius behind the Movement in Lagos. Though he was no longer the General Secretary, he continued to hold the reins of that office firmly in his hands through the agency of his faithful supporters, two of whom at different times occupied the office of General Secretary. It turned out that all the General Secretaries sponsored by Chief H. O. Davies did not possess anything like the calibre of their predecessors. For instance, the General Secretary in office at the time of Colonel Oliver Stanley's visit to Nigeria was not considered fit to be in the committee which prepared the memorandum submitted to the Secretary of State. In fact the incumbent at the time would have had a feeling of alarm and trepidation if he had been asked to serve on such a committee. Above all, it was Chief H. O. Davies who, through his agents, obstructed the implementation of the agreement reached at Ibadan on 9 August 1943. I now came very much to detest the tactics of the man whom I once adored. Some extracts from my letter of resignation dated 22 July 1943, addressed to the then President, Dr Maja, read as follows:

I have read with a mixture of sorrow and disgust the Nigerian Youth Movement Bulletin which was published in the *Daily Service* of today, granting amnesty to the 1941 traitors.

With all due deference to you and your Executive, I regard this decision as a most misguided and stupid act. It is even worse than all that. It is a shameless exhibition of lack of moral courage on the part of the leaders of the Movement in Lagos.

These people to whom you now grant amnesty were expelled

in 1941 for very good reasons. They flouted the authority of the Movement, outraged the principles for which the Movement stands, and vigorously and ruthlessly attempted to wreck the whole foundation and structure of the Movement. These people, as far as I know, have shown no signs of regret, penitence or contrition for their wicked acts. If they had, it would have been a different matter, and I would have joyfully joined those who recommend their re-admission. But since they remain unrepentant, it is more than outrageous to grant them amnesty without due consultation with the feelings and opinions of those who have stood loyally by the Movement all along the line. It is exactly like one of the Allies making a separate peace with the common enemy. . . . And I have no doubt in my mind that History will pronounce on those who are responsible for this amnesty the same verdict as is pronounced on Vichy France and the King of Belgium.

If we must re-organise the Movement, by all means let us. But we need not start to do so by going, like the dogs, back to our vomits. . .

The second incident consisted of a series of petty squabbles and intrigues among the leaders in Lagos, which disintegrated what was left of the Movement there, and damped our ardour in Ibadan. The following resolutions which were passed at the Western Regional Conference of the Movement held in Ibadan in 1944 speak for themselves, and give a clear picture of the mood and temper of those in attendance (I was also the organiser and Secretary of this Conference):

At the Second Session of the Western Regional Conference held at Ibadan from Friday January 14th to Sunday January 16th inclusive, 1944, the manner in which the Lagos Headquarters has up-to-the-present administered the affairs of the Nigerian Youth Movement is examined and found not only unsatisfactory but also most detrimental to the existence of the said Movement; it is therefore resolved that a vote of no confidence in the Lagos Executive is hereby passed, and that henceforth, the Lagos members of the Nigerian Youth Movement be regarded as constituting one Branch only of the Nigerian Youth Movement; it is further resolved that, forthwith, a Circular Letter embodying this resolution be sent round to all Branches of the Nigerian Youth Movement asking each Branch to send two delegates to a Representative Council to be held in Lagos during the Easter Week April 8, 9 and 10, 1944, for the purpose of reframing the constitution of the Movement and appointing a Central Executive for the better management and efficient administration of the Nigerian Youth Movement.

Resolved that Comrade the Rev. E. A. Odusanwo, M.A., etc. be empowered to set up a Provisional Committee, the terms of reference of which shall be:

(a) To conduct the affairs of the Nigerian Youth Movement during the interim period of reorganisation.

(b) Prepare a Draft Constitution which will be placed before the Representative Council in April.

(c) Convene an All-Nigeria Representative Council on the dates already fixed to set up effective machinery for the running of the Nigerian Youth Movement.

These resolutions provoked sharp reactions from Lagos, to which there were ripostes from Ibadan. From this time onward my faith in the NYM as a potent instrument of our nationalist struggles began to sag. As it was, the Ibadan Branch was left alone to whip up enthusiasm in the Movement only in parts of the Western Region. The Parent Body in Lagos, aside from the views it projected through the pages of the *Daily Service*, was practically inactive. I saw no future for the Movement. But if the Movement became moribund or extinct what followed? It was a baleful thought.

Four other resolutions which were passed at the 1944 Regional Conference were of national interest, and I reproduce them:

Resolved that the Western Regional Conference of the Nigerian Youth Movement hereby reaffirms the demands contained in the Memorandum submitted to the Secretary of State for the Colonies the Right Honourable Colonel Oliver Stanley during his visit to Nigeria in September, 1943, and respectfully urges that the reforms therein requested be pursued with all reasonable speed.

Resolved that the Second Session of the Western Regional Conference of the Nigerian Youth Movement associates itself with the activities of the Yaba Club as regards the industrial campaign launched by the Club, and pledges its fullest support to further its advancement in any way possible.

Resolved that the Nigerian Youth Movement pledges itself to co-operated wholeheartedly with the Nigerian Union of Teachers in submitting facts to the Elliot Commission.

Resolved that the Nigerian Youth Movement undertakes to

158

reawaken the interest of the people of Nigeria, especially farmers in the benefits of the Co-operative Movement, and to ensure that Government gives greater encouragement to the Farmers' Co-operative Societies.

When Chief H. O. Davies returned to the country in 1947, he made every effort to resuscitate the Youth Movement. Late in 1949 a Representative Council was convened with a view, among other things, to giving effect to the reform which the Ibadan Branch had strenuously advocated from 1941 to 1944. The Representative Council met, but all the elected Officers were Westerners. No Easterner or Northerner attended the meeting. Strenuous efforts were made thereafter to revive the NYM but they were belated and futile: this once powerful and promising organisation had already gone too far on the other side of the great divide.

CHAPTER 12

EVOLUTION OF A FEDERALIST

UNTIL 1951, when the Action Group proclaimed its slogan of 'Unity through Federation', the question as to what type of constitution Nigeria should have was not at all an issue in the country's politics. Since then it has become, and still is, a vexed question. In my considered opinion and in the view of the Action Group of Nigeria and of other parties in alliance with it, the present constitutional structure of Nigeria is not in accordance with some of the established principles and practice of true federalism.

In 1951 when the controversy on the form of Nigeria's constitution began, I had already been for more than eighteen years a convinced federalist. In the early thirties, I was a fanatical admirer of the Indian National Congress, and of three of its illustrious leaders—Mahatma Gandhi, Pandit Nehru, and Subha Bose. My acquaintance with the Congress and its leaders was, if I remember rightly, first made through the pages of the *Lagos Daily News* in 1928. This acquaintance deepened through other media. There was, in the early thirties, an enterprising gentleman of Ijebu extraction in Lagos who sold mainly Indian books on various subjects in a small bookshop. The most popular of them were books on English grammar and language by Indian authors. The ones that interested me were those dealing with Indian politics and Indian public men. They were booklets really, very cheap, and I bought such of them as my slender pocket could afford. By the time I returned to Wesley College as its clerk my knowledge of Indian politics had become fairly wide and my mental acquaintance with Gandhi, Nehru and Bose had grown into hero-worship. At Wesley College I was able to keep abreast of Indian political events. The Rev. E. G. Nightingale was a pastor with eclectic literary taste. The college library was full of masterpieces on various subjects; and the Common Room was regularly stocked with *The Times, Manchester Guardian, John Bull, John O'London's, Tit-Bits, Punch*, etc., alongside religious papers such as *Methodist Recorder* and *Christian Herald*. It was the secular journals which appealed to me, and I read them with unquenchable interest; especially as through their pages my knowledge of the activities of the Indian National Congress and its leaders grew. One of the pronouncements of the Indian Leaders which struck the right chord in me was the one relating to the revision of provincial boundaries along linguistic lines, in the reframing of the country's constitution. If this was done, it would mean that apart from the Indian Parliament, each linguistic group would have its own legislature and government to deal with matters of peculiar interest to the group and within the competence of a provincial government.

I tried to apply this proposal of the Indian leaders to Nigeria, and I became convinced that our protectorate boundaries were arbitrarily drawn. Why should there be Yorubas and other non-Hausas in the Protectorate of Northern Nigeria? Why were Ibos and other non-Yorubas grouped together with the Yorubas in the Protectorate of Southern Nigeria? I knew the answers. At the Berlin Conference in 1885, the imperialist powers had paid no regard to linguistic or ethnic affinities nor to geographical features or boundaries in their final share-out of the territories of Africa. The dominant note at the conference was the need to reach a compromise among the contending colonial powers, in order to ensure peace among themselves and a prosperous tenure for each in its newly acquired colonial territory. The result was that people belonging to one and the same linguistic group were split between two or more different colonial powers. In the organisation of the territories assigned to them, the over-riding considerations with the British government were the maintenance of law and order, and administrative convenience. The ethnic affinity of the people under their rule did not appear to interest them.

Though I knew the answers to the questions which the Indian Congress proposal stirred up in my mind, yet I did not feel myself qualified enough to say them aloud. At that time, much more than now, the public status of the person who said a thing counted far more than the intrinsic merits of what was said. On the other hand, I was not sure if the application to Nigeria of the proposed Indian constitutional pattern was an urgent proposition. There was no communal strife in Nigeria, as there was then in India. All the linguistic groups in Nigeria lived in harmony one with another, and linguistic distinctions did not appear as yet to be a matter of practical politics. What the country needed, I thought, for the immediate present and for quite a while to come was that Western education should spread widely enough to enable easier contact and understanding amongst the entire peoples of Nigeria. The issue of what constitution was best suited to the country would then be settled by Nigerians in their own good time. When the time arrived, however, I had no doubt on which side I would be— the federalist side.

Between 1938 and 1940, however, the partisan activities of Dr Azikiwe, and the changed attitude of his Western adherents from one of harmonious friendliness to that of cynicism and the occasional display of an air of superiority, drove me to the conclusion that there was a dangerous complacency in the attitude of Nigerian leaders towards the country's constitutional problem. They had all accepted the form of government laid down by the British for Nigeria; and all that the nationalists from Herbert Macaulay downwards had been doing was to fit themselves into this framework, and to accelerate the country's progress towards the attainment of Dominion satus within the British Commonwealth of Nations. I thought they were wrong for not applying their minds to the form of constitution best suited to the country.

By 1940 I had already made a name for myself, and I knew that if I spoke my mind in any influential circle, I would command audience if not support. Nevertheless, I was somewhat hesitant, because I knew that in the Nigerian context my ideas were novel and were likely to evoke acrimonious controversy. I decided to try them on my intimate friends first, and see how they reacted. I did, and in the hearing of two of them (both of them then and still now in government service) I argued that Nigeria should have as many provinces, zones, regions or states as there were linguistic or ethnic groups in the country, and that each region should have a legislature and government of its own. There would be a central parliament and government on which the various linguistic groups in the country would be represented. Under these arrangements each ethnic group could develop its own peculiar culture and institutions in accordance with its wishes, and the inter-tribal acrimony and jockeying for leadership which were rearing their heads would cease. The Government of each linguistic group would be led by one of their number, and Nigeria would be led by any Nigerian acceptable to all or to the majority of the peoples of the country. My views were shot down by my friends. They thought the ideas were bright and ingenious but highly explosive. As I could get no further with them, I dropped the matter.

After the 1941 election crisis in the Nigerian Youth Movement, I reopened the issue. I was now emboldened to argue my case before a larger number of friends and colleagues in the Ibadan Branch of the Nigerian Youth Movement. In addition to my previous argument, I pointed out that the sheer territorial size of Nigeria necessitated the adoption of a federal form of constitution and hence the division of the country into regions, even if the inhabitants of Nigeria were linguistically or ethnically homogeneous. The British, who had not given much thought to the heterogeneous character of Nigerian peoples in formulating their administrative arrangements, had been compelled to divide the Protectorate of Southern Nigeria into two—for administrative purposes—because it was becoming more and more enlightened and articulate. In the main, language lay at the root of racial differences: be they differences in culture and custom, in philosophy of life and political institutions, in national characteristics and social concepts and practices. I referred to some of the writings of Dr Azikiwe from which it appeared that he would abolish the institution of Obaship and Chieftaincy if he had the power. Whilst such a proposition might be acceptable to his followers in and from the Eastern Region where the British had experimented, with varying degrees of success and failure, with 'Warrant Chiefs', it would not do for the Western Provinces and the Northern Provinces where traditional chiefships had been established from time immemorial. The implicit and unshaken loyalty which the Ibos had shown to Dr Azikiwe during the Ikoli-Akisanya crisis, did not arise in my view from ideological faith but rather from linguistic affinity and ethnic self-assertion. This, I warned, was an ominous pointer to the future. Nigeria under a unitary constitution might be dominated by those, whatever their number, who owed greater allegiance to ethnic affinity than to principles and ideals.

The situation in the north, I also pointed out, was in no way reassuring. The powers-that-be appeared determined to administer the north in isolation from the south, and at all events to prevent Northerners from being 'contaminated' politically by educated Southerners. Southerners who had made efforts to start a newspaper in the north were unsuccessful. Educated Northerners who had visited the south had done so under the close supervision of white officials. No Northerner was allowed to take part in politics, and Southerners resident in the north were obliged to confine their political activities to the areas set aside for the abode of strangers. Above all, the average enlightened Northerner looked down on the Southerners as *Kafiris* (unbelievers). As between the various ethnic groups, I argued, there were differing standards of civilisation as well as uneven stages in the adoption of western education and the emulation of western civilisation. A unitary constitution with only one central government would only result in frustration to the more pushful and more dynamic ethnic groups, whereas the division of the country into regions along ethnic lines would enable each linguistic group not only to develop its own peculiar culture and institutions but to move

164

forward at its own pace, without being unnecessarily pushed or annoyingly slowed down by the others.

Finally, I emphasised that the spiritual union among Nigerians, and the assumption that they would readily accept common standards and common leadership, which had formed the basis of our nationalist activities hitherto, appeared to me to be grossly misconceived. A complete re-orientation of methods of approach to the constitutional problem of Nigeria became, to my way of thinking, of the utmost importance and urgency.

In the entire rank and file of the Nigerian Youth Movement, I did not have a single enthusiastic convert to my points of view. But after the Ikoli-Akisanya crisis, my friends in Ibadan no longer regarded my ideas as new-fangled and dangerous. Because of the general sympathy which they evinced, I made bold to state categorically, in paragraph 45 of a memorandum prepared by me and under cover of which I forwarded to the Chief Secretary to the Government the resolutions passed by the 1942 Western Regional Conference of the Nigerian Youth Movement, as follows:

What we of the Nigerian Youth Movement are visualising is a Nigeria in which the various linguistic units will federate to form a single nation. . . .

This was as far as it was permissible for me to commit the Nigerian Youth Movement on this momentous issue. If the issue had been expressly put as a question for debate and resolution, it would have been defeated.

But events subsequent to 1942 only helped to fortify rather than weaken my stand. In 1943 the Ibo Federal Union was launched, and Dr Azikiwe himself was not only a prominent member of it, but also its President. Both the Ibibio Union (now known as Ibibio State Union) and the Ibo Federal Union (now known as Ibo State Union), were able to arouse among their respective members such enthusiasm and selfless devotion as had never before been known in the country. I welcomed this phenomenon as a worthy means to a great end. If the members of each ethnic group feel happy among themselves; if they are free, within prescribed limits, to order their own lives and advance their culture as they like; and if the solidarity and devotion exhibited within their ranks can be sublimated to the cause of the nation, the federal unity of Nigeria would have been assured. But whilst there was an Ibibio Union and an Ibo Federal Union, there was no comparable all-embracing union for the Yorubas. Since the strength of a chain is that of the weakest link, I thought it would be in the interest of the federal unity of Nigeria if one was founded.

The Yorubas were a highly progressive but badly disunited group. They paid lip-service to a spiritual union and affinity in a common ancestor—Oduduwa. But in all their long history they had waged wars against one another. When the Portuguese and the British had visited their coasts in the course of their slave trade, the Yorubas had shown no qualm of conscience in conducting violent and merciless slave raids on one another. These inter-tribal wars and slave raids had come to an end under the so-called *pax Britannica*. But the mutual hatred and acerbity which were attendant on them lingered. Furthermore, the propaganda of Dr Azikiwe was already having a deleterious effect on a once dynamic group. The Yorubas now indulged in mutual recrimination and condemnation. The younger elements thought that the Yorubas were inferior to the go-ahead Ibo people, and that whatever might be their past glories they had become effete and decadent. To cap it all, it was freely bandied about that the Yorubas were no longer capable of leadership in any sphere of life. I thought that it was in the best interests of Nigeria that the Yorubas should not be reduced to a state of impotence, into which they were fast degenerating. They had something which was all their own to contribute to the common pool of Nigerian nationalism and nationhood. I decided, therefore, to do all in my power to infuse solidarity into the disjointed tribes that constitute the Yoruba ethnic group, to raise their morale, to rehabilitate their self-respect, and to imbue them with the confidence that they are an important factor in the forging of the federal unity of Nigeria.

Also in 1943, Dr Azikiwe wrote a series of articles in the *Pilot* entitled 'Political Blueprint Of Nigeria'. In the series he advocated, without saying so in so many words, a quasi-federal constitution for Nigeria, and the division of the country into eight protectorates. The articles were later published in pamphlet form with the same title. The following paragraph from the pamphlet at page 11 is relevant and of interest:

The exercise of executive power is concerned with the administration of the laws of the State for the maintenance of order and good government. To exercise it in accordance with the idea of democracy which animates our constitutional advance, Nigeria and the Cameroons should comprise eight Protectorates:

(1) Northern (Katsina, Kano, Zaria Provinces),
(2) Northwestern (Sokoto, Niger, Ilorin Provinces),
(3) Northeastern (Bornu, Bauchi, Adamawa Provinces),
(4) Central (Kabba, Benue, Plateau Provinces),
(5) Southern (Warri, Benin, Onitsha, Owerri Provinces),
(6) Southwestern (Onde, Ijebu, Abeokuta, Oyo, Lagos Provinces),
(7) Southeastern (Calabar, Ogoja Provinces),
(8) Cameroons (Southern, Northern Provinces).

These Protectorates shall form a Commonwealth of Nigeria. At the head of the Commonwealth shall be a Governor-General and Lieutenant Governor-General. At the head of each Protectorate shall be a Governor and a Lieutenant-Governor.

Two things struck me as significant in Dr Azikiwe's formula. First, all the Ibos in Benin and Warri Provinces of the Western Protectorate or Region were to be merged with their kith and kin in Onitsha and Owerri under Azikiwe's proposed 'Southern Protectorate', though similar consideration was not extended to the Yorubas of Ilorin and Kabba Provinces. Secondly, the Ibos were cleverly split into two Protectorates—Southern and South-eastern—where because of their numbers they would be in permanent dominance, having regard to their unique ethnic loyalty and solidarity which had been demonstrated during the Ikoli-Akisanya crisis, and which has been demonstrated several times since. I thought the formula was unscientific and partisan, not in accordance with precedent, and not capable of ensuring harmony among the diverse ethnic groups in Nigeria.

On leaving the shores of Nigeria in August 1944, I resolved that I would have nothing to do with politics until I had finished my studies and made some money. I also resolved that before I again entered into politics I would see to it that the Yorubas evolved an ethnic solidarity among themselves just as the Ibibios and the Ibos had done, in order to ensure a strong and harmonious federal union among the peoples of Nigeria. In less than a year after I reached the United Kingdom I set to work to translate my ideas into realities. A group of Yorubas, mostly students—Dr Oni Akerele, Chief Abiodun Akerele, barrister-at-law and Member of the House of Representatives, Mr Akintola Williams, chartered accountant, Chief Ayotunde Rosiji, Federal Secretary of the Action Group and Member of the House of Representatives and others—and I founded a Yoruba organisation in London named the Egbe Omo Oduduwa (meaning 'A Society of the Descendants of Oduduwa').

In view of the hostility and controversy which had marked the birth of the Egbe Omo Oduduwa, and of the general misunderstanding which has existed ever since about the real intentions of this organisation, I reproduce here in full the aims of the Egbe and its methods of approach as set out in its first constitution which was drafted by me with the collaboration of one of its founders.

The aims of the association are divided into two categories:

(a) *Yorubaland*
   (i) To study fully its political problems, combat the disintegrating forces of tribalism, stamp out discrimination within the group and against minorities, and generally infuse the idea of a single nationality throughout the region;
   (ii) To study its economic resources, ascertain its potentialities, and advise as to the wisest utilisation of its wealth, so as to ensure abundance and prosperity for its people;
   (iii) To plan for the improvement of educational facilities both in content and extent, to explore the means of introducing mass education promptly and efficiently

and to foster the study of Yoruba language, culture and history;

(iv) To promote the social welfare of Yorubaland, combat the cankerworm of superstitition and ignorance, spread the knowledge of medical relief and stimulate the provision of hospitals, maternity homes and suchlike amenities.

(b) *Nigeria*

(i) To co-operate in the fullest measure with other regions to see that the aims set out in (a) are applied to the whole country;

(ii) To aid and encourage similar groups in the other regions in every way possible to achieve these ideals.

METHODS OF APPROACH

(a) By studying problems affecting Yorubaland in particular and Nigeria in general through:
(i) Research.
(ii) Lectures.
(iii) Paper reading, and
(iv) Discussion.

(b) By disseminating the knowledge thus gained and conclusions reached among the people in Yorubaland and Nigeria by the following means:

(i) The propagation of the idea of a modern Yoruba state and a Federal State of Nigeria through the agency of reliable persons who share our ideals.

(ii) The issuing of magazines, booklets, and other publications in English and Yoruba.

(iii) The encouragement of the immediate setting up of Egbe Omo Oduduwa in Yorubaland provided the promoters give an undertaking that the first three years will be devoted to strengthening the organisation financially and studying local problems, while refraining from any direct political action.

Before the Egbe was founded in London in 1945, there was already a two-year old branch of the Ibo Federal Union there. Even so the reaction of practically all the students from the Eastern Region and of some from the Western Region to the formation of the Egbe was a hostile one. Being the most prominent among the founders, I was singled out for attack. I was accused of being tribalistic and of having a design to wreck the

169

unity of Nigeria. In the face of the aims and objects of the Egbe which were widely circulated among Nigerian students in the United Kingdom, these accusations did not make any sense to me. All the same, I seized every opportunity that offered itself to explain these aims and objects to my detractors. The Executive Committee of the Egbe also decided to hold a joint meeting with the Executive Committee of the London Branch of the Ibo Federal Union, with a view to making to the latter a full explanation of what the Egbe stood for, and to driving the point home that the Egbe was purely and simply the Yoruba counterpart of the Ibo Federal Union. I made contact with the Chairman of the Ibo Federal Union, Mr Chuba Ikpeazu (a law student) through my friend Mr G. Onyiuke (another law student), and a date for a meeting between the committees was fixed. Somehow, about twenty-four hours before the time of the meeting, Mr Ikpeazu sent a message to say that he and his officers had another important engagement which made it possible for them to attend the proposed meeting. He promised to let us have another date. He was unable to fulfil this promise before we all returned home to Nigeria.

When the Egbe was founded in London, copies of its constitution were sent to Obas, Chiefs and outstanding Yorubas, with an accompanying letter in which an appeal was made to them to found a similar organisation at home. Apart from His Highness Sir Adesoji Aderomi, the Oni of Ife and President of the Western House of Chiefs, and three other persons, there was no response from the scores of people to whom we had written, and nothing at all was done at home to start the Egbe or something similar to it. On my return home, I began in earnest to preach the formation of the Egbe. People listened to me either with concealed indifference or undisguised boredom. Then one day in 1948, I read in the papers that the Egbe Omo Oduduwa had been formed in Lagos by a group of outstanding Yoruba leaders. Sir Adeyemo Alakija, Dr Akinola Maja, Sir Kofo Abayomi, Chief Bode Thomas, Chief H. O. Davies, Dr Akanni Doherty and others too numerous to mention were among the foundation members. I was jubilant to read this report, and I quickly sent a telegram of felicitations to the Lagos founders of the Egbe. I also took immediate steps to inaugurate a branch in Ibadan. The aims and objects of the newly formed Egbe were identical with those of the one founded in London with but some slight modifications. The new organisation pledged itself (a) to encourage (especially by means of scholarship awards by the Society) the pursuit of secondary and university education among Yoruba boys and girls, (b) to recognise and maintain the monarchical and other similar institutions of Yorubaland, to plan for their complete enlightenment and democratisation . . . and (c) to strive earnestly to co-operate with other ethnical associations in matters of common interest to all Nigerians, so as thereby to attain to unity in federation.

The reaction of Dr Azikiwe and all his supporters to the newly formed Egbe was violent beyond compare. All the leaders of the Egbe were vilified in Dr Azikiwe's newspapers. The high-water-mark of the campaign was reached in the following extract from an editorial article in the *Pilot* of September 8, 1948:

> But now that the Egbe has made it clear that its battle is not really against Dr Azikiwe personally and even against Ibos as a group, but against the aspirations of the 27 million Nigerians backing up the NCNC, the time has come for real action. . . . Henceforth the cry must be one of battle against the Egbe Omo Oduduwa, its leaders, at home and abroad, up hill, and down dale, in the streets of Nigeria and in the residence of its advocates. The Egbe Omo Oduduwa is the enemy of Nigeria; it must be crushed to the earth. . . . There is no going back, until the Fascist organisation of Sir Adeyemo Alakija has been dismembered.

Apart from newspaper attacks, there were also physical assaults on the persons of the leaders of the Egbe, and damage to the houses and other property of some of them. It was absolutely impossible on nationalist grounds to reconcile Dr Azikiwe's insensate hostility to the Egbe with his presidentship of the Ibo Federal Union and his obvious condonation of the existence of a similar organisation founded in the Northern Region in May 1948 and called Jamiyyar Mutanen Arewa

171

(Northern People's Congress). Besides, in spite of his protestations to the contrary, Dr Azikiwe was himself an unabashed Ibo jingoist. And he gave the game completely away when he said inter alia in his presidential address to the Ibo Federal Union in 1949, as follows:

. . . It would appear that the God of Africa has specially created the Ibo nation to lead the children of Africa from the bondage of the ages. . . . The martial prowess of the Ibo nation at all stages of human history has enabled them not only to conquer others but also to adapt themselves to the role of preserver. . . . The Ibo nation cannot shirk its responsibility. . . . Politically, you have seen with your own eyes how you were disfranchised by the British. . . . The Ibo nation has never been represented in the Executive Council. . . .

Economically, the Ibo nation has laboured under onerous taxation measures, without sufficient social amenities to justify same.

We have been taxed without representation, and our contributions in taxes have been used to develop other areas, out of proportion to the incidence of taxation in those areas.

It would seem that the Ibo nation is becoming a victim of economic annihilation through a gradual but studied process.

In 1948 another Ibo leader and a member of the Nigerian Legislative Council had declared the domination of Nigeria by the Ibos is a question of time.

It was clear from these statements and from the general political and journalistic manoeuvres of Dr Azikiwe over the years that his great objective was to set himself up as a dictator over Nigeria and to make the Ibo nation the master race. It would appear according to his reckoning that the only obstacle in the path of his ambition was the Yoruba intelligentsia, and these must be removed at all cost. A situation in which one ethnic group would dominate the others does not accord with my conception of a united and happy Nigeria. I am implacably opposed to dictatorship as well as the doctrine of *Herrenvolk* whether it was Hitler's or Dr Azikiwe's.

In the same year (1945) as the Egbe was founded in London a White Paper entitled *Proposals for the Revision of the Constitution of Nigeria—Cmd* 6599, was published simultaneously in Nigeria and London. The objects of the proposed Constitution as contained in the White Paper were:

to promote the unity of Nigeria; to provide adequately within that unity for the diverse elements which make up the country; and to secure greater participation by Africans in the discussion of their own affairs.

The Governor of Nigeria at the time this constitution was introduced was Sir Arthur Richards (now Lord Milverton), and the constitution is popularly known as the Richards Constitution. I welcomed the constitutional proposals in principle but criticised some of its detailed features. I wrote a long open letter to Sir Arthur Richards which was published in about ten articles in the *Daily Service*. I followed this up in my book *Path to Nigerian Freedom* (Faber & Faber) which I wrote in the same year, 1945, but which was published in 1947. The only chapter which is relevant to the topic with which I am now dealing is the one headed 'Towards Federal Union'. The following passages from this chapter are of interest because, in broad terms, they correctly represent my stand then and now on this very important issue:

Since the amalgamation (of Northern and Southern Protectorates of Nigeria) all the efforts of the British Government have been devoted to developing the country into a unitary State. This is patently impossible; and it is astonishing that a nation with wide political experience like Great Britain fell into such a palpable error.

In the White Paper (Cmd 6599) to which we have already referred, some attempt is being made to rectify this original mistake. But it is only a partial attempt; and in many respects falls short of effectively checking the retarding influences of the existing unitary Constitution. The division into three Regions was arbitrary, and made only for administrative convenience. The proposed Constitution maintains the present division. It goes further, to devolve autonomous legislative and administrative functions on each Region, and thus to strengthen the existing decentralisation. There are a few sentences in the White Paper which indicate rather vaguely that the British Government now recognises the federal character of Nigeria. But nothing is done beyond this paper recognition. . . .

If the idea of a federal constitution for Nigeria is accepted, and if it is sincerely desired by the British Government to create 'a system within which the diverse elements may progress at varying speeds, amicably, and smoothly, towards a more closely integrated economic, social, and political unity, without sacrificing the principles and ideals inherent in their divergent ways of life' then the present administrative boundaries within the country must be redrawn.

. . . The present three Regions were constituted without regard to ethnological factors. The Yorubas of Ilorin, Offa, and Kabba are included with the Hausas in the Northern Region. Ibos who properly belong to the Eastern Zone are grouped with the Yorubas in the West. There is no justification whatsoever for this arbitrary grouping. Certainly these minority groups are at a considerable disadvantage when they are forced to be in the midst of other peoples who differ from them in language, culture, and historical background.

But readjustment of the boundaries of the three administrative Regions will not solve all the problems. In that event, the Western Region would be the only area inhabited by people who all belong to the same ethnical stock, and speak the same language. In the Eastern Region there are three main national groups, namely, the Ibos, Ibibios, and Ijaws; and in the North there are five—the Hausas, Fulanis (who form the ruling class), Kanuris, Munshis, and Nupes. . . . There are a number of other national groups which are not recorded separately in the 1931 census.

Under a true federal constitution each group, however small, is entitled to the same treatment as any other group, however large. Opportunity must be afforded to each to evolve its own peculiar political institution. Each group must be autonomous in regard to its internal affairs. Each must have its own Regional House of Assembly. Just now, however, it would be difficult to provide enough administrative staffs to handle the affairs of well over ten Houses of Assembly throughout the country. Even if such staffs were available the revenue of the country is unable to bear the expense. For the present, it is enough if it is borne in mind that this is our ultimate goal, and if we begin forthwith to take steps which would ensure the speedy attainment of this end.

We need not be alarmed at the number of autonomous States which would thus emerge. The population of Switzerland is about 4,000,000; just about one-sixth of that of Nigeria. This country consists of four racial groups. These are divided into twenty-two cantons, each of which has its own Parliament and Government. The Romansch, who form the fourth racial group, are only 44,000 in number. They, too, have regional autonomy with a Parliament and Government of their own. Canada, with a population of about half of that of Nigeria, has nine Provinces, each of which has its own Legislature. According to these and other well-known and well-tried constitutional precedents, even as many as thirty to forty Regional Houses of Assembly would not be too many in the future United States of Nigeria.

In 1947, Sir John Macpherson succeeded Lord Milverton as the Governor of Nigeria. Barely two years after his assumption of office Sir John Macpherson decided that the Richards Constitution should be reviewed. Sir John's Chief Secretary was Sir Hugh Foot, the present (1960) Governor of Cyprus. Strangely enough, Sir Hugh Foot was an official very much after my heart. He was a very honest and affable person; an exceptionally able and brilliant administrator, and a powerful and almost irresistible orator whom I once described in a newspaper article as a 'verbal sorcerer'. For the review of the Richards Constitution Sir Hugh framed a series of questions, the first two of which were:

1. Do we wish to see a fully centralised system with all legislative and executive power concentrated at the Centre or do we wish to develop a federal system under which each different region of the country would exercise a measure of internal autonomy?
2. If we favour a federal system should we retain the existing regions with some modification of existing regional boundaries or should we form regions on some new basis such as the many linguistic groups which exist in Nigeria?

These and other questions were to be answered by the people at various levels—local government (then Native Authority) level, Provincial level, Regional level, and all-Nigeria level. Interested bodies were free to submit memoranda to the government.

Apart from having a number of private meetings with Sir Hugh (then Mr) Foot in Ibadan and Lagos, I was able to project my views through the Ijebu Remo Native Authority, the Ijebu Provincial Conference, the Nigerian Youth Movement and the Egbe Omo Oduduwa. I was the chairman of the committee which the NYM set up to draw up a memorandum

175

and I was ex-officio Secretary of the Egbe Omo Oduduwa's committee for the same purpose. In a foreword to the memorandum submitted by the Egbe Omo Oduduwa, I wrote as follows:

We advocate the grouping of Nigeria into various autonomous states or regions, purely on ethnical basis. Experience of other countries shows that this basis is more natural, and invariably more satisfactory than any other basis. For this reason we urge that the Yoruba-speaking people in the Northern Region, and the Ibo-speaking people in the Western Region, should be grouped respectively with the Western and the Eastern Regions. Where necessary, a plebiscite may be conducted to ascertain the wishes of the people concerned.

I hasten to add, however, that we advocate ethnical grouping only as the ultimate objective. We realise that if this basis is strictly adhered to at present throughout the country, some states would emerge which would be totally incapable of finding money to run their own affairs. We consider it desirable, therefore, that for the time being such ethnical groups as are unable financially to maintain their own separate states should be amalgamated with other larger and neighbouring groups until they are able to maintain their own separate autonomous states. Such smaller ethnic groups should be free to decide with which larger groups they are willing to be temporarily amalgamated.

With the Committee of the NYM it was somewhat difficult going for me. Some people developed a pain in the neck whenever they heard me talk of the division of the country into states or regions along ethnic or linguistic lines, as the ultimate aim for the Federation of Nigeria. After a good deal of verbal duelling and mental chafing, the Representative Council of the NYM on the recommendation of my committee gave an answer to the two questions quoted above. The NYM's answer, as will be seen presently, was rather elastic. It was the result of a compromise between those who belonged to my federalist school of thought on the one hand, and those who belonged to and had to be drawn away from the unitary school, on the other. The relevant passage is as follows:

It is a matter of general agreement that a lasting unity of the peoples of the vast country can only be achieved through federation and not fusion. Consequently it is absolutely necessary to lay the foundation for federation now by dividing the country into the regions that will form the units of the proposed federal constitution. This undoubtedly is the reason why regionalisation has been about the only acceptable feature of the Richards Constitution.

Nigeria is a country of various tribes, some of which have lived together in harmony for many years before the advent of the British, some were unknown to one another in the past and were only brought together for the first time by British administration. Some share similar customs, traditions and culture and are traceable to the same ethnic origin while others differ from each other as the Aborigines of Australia from the Zulu of South Africa. In dividing Nigeria into regions it is therefore necessary to group together only people who, through affinity or general experience, are known to be capable of working together harmoniously. The guiding principles in the division of the country into regions must therefore be: ethnic classification, cultural affinity, common problems and, perhaps, administrative convenience.

In the present Regional division of Nigeria, it is evident that regard has been had to some but clearly not to all of the principles of regionalisation already given. The Nigerian Youth Movement believes that a proper and acceptable division can only be made after the fullest consideration has been given to all these principles.

The answers of the three Regional Conferences to Sir Hugh Foot's first two questions are of interest because they represented more or less accurately the stand which their protagonists take even today on the structure of Nigeria's constitution. The Northern Regional Conference recommended that there should be a federal system of government in Nigeria, and that in addition to a central legislature there should be regional legislatures with powers to legislate on a number of specified subjects and also on such other matters as may, by legislation enacted by the central legislature, be vested in the regional legislatures. The Eastern Regional Conference also recommended that there should be a federal system, with a central legislature and regional legislatures. But it also recommended that the regional legislatures should exercise only such powers in any matter as the central legislature may delegate to them. The Western Regional Conference, of which I was a member, recommended that there should be a federal government consisting of states formed on an ethnic and/or linguistic basis, but that for the time being there should be only three states, namely, Western, Eastern and Northern. It further recommended that there should be a federal parliament and state parliaments, and that the state parliaments should be competent to legislate on all residual matters not specifically included within the legislative powers of the Federal Parliament.

The All-Nigeria Conference (styled the General Conference) for the review of the Richards Constitution met in Ibadan from 9 January 1950 to about the end of the month. I was not a member of the General Conference. When I was elected as one of the representatives of the Western Region to the General Conference, I declined for reasons which I will give in the next chapter. Dr Azikiwe did not participate in the review at any level. He was elected as one of the representatives of the Eastern Region to the General Conference, but he was absent throughout its proceedings. The General Conference did not expressly resolve that it agreed to a federal system. It merely recommended to the Secretary of State for the Colonies through the Governor that 'there should be three Regions—the Northern, Eastern and Western Regions—with the independent municipality of Lagos.' This recommendation was varied by the Secretary of State for the Colonies on the advice of the Legislative Council of Nigeria by merging Lagos with the Western Region. Two other relevant recommendations of the Conference relating to regional legislatures which were accepted by the Secretary of State were as follows:

1. *FUNCTIONS:*
   The Regional legislature should have power:
   (a) to enact legislation to be effective within the boundaries of its own region on the subjects of:
   > Local Government; Town and Country Planning; Agriculture and Fisheries; Education; Public Health; Forestry; Veterinary Services; Land; Welfare; Local Industries; Regional Public Works; Native Courts (subject to Central Legislation regarding appeals); Direct Taxation (other than Income Tax and Company Tax); Any other subject specifically delegated by the central legislature.

2. *OPERATION OF LEGISLATION*:

Regional legislation should not be subject to the approval of the House of Representatives but should be laid on the Table of the House of Representatives. Such legislation may be debated in the House of Representatives on the proposal of the Governor-in-Council. . . . If the motion is passed by a majority of all the members of the House of Representatives present the legislation should be referred back to the Regional House or Houses for reconsideration and in the event of continued disagreement thereafter no Regional legislation which is opposed by a majority of all the members of the House of Representatives present should take effect.

I thought that the country had been badly let down by the General Conference on the issue of federalism. For want of a specific recommendation on the point, it would appear that the attitude of the Conference was that it favoured a pseudo-federal system under which the existing regions were retained. I held and still hold that there are three differentiae by which a federal constitution must be distinguished from a quasi-federal or a unitary constitution. First, there must be a central government as well as regional or state governments, which must be co-ordinated in their relationship with one another and with the central government. Second, the residual functions must be vested in the constituent states or regions in the federation. Third, no one state or region in the federation must be so large that it can override the wishes of all the other states or regions put together. What had been decided upon by the Conference was a wretched compromise between federalism and unitarianism. Furthermore, the Conference was absolutely silent as to the constitutional objective towards which the country should work. It seemed to regard the structure it had recommended as the end of the road, at least for five years after the formal introduction of the new constitution. However, I welcomed the fact that under the new arrangements, Nigerians would become ministers, and that as such they would be in a position to participate not only in the discussion but also in the actual administration of the affairs of their country. Here was a golden opportunity long-awaited. Backed by a well-organised and disciplined party, the new ministers and their fellow-party men could from within and without bring pressure to bear to effect a drastic change in the structure of the new constitution as well as accelerate our pace towards the attainment of independence. I decided, therefore, that instead of attacking the new proposals and the eventual constitutional provisions based on them, I should strive to place myself and those who shared my views in a position of political influence whereby we could continually and effectively project those views until they eventually prevailed.

When the Action Group proclaimed its slogan of *Unity Through Federation* in 1951, and declared support in principle for the new constitution, popularly known as the Macpherson Constitution, Dr Azikiwe and his lieutenants made venomous attacks on my colleagues and me. Dr Azikiwe and the NCNC took the view that the country should have a unitary constitution with one strong government at the centre. According to Dr Azikiwe, the Macpherson Constitution, like the Richards Constitution before it, was designed to break the unity of Nigeria. It was argued, most preposterously, by the NCNC that if the idea of federalism was accepted, and the Macpherson Constitution was allowed to operate, it would become necessary for people moving from one Region to another to obtain passports or travel certificates. Accordingly the NCNC called, though unsuccessfully, for the boycott of the new Constitution. For our part, we stuck firmly to our guns.

On 31 March 1953 the Action Group precipitated a constitutional crisis, as a result of which a conference for the review of the Macpherson Constitution was held in London from 30 July to 22 August 1953. Before we went to London for the conference, an alliance was concluded between the Action Group and the NCNC in unexpected and most dramatic circumstances. The move for this alliance came from Dr Azikiwe, who of his own volition came to embrace me in front of the House of Representatives buildings on 31 March 1953 after the members of the NCNC in the House had joined those of my party to walk out of the House. It was stipulated by the

Action Group before this alliance that the two parties should first of all reach agreement on those issues of fundamental importance which divided them. At our first joint meeting we took up the question of federalism. It did not take us any time to persuade Dr Azikiwe. It must be said to his credit that he is himself a believer in federalism. Indeed he is a believer in many a good cause. The only puzzling thing about Dr Azikiwe is that more often than not there is a wide gap between what he believes and what he preaches, and between what he preaches and what he practises. In any case, though the alliance was short-lived, it did help to settle to my satisfaction some of the burning issues of the time. In regard to one of them, Dr Azikiwe declared at the 1953 constitutional conference that 'federalism is imperative'. The conference altered the structure of the Macpherson Constitution most drastically: specific powers were vested in the Federal Government, concurrent powers were also specified, and all the residual powers were vested in the Region. We of the Action Group, as a result of the agreement reached with the NCNC, did not press for the revision of regional boundaries; though the NCNC, contrary to this agreement, teamed up with the NPC to demand that Lagos should be separated from the Western Region and declared a federal territory, which was done. Notwithstanding the loss of Lagos to the West, an important step had in my view been taken at this conference towards the achievement of true federalism in Nigeria. The central and regional governments now equal in status in their internal relationship, and residual functions were vested in the regional governments. The Northern Region, which has 19 million out of the 34 million population of Nigeria, and 264,300 square miles out of Nigeria's total area of 340,000 square miles, was not yet in a position to dominate all the others put together. Under the Macpherson Constitution and its revised version, the seats in the House of Representatives were shared fifty-fifty between the Northern Region on the one hand and the Western and Eastern Regions on the other. Besides, there were official as well as unofficial members in the Central Legislature who were nominated by the Governor or the Governor-General, as the case might be, to represent interests not already adequately represented.

When the review of the Richards Constitution commenced, some of the leaders of the people of Benin and Warri (now Delta) Provinces in the Western Region demanded that these two provinces should be created into a separate region under the proposed constitution. I wholeheartedly supported this demand in principle, but I doubted the viability of the proposed State. I did not at that time know enough about the finances of the Benin-Delta Provinces, commonly referred to as the Mid-West, to be able to express a categorical opinion in support of the demand. I was the first speaker at the Western Regional Conference for the review of the Richards Constitution, and I gave clear and unequivocal expression to the view which I have just stated. I did make it clear also that as soon as the revenue of the area was judged adequate to sustain it, the proposed Mid-West State should be created. Some of the representatives from the Mid-West argued strenuously at the Conference in support of their demand, but it did not receive any sympathy even in principle from the majority of the members of the conference. The Midwestern representatives assumed, without giving any facts or figures in support, that the new region would be viable. I was not prepared to go the whole hog with them on a mere assumption which might afterwards prove to have been gravely misconceived. As the review proceeded from stage to stage, this demand received less and less attention until it finally faded out completely at the General Conference.

But the agitation for the creation of the Mid-West State was by no means dead. It gathered momentum after the Macpherson Constitution came into operation in 1952, and had as its mighty advocates the Oba of Benin, His Highness Akenzua II, and Dr Azikiwe. I was now the Minister of Local Government as well as the leader of the party in power in the Western Region. On 1 October 1954 I became the Premier, also holding the portfolio of Finance in the Western Region. My support in principle for the creation of the Mid-West State had never flagged. By virtue of my position in the government I had access to information which was not hitherto available to me about the finances of the Region, and in due course I was able to satisfy myself that the Mid-West if constituted into a separate state would be viable. I, therefore, made up my mind finally that the Mid-West should be allowed to go. But there were formidable forces within the Action Group which did not support my stand. The creation of the state, they argued, would mean the sacrifice of the people of the Mid-West to the domination of the Edo-speaking group. In any case such a state would be ruled, at least for some years to come, by the NCNC. Why should we gratuitously widen the area of our opponents' influence by offering them another state practically on a platter? Why should the Western Region alone and the smallest region at that, of all the three regions in the federation, be dismembered?

The arguments went forwards and backwards, and I was always in the minority within the party until 1955, when the agitation for the creation of the COR State, consisting of the Calabar, Ogoja and Rivers Provinces of the Eastern Region, became very intense. In that year the party agreed to support the creation of the Mid-West State provided Dr Azikiwe was prepared to agree to the creation of the COR (Calabar, Ogoja and Rivers) State. It was argued that it would be most impolitic for the Action Group to surrender to the protagonists of the Mid-West who were mostly NCNC, whilst the NCNC refused to make a similar concession in the Eastern Region. It would be a triumph for the NCNC over the Action Group if the Mid-West State were created, and the COR State were not. My view was that such a triumph could only be temporary. The creation of the Mid-West State was bound to have the effect of sustaining the agitation for and bringing about the creation of the COR State. Minority elements in the other regions of the country would sooner or later say to themselves 'if it can be done in the Western Region, why can't it be done here too?' About the same time as the demand for the COR

State was made, the demand for the creation of a Middle Belt State consisting of the non-Fulani, non-Kanuri and non-Hausa ethnic groups of the Northern Region was also made. By the end of 1955 the demand by the minority ethnic groups in each region to be constituted into a separate state had become very clamorous. I was an ardent supporter of all of them. First because I was now convinced that each of the proposed new states (Mid-West, COR, and Middle Belt) would be viable. Secondly, because I felt the time had come when the North should be broken into at least two separate states. But whilst I succeeded in carrying the party with me on the issue of the Mid-West and COR States, on condition that the two were created simultaneously, I did not succeed in regard to the Middle Belt State. There was at that time a good deal of friendship between the Action Group and the NPC. For myself, I nursed this friendship, but not out of conviction. There was, in my considered opinion, a yawning gulf of fundamental principles which lay between the Action Group and the NPC. But prudence dictated that I should toe the party line, and I did.

CHAPTER 13

THE DEBATE CONTINUES

THE tactics which the Action Group employed up to the commencement of the 1957 London Conference on Nigeria's Constitution, concerning the demands for the creation of the Mid-West State, the COR State, and the Middle Belt State, led to all sorts of compromises, complications and disappointments—all of which I frankly admit are concomitants of political life. Early in 1957 when preparations for the 1957 constitutional conference were being made, the line-up of each of the three major political parties (Action Group, National Council of Nigeria and the Cameroons and Northern People's Congress) on the issue of new states was separate and distinct. The Action Group wanted the creation of the Mid-West and COR States, provided the two were created simultaneously. It was also willing to support the demand for the creation of the Middle Belt State, but was at the same time anxious not to offend the NPC which was deadly opposed to the creation of any state, and in particular the Middle Belt State. As for the NCNC, it was keen on seeing the Mid-West State created. It also wanted the rest of the Western Region to be carved into three states: Lagos and Colony State (consisting of Colony Province of Western Region and the Federal Territory of Lagos); Central Yoruba State (consisting of Oyo, Ibadan and Ondo Provinces of the Western Region); and Kolanut and Cassava State (consisting of Abeokuta and Ijebu Provinces). It was, however, opposed to the creation of the COR State, and silent on the demand for the creation of the Middle Belt State.

The NPC and its leader, the Sardauna of Sokoto, made certain moves before the 1957 conference by means of which the Action Group was rendered almost hors de combat and splendidly out-manoeuvred, when the question of new states came up for discussion at the conference. On its own motion the NPC suggested to the Action Group that a meeting between the leaders of the two parties was desirable in order that both of them might exchange ideas in regard to proposals to be made by the NPC and the Action Group at the coming constitutional conference. It was thought that such an exchange of ideas would facilitate proceedings at the conference, and might lead to closer collaboration between the two parties. In order to ensure secrecy for the proposed meeting the venue chosen was the house of Alhaji S. O. Gbadamosi, one of the outstanding leaders of the Action Group, in his home-town Ikorodu, some twenty miles from Lagos. The meeting was held on 3, 10 and 17 March 1957. Neither the Sardauna nor I attended, but agreed to be bound by the conclusions reached there. Consequently, the Action Group and the NPC teams at the meeting were respectively led by Chief S. L. Akintola and Sir Abubakar Tafawa Balewa. Each of them is the Deputy Leader of his party. On the issues of creating new states and revising regional boundaries the following conclusions, which were recorded in the minutes of the meeting, were reached:

Creation of new States: It was agreed that all claims for the creation of new states should be referred to a commission of independent men who will be appointed by the Secretary of State. The commission would consider, in the first instance, whether the proposed new state is viable on the basis of existing services provided in the area. If the commission is satisfied that the proposed state is viable, then it will hold a plebiscite in the area in order to determine whether the majority of the people want the new state. If the majority of any ethnic group within the area vote against the creation of the State it will not be included, provided that its separation from the new State is geographically possible; but if it is an 'island' within the proposed new State, then it must form part of the new State.
Revision of Regional Boundaries: It was agreed by both sides, after some discussion, that any ethnic group within an existing Region can join a neighbouring Region if the majority of such ethnic group desired it and provided that the Region which it seeks to join is willing to accept it.

Shortly after this Ikorodu meeting between the Action Group

186

and the NPC, the Sardauna of Sokoto, Premier of the Northern Region, personally visited me at Ibadan. Now that the Action Group and the NPC had reached agreement on a wide variety of vital issues it would be an excellent thing, the Sardauna suggested, if the concurrence of the NCNC could be secured to as many points as possible. He thought the best approach would be for him to convene a Summit Meeting of the three Premiers (that is himself, myself and Dr Azikiwe) together with their advisers. I supported the Sardauna's proposed Summit Meeting because I saw in it the potential instrument by means of which Dr Azikiwe and the NCNC might be brought to heel on a number of tricky issues. I also thought that if the three of us who were leaders of our respective delegations to the conference could reach agreement on any matter, we would be able to present a united front on such a matter to the Secretary of State for the Colonies and the United Kingdom delegation. The Premiers' Summit Meeting was duly convened and it was held in Lagos on 16 and 17 April 1957. On April 15, that was the day before the commencement of the Summit Meeting, there was a preliminary meeting of the Premiers' advisers. The purpose of this meeting of advisers was to recommend to the Premiers subjects to be discussed and the procedures to be followed at their meeting. Those present at the preliminary meeting of advisers were Dr K. O. Mbadiwe and Chief Kola Balogun for the NCNC; Chief S. L. Akintola for the Action Group; and Alhaji Aliyu Makaman Bida and Sir Abubakar Tafawa Balewa for the NPC. One of the procedures recommended, and which was accepted by the Premiers' Summit Meeting, reads as follows:

That it was the view of the advisers that the Premiers' Conference should try to reach agreement on all the matters to be discussed, and that the agreement reached should be binding on the parties concerned.

Of the agreed decisions taken at the meeting of 16 April 1957, the one on the creation of new states is of great importance and relevance. I am quoting from the minutes of the meeting which were duly signed by the three Premiers in confirmation of the accuracy of the records contained in them:

Creation of new States: The Conference agreed that the creation of new States should be based on the following principles:
   (a) The wishes of the people of the area should be determined by a plebiscite or a referendum.
   (b) The creation of the new States should be consistent with the principles of viability.
   (c) The component units of the new States should be geographically contiguous.
   (d) No ethnic group should be split into new States except with the express wishes of a two-thirds majority of the people in the ethnic group, determined by a plebiscite.

It was further agreed that a State Boundary Commission should be appointed by the Secretary of State, in the first instance, and by the Government of the Federation after independence, to determine the creation of new States.

Three decisions, among others, were also taken at the meeting of 17 April 1957, which I think ought to be reproduced in order that some of the events which followed, and some of the comments and observations which I make later may be correctly appraised. They are:

(1) It was agreed that a joint memorandum or memoranda on all the points on which agreement had been reached should be prepared by me for signature or initialling by the three Premiers.
(2) It was agreed that, while in London, the Premiers should meet leaders of minority groups and try to infuse in them the spirit of unity and independence of Nigeria which was the keynote of the Premiers' Conference.
(3) It was agreed that the Premiers should hold further meetings after their arrival in the United Kingdom.

After we had all arrived in London, the Sardauna convened a further meeting of the Premiers, to which Dr E. M. L. Endeley, former Premier of the Southern Cameroons, was invited for the first time. At some inconvenience to myself, I saw to it that memoranda on the decisions taken at the Premiers' meeting in Lagos were prepared ready for signature at the London meeting, if approved. To the utter astonishment of my colleagues

188

and me, and quite contrary to the agreement reached at the Summit Meeting in Nigeria, the NPC declared that they would not support any of the decisions taken at the Summit Meeting, save the one on the independence of Nigeria in 1959. They remarked that they had adopted this attitude in clear and un-compromising resentment that the NCNC had submitted a welter of memoranda on the creation of new states, the con-tents of which were diametrically opposed to the principles agreed to at the Premiers' conference in Lagos. Throughout the resumed Premiers' meeting in London, the NPC remained adamant, and the NCNC uncommunicative.

After this meeting, the Action Group party line on the issue became rather jagged and disconcerted. In a series of meetings which followed, there was a long debate as to whether we should as a party press the issue at the conference table or not. The majority view which prevailed was that delegates of the Action Group from the minority areas should submit memoranda to the conference on the subject, strictly in their capacity as members of their respective minority groups. I was, however, totally dissatisfied with this arrangement. There was a struggle within me between what I as an individual believed and cherished and what the delegation which I led decided upon as the correct line of conduct in the prevailing circumstances. I thought that if the Action Group as a party was precluded from submitting a memorandum on the subject in order not to offend the NPC, I as a delegate and as a Nigerian should be permitted to make my contributions to the discussions on the subject. I convened a meeting of the Action Group delegates and told them my mind. I assured them that whilst I was prepared to argue as forcefully as I could a case for the creation of the three proposed states, I would try to be objective and not to say anything that would be offensive to the NPC. I was given unanimous approval to do this on condition that an advance copy of my speech was given to the NPC at least a day before I delivered it at the conference. As a matter of fact, I was able to let the Sardauna have a copy three days before I delivered it.

At the conference table the NPC insisted on the three Regions remaining as they were, and opposed the incorporation in the constitution of any provisions which would make possible the creation of more states at any future time. Such provisions in our constitution, the NPC argued, would only help to encourage and keep alive the agitation for more states, and more and more states. The NCNC adopted a more devious approach. They demanded that right there in the conference room the country should be divided into seventeen states which were named by them. The argument of the NCNC was that the smaller the states the better for the federal unity of Nigeria. It was my view that in the existing economic, financial and administrative conditions of Nigeria, the creation of seventeen states would make nonsense of federalism, and indeed would amount to a backdoor reversion to a unitary system. Each of the seventeen states would be so weak that it would perforce be subordinated to the federal government in practically all the major functions which the Regions now performed. In that event, the so-called states would be nothing more and nothing less than glorified Local Government Authorities.

Speaking for myself and for the Action Group delegation, I advocated the incorporation in our constitution of provisions for the creation of states in the future, and the immediate creation of the COR State, the Mid-West State and the Middle Belt State. I proffered four principles which I thought should govern constitutional provisions for the creation of states in the future. They are:

1. New states may be created in the Federation of Nigeria; but no new state shall be created within the jurisdiction of any other state nor any state be created by the junction of two or more states or parts of states without the consent, signified by a two-thirds majority, of the legislatures of the states concerned as well as of the Federal Parliament.

2. No ethnic or racial group in any of the existing Regions should be split in the process of creating new states.

3. Any ethnic group which does not elect to join a proposed state should be permitted to stay out and remain with the original

state, unless such a group is not geographically contiguous to the original state.

4. The creation of a new state should satisfy the test of viability.

In regard to the proposed COR, Mid-West and Middle Belt States, I argued that these three (and only these three) should, after due inquiry, be created immediately, for reasons which I gave. First, the demand for the three was much older in order of time than that for the new ones, and had formed part of election issues in the areas concerned, with a measure of success at the polls for their protagonists; and secondly, the demand for the three states appeared to be more in accordance with what was practicable, having regard in particular to the fact that we wanted each state in the federation to be viable both financially and administratively. I emphasised that in regard to the three proposed states the first principle enunciated by me should not be applicable. The reason for this was obvious. If the three states were to be created immediately, their creation must not be made subject to the consent of the Regional Governments, two of whom (the Northern and Eastern) were unyieldingly and unconditionally opposed to the carving out of new states from their respective jurisdictions. Furthermore, I thought it was ridiculous to suggest as the NCNC had done that the question of creating new states, whether three or seventeen, could and should be tackled at all, much less settled with finality at the conference table. The delimitation of the boundaries of the new states, the determination of the viability of each of them, the ascertainment of the wishes of the people and so on and so forth were matters which only a high-powered commission could investigate and report upon.

After a long spell of spirited and heated debate which lasted for some days it was agreed that a commission should be appointed. The terms of reference of the commission were agreed upon only after a protracted and nerve-racking negotiation. About three different drafts were made by the Secretary of State, Mr Lennox-Boyd. It was the third draft that was accepted as a compromise. I did not very much like it. But Action Group delegates from the minority areas thought the commission would afford them a forum for ventilating their grievances, and that having regard to the facts at their disposal they very much hoped to win. In September 1957, a Commission of Inquiry known popularly as the Willink Commission, and officially as 'the Commission appointed to enquire into the fears of Minorities and the means of allaying them', was appointed by the Secretary of State and its terms of reference were as follows:

1. To ascertain the facts about the fears of minorities in any part of Nigeria and to propose means of allaying those fears whether well or ill founded.

2. To advise what safeguards should be included for this purpose in the Constitution of Nigeria.

3. If, but only if, no other solution seems to the Commission to meet the case, then as a last resort to make detailed recommendations for the creation of one or more new states, and in that case:

(a) to specify the precise area to be included in such state or states;

(b) to recommend the governmental and administrative structure most appropriate for it;

(c) to assess whether any state recommended would be viable from an economic and administrative point of view and what the effect of its creation would be on the Region or Regions from which it would be created and on the Federation.

4. To report its findings and recommendations to the Secretary of State for the Colonies.

The Commission came, made its investigation, and submitted a report which, in my first reaction, I described as bad and astonishing.

At the beginning of the 1958 constitutional conference, the positions taken by the Action Group, NPC and NCNC on the issue of states (and hence on the recommendations of the Minorities Commission) were different from those from which they gave battle in 1957. The Action Group rejected the recommendations of the Commission in their entirety, and demanded, without any reservation, the creation of the three proposed states. For the first time, it had the courage to tick off the NPC on the question of the proposed Middle Belt

State. The Action Group submitted to the conference memoranda in which, among other things, it urged that provisions
should be made in the constitution which would make it
possible for new states to be created in future. The NCNC as a
party was more devious than ever. It accepted the recommendations of the Minorities Commission and was opposed to
the creation of any states before independence—the Mid-West
State not excepted. It was also opposed to the consideration
at the conference of any provisions in the constitution which
would enable states to be created in future. After independence,
the NCNC argued, a constituent assembly should be convened
which would deliberate and decide on all the outstanding
problems of the country, including the question of new states.
It was interesting to note that at the 1958 Conference, the
NCNC was hand in glove with the NPC. As a matter of fact,
the NCNC did not disguise its fawning and unrelieved subordination to the NPC on all matters. This in my view was
responsible for the unashamed *volte face* of the NCNC on the
issue of the Mid-West State, the immediate creation of which
it had demanded in 1957 as well as during the inquiry by the
Minorities Commission. The NPC also accepted the recommendations of the Minorities Commission and was as adamant
as ever in its opposition to the creation of any state. It was,
however, prepared to support the proposals made in the
memoranda submitted by the Action Group and the United
Kingdom delegations concerning provisions for the creation
of states after independence. Its support was subject to the
proviso that such provisions would be so stringent as to make
the creation of new states a very difficult proposition.

When the Commission's Report came up for consideration,
it proved to be the most controversial matter dealt with by the
1958 conference. It was debated at great length and with
unparalleled vigour by all the Nigerian delegations. On one
side were the Action Group and the representatives of the
minority groups; and ranged against them on the other side
were the NCNC and the NPC, adroitly supported by the
United Kingdom delegation. In the course of the gruelling

and long-drawn discussion, the Secretary of State, Mr Lennox-Boyd made a statement in which he attempted to impale the Action Group on the horns of a dilemma. I quote his own words as recorded in the Report of the 1958 Conference:

The Secretary of State said that the Conference seemed to have two choices: on the one hand to abandon the request for independence in 1960 and instead to put the question of new states to the test at the next elections or at a series of plebiscites next year, followed by a fresh conference thereafter to consider whether new states should be created and, if so, what provision for them was needed; on the other hand to accept that if there was to be early independence no new states could be created either now or as a result of next year's elections, so that the present structure of the Federation would continue in existence at least until after the strains of independence had been taken. But he recognized that the present regional boundaries and number of Regions could not be regarded as standing for all time and accordingly commended to the Conference proposals which he tabled for a procedure to be included in the constitution for independence for effecting boundary changes and creating new Regions.

Between the end of the 1957 Conference and the beginning of that of 1958, the spokesmen of the minorities had become more insistent on their demands: they wanted the new states created before the grant of independence. They even went so far as to declare that unless these states were created they would oppose the grant of independence. Their slogan was 'no states, no independence'. Since the Action Group was the only advocate of the creation of states before independence, there was no doubt that Mr Lennox-Boyd was determined to disarm or disarray my delegation on the issue. He went about it in a most skilful and remorseless manner. If the Action Group delegation opted for the postponement of the date of independence, it would be discredited for ever and ever in the eyes of Nigerians and of the world. If on the other hand we insisted on the attainment of independence by Nigeria in 1960, then the issue of creating new states would have to be postponed until after that independence. I had a tough time in rallying the leaders of the minorities in my delegation to my unmistaken standpoint. Cablegrams poured in to them and to me from supporters of the proposed states in Nigeria calling upon us to press for the postponement of the date of independence, so that new states might be created. I, however, stood absolutely immovable. As far as I was concerned there could be no question of postponing the date of independence. In my presidential address to the Action Group Congress delivered at Calabar on Monday 28 April 1958, I had said:

You have probably noticed that two basic assumptions underly my thoughts and ideas and the views which I have expressed in this address. Firstly, I have assumed the inviolability of Nigeria's unity. Secondly, I have assumed that Nigeria will become independent before or by April 2, 1960. There are a number of well-meaning and undoubted nationalists who, incensed by the dishonest tactics of some of our political leaders, have been compelled to doubt the future unity of Nigeria and to declare that they would not support independence in 1960 unless the COR State, the Midwest State and Middle Belt State are created, and Regional boundaries are adjusted, before then.

My appeal to these outraged nationalists is that, whatever we do, we must on no account retreat from our legitimate and long-standing demand for independence. Nor must we destroy the great heritage of a united Nigeria which the British will bequeath to us on their surrender of power.

Let us all therefore hope and pray that God Almighty may guide the resumed conference to come to those conclusions which we know are the only right ones for the peace, happiness, and prosperity of the diverse peoples of this country. If the resumed conference fails in this regard, the fight for the creation of states and the adjustment of boundaries will have to be resumed by us with increased intensity. And I have no doubt at all in my mind that if our cause is just, it will, with hard work and faith in God, triumph in due course of time.

In regard to Mr Lennox-Boyd's statement quoted above, I pointed out at the conference that if the choices were indeed *alternative* as stated by him, the preference of the Action Group and its allies was clear and unequivocal. We took our stand unwaveringly on the demand for independence on 2 April 1960. It was on record, I said, that the Action Group was the spearhead of the demand for a target date for Nigeria's independence. When we first made the demand we were ridiculed and vilified by many people; but now that our dream was about to become a reality we were filled with joy. I expressed the belief that from the hints which Mr Lennox-Boyd had dropped, 1960 would be the year of Nigeria's independence. I declared, however, that the choices open to the conference were not the alternatives as stated by Mr Lennox-Boyd. I argued that it was possible, if the will were there, for the three proposed states to be created before the date of independence in 1960.

After all the arguments which could be urged for and against the creation of new states had been advanced and exhausted, the recommendations of the Minorities Commission were accepted by the conference with minor modifications. In view of the alternative choices placed before the conference by Mr Lennox-Boyd, and which were obviously directed against my delegation, I felt myself under compulsion, and, thank God, I succeeded in carrying all my colleagues with me, to make the best of a bad situation in order to ensure that Nigeria attains to independence in 1960. But the nearer we are to the day of Nigeria's independence, the firmer I become in my conviction that the remedies proposed by the Willink Commission are inappropriate and inefficacious and that Britain has let down the minority ethnic groups in Nigeria by the refusal of Her Majesty's Government to create the three proposed states before its handing over of power.

Before I proceed to deal with the main recommendations of the Commission, I would like to make some preliminary remarks. In the first place the minority groups in each Region rightly or wrongly accuse the government of the Region of oppression, victimisation and tyranny. They fear that their sufferings will be aggravated after Nigeria shall have attained independence, and the restraining and liberalising influence of the British Government has been withdrawn. Consequently, the Nigerian minorities, particularly those of the Northern Region, contemplate the attainment of sovereignty by Nigeria on 1 October 1960, with a feeling of trepidation. At page 87 paragraph 2 of its Report, the Commission itself observes as follows:

In each Region, we came to the conclusion that—on its own merits—a separate state would not provide a remedy for the fears expressed; we were clear all the same that there remained a body of genuine fears and that the future was regarded with real apprehension.

This is one of the findings of the Commission, and I am strongly of the opinion that by failing to create the three proposed states before independence, we have omitted to do the one and only thing that would have given the minority ethnic groups a feeling of security, in a new and free Nigeria.

It is Aristotle who says that courage is the facing of a known danger for a noble purpose. I admit that independence for Nigeria involves many risks and that all the citizens of the country must be prepared to meet those risks. After independence we will have to stand on our own and rely on our own resources. The unifying force—'the cement' to borrow Lord Chandos's expression—which had hitherto been supplied by the United Kingdom Government will be removed, and will have to be replaced by new virtues of our own which must be capable of keeping all the diverse elements of the country together in mutual trust and harmony and with a common national purpose. Internal and external problems, of a new complexion and variety, will press themselves upon us, sometimes demanding an urgent and always a judicious solution. Our government might be good and benevolent or it might be bad and tyrannical. In all the circumstances of a new and independent Nigeria, we must be prepared to fend for ourselves. It would be idle, and a negation of our sovereignty, for us as a nation or as individual citizens to look to Britain or to any other country for succour or for the solution of our problems. Whilst political independence for our country, like all great ventures, involves risks, it is nevertheless a noble purpose. The yearning for independence is a natural instinct embedded in the breast of man by Nature. Had it been natural for man to live in slavery or under the domination of others with perfect contentment, the human race would have long ago been exterminated.

As we approach independence, however, we must not mistake foolhardiness for courage. While it is necessary, for human evolution, to take risks, it does not follow that steps should not be taken to minimise such risks, so as to reduce the dangers of the venture on which we propose to embark. When Sir John Hunt, Sir Edmund Hillary and their associates were invited to make an attempt on Mount Everest they knew they were taking risks because others before them had failed and perished in the attempt. Nevertheless they took all the precautions which common sense and modern science dictated. Furthermore, their aim was not merely to climb to the top of the mountain, but in the process to acquire information which would enable them to make a valuable contribution to knowledge. Similarly, I am of the opinion that as we approach and enter into independence, we must take such steps as prudence and foresight dictate to minimise the risks involved in our noble venture. In this connection we must never lose sight of the fact that the attainment of independence is not an end in itself. It is a noble means to a great end. It must be our aim to maintain the existing unity of the country, guarantee individual liberty for the people, promote harmonious relations between the different groups, nurture the democratic way of life, and generate wholesome influences on other parts of the world. It has been said that bad self-rule is preferable to benevolent foreign rule. Well said; but we must not on that account deliberately, carelessly or spitefully do anything which to all intents and purposes is bound to operate to the prejudice of good government. In ushering in a new and free Nigeria, it is imperative that we take those steps which wisdom and the empirical facts of history proclaim to be essential and prerequisite to harmony and happiness among the diverse peoples of our land.

In the second place, I have been accused by my political opponents of supporting the creation of new states in order to catch votes from the minority areas with a view to winning the last federal elections. I make no apologies for aspiring to win the federal elections. This is a legitimate objective which I strove and I am still striving after. But my support for the creation of new states is not motivated by a mere desire to attract votes. As has been amply demonstrated in the last chapter, my support springs from a long-standing and deep-rooted conviction. With me, federalism and the creation of more states is an article of faith.

Now to the Report of the Minorities Commission. I will only refer to two features which I consider to be crucial and fundamental. In the one, the Commission recognised the fact but failed to direct itself as to the consequences which would of a necessity flow from the existence of such a fact. In the other the Commission made, as the very foundation of its recommendations, an assumption which itself requires rigorous proof over a period of years after Nigeria's attainment of independence.

At page 3 paragraph 11 of its report, the Commission admits that the Federation of Nigeria is 'unusual in the relative size of the units which make it up.' This is an incontrovertible statement of fact. In this connection, I would like to refer to a passage in Professor Wheare's illuminating book entitled *Federal Government*. 'The capacity of states to work a federal union', says Professor Wheare, 'is also greatly influenced by their size. It is undesirable that one or two units should be so powerful that they can overrule the others and bend the will of the federal government to themselves.' The Professor continues: 'The size of the units concerned—in wealth, area and population—is therefore of prime importance. There must be some sort of reasonable balance which will insure that all the units can maintain their independence within the sphere allotted to them and that no one can dominate others. It must be the task of those who frame and work a federal government to see that no unit shall be too large, and, equally important, none too small.'

It is obvious that when the Willink Commission described the Federation of Nigeria as 'unusual in the relative size of the units which make it up', they were well aware of the above quoted principles enunciated by Professor Wheare, and that they were implicitly adverting to the Northern Region, whose size, population and potential wealth are greater than those of the other Regions put together. It is strange and accordingly detracts irreparably from the value of its recommendations that the Commission gave no thought at all in its report to the danger to the entire Federation of Nigeria inherent in the size and population of the Northern Region. The slogan of the NPC (the ruling party in the North) is 'One North, One People'; and significantly enough this party has so far refused to change its name and constitution to enable Nigerians other than those who are indigenous to the Northern Region to become its members. Nevertheless this political party which is exclusive to Northerners not only insists on maintaining the feudal aristocracy of the North but also seeks to dominate the government of the Federation. There is no doubt that the Northern Region as at present constituted is determined to bend the will of the Federal Government to its own and, if it can, to make the other Regions live in permanent subordination to it. During the 1958 Conference, I warned that with the harsh feudal system operating in the area, the NPC stood a chance of winning all the seats (174 out of a total of 312 for the whole of Nigeria) allocated to the Northern Region. Alternatively it might win so many of these 174 seats that it would only require a few political satellites from the South to enable it to control the affairs of the Federal Government. In support of my warning, I referred to a newspaper article in which the writer, who himself had spent many years in the Northern Region, said: 'As long as the Middle Belt areas lie within the zone of Northern Regional Government and control, so long will the NPC have a special electoral influence.' My warning which was unheeded at the time has been fully vindicated.

Again at page 30 paragraph 9 of the Report, the Commission says:

If therefore grievances and fears were the sum total of the case for a separate state we should have no doubt that those recounted to us—all of which proved to contain large elements of exaggeration

—so far from justifying the creation of a new state could in fact be better remedied by other means. There are however intangible qualities such as national pride and love for a national language which contribute to the desire for a separate political organisation, and we think it necessary to examine in detail the feeling of the various sections of the area in relation to the proposal.

After studying the report with great care I have failed to see a single passage which indicates that the Commission has given due consideration to the 'intangible qualities' to which it refers in the passage quoted above. What are these 'intangible qualities'? According to Professor Wheare there are certain factors which produce in communities the desire for separate existence within a federal union. These factors which the Commission described as 'intangible qualities' include (1) previous existence, (2) geographical differences, (3) differences in language and religion, and (4) dissimilarity of social and political institutions. All these factors are very much present in Nigeria, and they create in each Region a sharp and bold line of demarcation between the majority ethnic group on the one hand and the minority ethnic groups on the other.

In sum, the Commission has found (a) that genuine fears exist among the minorities towards the majority ethnic groups; (b) that the Federation of Nigeria is unusual in the relative size of its units; and (c) that there are 'intangible qualities' which induce people to want separate states. In its recommendations, however, it only deals with the fears, and ignores its other two major findings. Even so, the recommendations which it made for allaying those fears are, as I said before, absolutely irrelevant and inappropriate. Broadly speaking, there are three of them. The Commission recommends, first the incorporation in our constitution of fundamental human rights; second, the ultimate control by the federal government of the Nigeria Police Force; and third, the creation of Special and Minority Areas in the Western and Eastern Regions only. Surely the Commission did not expect any reasonable and unbiased person to take these recommendations seriously. Fundamental human rights are ordained not for the protection of ethnic minorities as such but for the protection of the citizens at large against executive and legislative tyranny or excesses. In other words, even if Nigeria was divided into states on an ethnic basis, or even if it consisted of one homogeneous ethnic group, it would still have been necessary to entrench fundamental human rights in our constitution. As a matter of fact discussion on the entrenchment of these rights in our constitution first took place in 1953 at the instance of the Action Group-NCNC alliance, and were reopened in 1957 when the Action Group submitted a memorandum to the Conference on the subject. On each occasion, the subject was discussed without relating it to the fears of minorities in the Federation. The same is true of police. When the 1953 Conference decided that police should remain an exclusive federal subject, the question of states and the fears of minorities were not at all in issue. When the matter was again raised by the Action Group in 1957, and police was removed from the exclusive federal list and placed on the concurrent list, there was no question that this was being done to allay or aggravate the fears of minorities which were still then to be investigated.

The recommendation that certain areas in the West and East should be declared Special and Minority Areas is a very poor and unsavoury sop. In spite of the acceptance by the 1958 Conference of this recommendation, the minorities in the areas concerned continue to clamour for the creation of new states. Paragraphs 52, 53 and 56 of the report of the 1958 Constitutional Conference succinctly and explicitly set out the decisions of the Constitutional Conference concerning the creation of Special Area and Minority Area.

The Conference noted the recommendation of the Minorities Commission that there should be established a Special Area Board for the delta area on the coast between Opobo and the mouth of the Benin River, and agreed as follows:
(a) There should be constitutional provision for the establishment of a Niger Delta Development Board for an initial period of 10 years, after which the Federal and Eastern and Western Regional Governments should consider, in consultation with

202

the Board itself and the local authorities in the area, whether it should continue in existence.

(b) The Board should consist of a Chairman appointed by the Federal Government, one representative each of the Eastern and Western Regional Governments, and a number of representatives of the inhabitants of the area. The number of representatives from the Eastern and Western parts of the area should be roughly in proportion to the number of people living in the area belonging respectively to the two Regions. The Chairman and Secretary of the Board should be full-time and the other members part-time.

(c) The Board should be concerned solely with the physical development of the area. . . . It should carry out a survey of the area to ascertain what development is needed in land improvement and drainage and in the improvement of communications; it should investigate questions of agriculture, fisheries, land tenure and forestry involved in this survey; and should advise the Federal and the Eastern and Western Regional Governments as required on the planning and execution of development in the area.

(d) The funds for carrying out these functions should be provided by the Federal Government.

The Conference considered the recommendations of the Minorities Commission for the establishment of certain Minority Areas as one means of allaying the fears of minorities, and agreed that:

(a) A Minority Area should be created in the Western Region and should consist of the whole of the Benin and Delta Provinces, excluding Warri Division and Akoko-Edo District, on the understanding that the position of Warri Division in relation to the proposed area should be further considered locally by the Government of the Western Region.

(b) The proposed Council should be composed of members of the House of Assembly, House of Representatives and House of Chiefs elected or appointed from within the area.

(c) The functions of the proposed Council should be broadly to foster the well-being, cultural advancement and economic and social development of the Minority Area, to bring to the notice of the Western Regional Government any discrimination against the Area and to exercise such executive powers as might be delegated to it from time to time by the Regional Government.

The Commission had also recommended that the former Province of Calabar should be made a Minority Area and that a Calabar

Council should be appointed. The Conference agreed that there should be a Calabar Minority Area consisting of Calabar Province, subject to subsequent enquiry by the Governor of the Region and decision in his discretion as to whether any or all of the Annangs and Aro-Ibos should for this purpose remain in or be excised from the Area. The Conference also agreed that the principles governing the functions and composition of the Calabar Minority Area Council should be the same as those agreed in respect of the Mid-West Council in the Western Region.

Having regard to the fact that final decisions as to what legislative or executive action should be taken on the proposals of the Special Area Board and of the Minority Area Councils rest with the Western and Eastern Regional Governments, the minorities concerned have been left in pretty much the same plight as the Commission found them. The additional forums provided for the minorities to ventilate their grievances and formulate proposals for their advancement and happiness would only lead to more acute frustration unless the Regional Governments concerned are willing as well as financially able to redress the grievances and implement a substantial part of the proposals. In regard to the Eastern Government *vis-à-vis* its Special and Minority Areas there is neither the willingness nor the financial capacity to do what may be required. The Federal Government on the other hand, controlled as it is by the NCNC and the NPC, would not be likely to show that earnestness, initiative, leadership and financial generosity which the Commission had presumed in its favour, in the development of the Special Area.

On page 89 paragraph 10, the Commission laid the foundation for its recommendations in the following words:

As to the assumption that power will only be used to the exclusive advantage of the party in office, it would be a rash Commission that made prophecies. But, as we have said, there are possibilities in the political scene that would make it to the interest of any party to woo the minorities, and there is one further point. The whole structure of the proceedings leading to independence is based on the belief that Nigeria means to follow the road of liberal democracy and parliamentary government; to base parts of the structure on the opposite assumption is to invite governments to do their worst. But if that road is followed, votes will count and in the last resort it is the votes that will win fair treatment for minorities.

'But if that road is followed. . . .' It is on the supposition that this imponderable hypothesis might materialise that the Commission came to the conclusion that means other than the creation of states were sufficient to allay the fears of Nigerian minorities. I have already said that the means proposed by the Commission and accepted by the Conference are inappropriate. I now wish to add that the supposition on which the recommendations are based is rash and reckless in the extreme.

In paragraph 11 of page 89 of its Report the Commission quotes Churchill's graphic definition of liberal democracy:

We have spoken of liberal democracy and have used such words as freedom and fair treatment. If we are asked to define these concepts, we cannot clarify them better than by the following quotation:

'. . . It has been said that the price of freedom is eternal vigilance. The question arises, What is freedom? There are one or two quite simple, practical tests by which it can be known in the modern world in peace conditions, namely:

Is there the right to free expression of opinion and of opposition and criticism of the Government of the day?

Have the people the right to turn out a Government of which they disapprove, and are constitutional means provided by which they can make their will apparent?

Are their courts of justice free from violence by the Executive and from threats of mob violence, and free of all association with particular political parties?

Will these courts administer open and well-established laws which are associated in the human mind with the broad principles of decency and justice?

Will there be fair play for poor as well as for rich, for private persons as well as for Government officials?

Will the rights of the individual, subject to his duties to the State, be maintained and asserted and exalted?

Is the ordinary peasant or workman who is earning a living by daily toil and striving to bring up a family, free from the fear that some grim police organisation under the control of a single party . . . will tap him on the shoulder and pack him off without fair or open trial to bondage or ill treatment?'

The truth is that apart from the High Courts and Magistrates' Courts presided over by British-trained barristers or solicitors of requisite post-call experience, the conditions which obtain today and will persist for some years to come in the Northern Region of Nigeria are the very opposite of the concepts defined in Churchill's inimitable words. What is more, the policy-making elements in the NPC, which now dominates the affairs of the Federal Government, are strong believers in the sacrosanct nature of the feudal system from which they draw their inspiration and main support.

Nigeria is a young country by modern standards. In the art of democracy it is still an infant. In this art it has been made to stand on its feet and walk thus far mainly by the help of the British Government which has up to now been the tutelary power. But after 1 October this year, Nigeria will be left to stand and walk on its own in the realm of democratic concepts and practices. Will it succeed? Will it faithfully follow the road of liberal democracy and parliamentary government? These are the big questions; and the answers to them are in the womb of the unknown and unfathomable future.

It is my unshaken belief that Nigeria's feet would have been firmly and unswervingly set on the road of liberal democracy if the three proposed states had been created by Britain before she surrenders sovereign power over Nigeria on 1 October 1960. True enough, the heterogeneous character of the peoples of Nigeria is in itself a potential check on the emergence of a totalitarian form of government. It is most unlikely that all the ethnic groups in the country will succumb at one and the same time to the charm and hypnotism, or the blustering and bludgeoning of a dictator. It is not going to be easy for any leader however powerful he may be to regiment Nigeria's diverse peoples into a uniform mass either of terrorised subjects or of blind fanatical followers. Here then are Nigeria's natural and formidable factors in favour of democracy. But if a Northern leader were to emerge who had or crazily believed he had the whole of the Northern Region under his heel, the factors already mentioned will not of themselves be an effective enough deterrent to an attempt on his part to tyrannise over the remaining lesser half of the Federation. If such an attempt as this were made, it would invite chaos and disaster. On the other hand, if the three proposed states (particularly the Middle Belt State) had been created, such an attempt would have been rendered a remote possibility.

When Britain brought together all the ethnic groups in Nigeria, she had done so in the pursuit of her national self-interest and without the consent of the peoples concerned. On the eve of her surrender of sovereignty over them, therefore, she owes it a duty to them to give them a right of self-determination. In my candid opinion, the Minorities Commission, far from vindicating Britain's stand on the issue, only proclaims her as an unabashed betrayer of Nigeria's minority ethnic groups. The terms of reference of the Commission were too narrow to start with, and the recommendations made by the Commission leave me in no doubt that the Inquiry had been deliberately staged in order to provide an authoritative excuse for Britain to wash her hands of the matter and transfer responsibility for creating the three proposed states, or any states for that matter, to the majority ethnic groups. As far back as 1955 Mr Lennox-Boyd himself declared publicly in Nigeria that it was unwise and not in the interest of Nigerian unity to demand the creation of additional states or regions. Before the Commission ever arrived in Nigeria all the high-ranking British officials without exception (from the Governor-General downwards) had made up their minds that the creation of more states was detrimental to Nigeria's unity. During the 1957 Constitutional Conference, the Secretary of State and Nigeria's Governor-General made certain clever moves, the import of which was not understood by me until I saw the report of the Minorities Commission. My party and the NPC had advocated the regionalisation of the police force. That is to say, each Regional Government should have its own police force whilst the Federal Government would have its own for federal purposes. The case of my delegation in this connection was simple. Each Regional Government is charged with responsibility for law and order in the area of its jurisdiction. I thought, therefore, that it was only right and proper that the Regional Governments should have at their disposal all the means for effectively discharging their responsibility. To deprive them of the operational control of the police force was to render them impotent in the face of challenge to or a serious breach of law and order. After a long argument, and a good deal of persuasion by the Secretary of State and the Governor-General the Conference was made to agree, among other things:

that no police force in Nigeria should, so far as its use and operational control were concerned, at any time come under the control of political parties . . .;

that the Federal and Regional Governments would always have a concurrent responsibility for law and order throughout the Federation and that after independence the ultimate responsibility for this, at present vested in the Secretary of State, would be inherited by the Federal Government;

that, in the meantime, Police should be deleted from the Exclusive Legislative List and an item on the following lines be inserted in the Concurrent Legislative List.

'Police, provided that the Legislature of any Region shall not enact any law in pursuance of this item unless the Secretary of State has, after consultation with all the Nigerian Governments, decided that Regions should set up their own police forces.'

During the same Conference, the Action Group submitted a memorandum requiring the Conference to agree that fundamental human rights should be entrenched in our constitution. These rights were set out in outline in the memorandum. Discussion on this subject was accordingly commenced; but in the course of it the Secretary of State made a suggestion which led to the following conclusion which was recorded in the Report of the Conference:

The question of the inclusion in the constitution of provisions to safeguard fundamental human rights was discussed. It was agreed that such provision should be made, but that because of the complexity of this important subject the Secretary of State's legal advisers should first prepare, in the light of the memoranda submitted to the Conference and the discussion on them, draft clauses for insertion in the constitutional instruments. These clauses should be submitted to all Nigerian Governments and considered at a resumed Conference.

It was passing strange that two of the three main recommendations made by the Commission concerned the control of the Nigeria Police and the entrenchment of fundamental human rights in our constitution. It remains for me to say that the draft Bill of Rights promised by the Secretary of State was never circulated, as agreed, to the Nigerian Governments, nor was it prepared until more than a year after the recommendations of the Minorities Commission had been accepted.

The oft-repeated argument that the creation of more states will impair the unity of Nigeria or make for a weak Federal Government has never impressed me. There are twenty cantons or regions in Switzerland and yet the country is as united and its federal government as strong as can be. In Canada there are nine Provinces, but no one in his senses will say that Canada is not united, or that its federal government is weak. Furthermore, in Switzerland and Canada the linguistic units are grouped in different Cantons and Provinces respectively. There is no overlapping between one linguistic group and another. As far as I know, all these arrangements have earned for Switzerland the praise of being the most democratic country in the world. The Minorities Commission held the view that if new states were created as demanded, there would still be minority groups within them. This is granted. But it is incontestable that if such states were created after a plebiscite the minority ethnic groups within them would be consenting minorities, unlike the minorities in the present Regions. The Commission also expressed the fear that the creation of new states would emphasise tribal feelings which it was their duty to moderate. My own comment on this is that the groups to whom the Commission referred were not tribes at all. The English, Scots or Welsh will resent being described as tribes. They are ethnic units in Britain. According to *The Times* of 13 December 1957, Mr Harold Macmillan, Britain's Prime Minister, sent a letter to the Welsh Advisory Council in which he spoke of 'the majority of the Welsh nation'. In that letter, he acknowledged that Wales not only had her own language but also her own distinctive needs and culture, and that any system of government must be based on a full recognition of these facts. He, however, expressed the belief that the majority of the Welsh nation were in agreement that their interests could best be furthered by a continued association with England and the English people. It is significant to observe that the British Prime Minister could address the Welsh people in this way after almost 700 years of association between England and Wales. It may be stated in passing that Nigeria is not yet one hundred years old, and Nigerian peoples are still to learn to live together on their own, without outside surveillance and guidance, after 1 October this year.

The Premiers' Summit Meeting, to which I have previously referred, recognised that the most prominent rock on which the ship of Nigeria's unity, welfare, progress and happiness might founder was the issue of new states. We took cognisance at that meeting not only of the existing strong demands for new states, but also of the possibility of similar demands after independence. It was in this understanding spirit that the subject was fully examined, and the principles which I have already stated were enunciated. It is noteworthy that the Premiers' Meeting did not deal with the issue of Nigeria's independence until after this subject had been disposed of. It must be noted that when the Sardauna of Sokoto, Sir Abubakar Tafawa Balewa and their colleagues agreed to these principles at the Premiers' Summit Meeting they were doing so for the second time, as they had previously agreed to exactly the same principles at Ikorodu. Furthermore, my colleagues and I consider the principles laid down for the solution of the minorities problem by the Premiers' Meeting as sound, and as being capable, in their faithful application, of satisfying the insistent clamour for more states. If the wishes of the people of the area concerned were consulted through a plebiscite and the majority of them voted against the creation of the proposed state, or alternatively if the majority voted in favour but the proposed state, after due inquiry, proved not to be viable, it would have been untenable for the leaders of the agitation, in either case, to continue to press for the immediate creation of the proposed state. By going through the processes laid down in the principles, they would have felt that they had been given a square deal. They would certainly have contented themselves with waiting until such a time in the future when the proposed state would both be viable and enjoy the support of the majority of the people in its area.

The NPC and the NCNC having mystifyingly failed to abide by the principles agreed to at the Premiers' Summit Meeting, it was left to the 1958 Constitutional Conference to formulate a procedure for incorporation into the constitution for the creation of states after independence. The procedure is as follows:

An area forming part of one or more Regions may be converted into a new Region by means of the following procedure:

(i) Each House of the Federal Legislature must pass by a two-thirds majority of all the members a resolution approving a proposal that the procedure for creating a new Region should be set in motion.

(ii) The proposal must then be submitted to each House of all the Regional Legislatures and must be approved either (1) by resolution passed by each House of the Legislatures of two Regions, provided these include the Region or Regions out of which the new state would be created, or (2) by resolution passed by each House of the Legislatures of a bare majority of the Regions.

(iii) The Federal Legislature may then enact a law providing for such constitutional amendments as are necessary or expedient to give effect to the proposal. This law should then be submitted to the Legislative Houses of all the Regions and should require the approval by resolution of the Legislative Houses of at least two Regions.

(iv) Thereafter before the law can come into operation a referendum must be held in the area which it is proposed to convert into a Region, at which all inhabitants of that area who are entitled to vote at elections to the House of Representatives shall be entitled to vote, and at which at least 60 per cent of those who in fact vote are in favour of the proposal.

From present trends and indications, it does not look as if the present Governments of the Federation and of the Eastern and Northern Regions will approach and discharge the responsibilities laid on their legislatures fairly and equitably. Out of spite towards the Action Group (which is the party in power in the Western Region), and under pressure from the NCNC, the three Governments may take steps to create the Mid-West State only. At the same time, because of the inexorable opposition of the NPC and the NCNC, the three Governments will refuse to consider much less take steps towards the creation of the Middle Belt State, the COR State, or any other state which will have to be carved out of the Northern Region or Eastern Region. Be it so. Speaking for myself, I shall always welcome the creation of the Mid-West State. For I am quite convinced that the creation of this state will be bound to exacerbate the feelings of minorities in the other Regions, and the agitation for more states in those regions will be much more intense than before. The new Mid-West State will be a living tangible symbol of hope for other minorities. The more enlightened and educated and the more politically conscious these other minorities become, the clearer to them will be the grave injustice of carving a new state from the smallest Region for the minorities there, while at the same time turning a deaf ear to the demands of other minorities who from all accounts have a much stronger case. Indeed, the creation of the Mid-West State will be the beginning of a journey which may be short or long but which will, in my considered judgment, irresistibly bring Nigeria to the goal of true federalism and more states, and of individual freedom and happiness for all our people.

CHAPTER 14

THE ACTION GROUP

THE announcement in Nigerian newspapers on the 21 March 1951 of the birth of the Action Group took the country by storm. Those who later became covert and overt adversaries of the party heralded its debut in glowing terms. The *Daily Times*, in an editorial comment headed 'Awakening In The West', hailed it as 'first in the field with a definite plan for winning seats under the new Constitution.' The paper described the objective of the Action Group as 'admirable and deserving of support', and concluded its comment in the following words:

The CPP in the Gold Coast has proved that party organisation pays big dividends.

We therefore welcome the Action Group to the Nigerian political scene. And may other organisations follow its lead. Several strong parties are required if the new Constitution is to function effectively.

The *West African Pilot* of 29 March 1951 (under the Managing Editorship of Dr Azikiwe), in an editorial comment wished the Action Group the best of luck, and said of the new party as follows:

Its aims and objects are laudable and its programme of action is varied and wide.

From all appearances it is an awakening consciousness in the West. . . . It agrees in some aspects with the Gold Coast Convention People's Party in being a party organisation.

By the time the formation of the Action Group was announced, it was already one year old. Early in March 1950, I had issued a circular to about sixty persons drawn from different parts of the Western Region, inviting them to a meeting which was to take place in my house at Ibadan on Sunday 26 March 1950, at 9 o'clock in the morning. Over a period of some six months previously, I had made personal contacts and had held discussions with every one of those who had been invited to the meeting. In the letter of invitation, I reminded them as follows:

You have already had a hint of the object of the meeting. Put in a nutshell the object is to devise plans for organising the people of the Western Region so that they may be able to play an influential and effective role in the affairs of Nigeria under the New Constitution.

In spite of my personal contacts with them and the circular letter only seven out of the over sixty persons invited attended the meeting.

These seven persons are still staunch and leading members of the Action Group and they are:

(1) Mr S. O. Shonibare, then Manager UAC (Technical) Limited, Lagos; now Federal Publicity Secretary of the Action Group and Managing Director of the Amalgamated Press of Nigeria Limited;

(2) Chief Abiodun Akerele, Barrister-at-Law; now Member of the House of Representatives and Balogun of Oyo;

(3) Mr S. T. Oredein, then Shorthand Typist in the employ of the British-American Tobacco Company Limited and Secretary of the BATC Workers Union; now Principal Organising Secretary of the Action Group, Western Region;

(4) Mr Olatunji Dosumu, then Journalist in the employ of the Service Press Limited; now Administrative Secretary of the Action Group, Western Region;

(5) Mr J. Ola Adigun, then Editor of *Morning Star*; now Minister of Health and Social Welfare, Western Region;

(6) Mr Adeyiga Akinsanya, now Law Student, but formerly Manager of the African Press Limited—Printers and Publishers of the *Nigerian Tribune*; and

(7) Mr Ayo Akinsanya, Chemist and Druggist, now Executive Director of the Western Nigeria Development Corporation.

Nothing daunted, I proceeded to address my audience of seven.

The performances of the people of the Western Region at

214

the Regional and General Conferences for the review of the Richards Constitution had shown that they were unorganised, and were lacking in concerted programme and effective leadership. At the Western Regional Conference the spectacle of the motley crowd which our representatives presented so nauseated me that I declined election to the General Conference. I continued, however, to project my views on the constitutional review through my friends and NYM colleagues like Chief Bode Thomas, Mr S. O. Awokoya, and Dr A. S. Agbaje with whom I had constant meetings throughout the period of the review. In an article entitled 'Sidelights on Enugu Legco', Chief (then Mr) Anthony Enahoro deplored the weakness of the Western members of the Legislative Council. The Easterners, he pointed out, knew how to get things done; the Northerners believed in the leadership of Tafawa Balewa (now Sir Abubakar); but none of the Western representatives in the Legislative Council knew what the other man was going to do. I thought it would be a tragedy if the Western Region, which like other Regions was going to have its own parliament and a ministerial system of government, were to enter the new dispensation in its present unorganised and undisciplined state. To this end, it was in my view imperative that the complacent, individualistic, reactionary and conservative politicians who were then in the House of Assembly and some of whom were representing the Western Region in the Legislative Council should not be allowed to get elected into the new House of Assembly. If they were, they would become ready and willing tools in the hands of British Administrative Officers, most of whom were not at all pleased with the new Constitution, and who would therefore be only too happy if the ministerial experiment under the constitution failed. Instead, everything possible should be done to get elected into the House of Assembly a group of progressive elements in the Region who shared the same political views and ideals, were prepared to work together as a team in pursuance of agreed policies and programmes, and were willing to submit themselves to party discipline.

The new Constitution would be a test of the readiness and fitness of Nigerians to manage their own affairs. In order to pass this test, it would be of paramount importance for the new ministers to run and maintain an efficient as well as a stable government. There could be no such government, unless there was a dynamic and well-disciplined political party with a majority in the new House of Assembly, and with a definite programme which that party would set out to fulfil during its term of office. If it was agreed that an organised body was a desideratum to the success of Nigerian political leaders under the new Constitution, then as soon as such a body came into being, it must appoint a Shadow Cabinet. I pointed out that a political party that was worth its salt should have a permanent Shadow Cabinet when it was not in office. In the present case, the duty of the Shadow Cabinet of the new organisation would be

(1) to make a detailed study of all the problems affecting the various departments of the Nigerian Government, so that if the Cabinet eventually acceded to office its members would have a proper and self-reliant grasp of the subjects of their respective portfolios; and
(2) to formulate policies and programmes in respect of all such departments, which would be put to the country as the objectives which the party pledged itself to achieve during its tenure of five years.

When these had been done, it would be the duty of the party, if it won a majority of seats in the House of Assembly and formed the government, to embark on the execution of its policies and programmes in an organised manner and with the utmost despatch.

At present there was no political party in existence dedicated to operating in the manner which I had outlined. The NNDP was for all practical purposes a Lagos organisation and was not therefore suitable for the end in view. The NCNC was not sufficiently organised to present an effective programme. It was not even a political party, but an amalgam of various unions and associations which had very little in common save the proclaimed common objective of the unity of the country, and of opposition to British imperialism. In spite of this claim, however, and in spite of the miscellany of unions constituting it, the influence of the NCNC was not felt at all during the review of the Richards Constitution. Dr Azikiwe himself, the President of the NCNC, was not in the country during the review and took no part at all in it. Besides, with all its shortcomings the introduction of the new Constitution would *ipso facto* demand of Nigerian leaders a change of tactics and the cultivation of a new phase of nationalism, namely the constructive phase. The NCNC and its leadership did not appear to me to be consecrated to this novel, momentous and inevitably trying phase. As for the NYM, its activities and following, like those of the NCNC, were confined to urban areas and the working-class alone. Any organisation that did not appeal to and cater for the interest of the peasantry could not reckon on winning a majority of seats in the coming election. Besides, the NYM was a dying organisation; and much more effort would be required to revive it than would be needed to start a new organisation with an entirely clean slate, The National Emergency Council was, as its name suggested, an *ad hoc* organisation which was established to deal with the shooting incident at the Enugu Coal Mines in 1949. It had, been envisaged that the NEC would devise ways and means of establishing a new nationalist movement which would absorb all existing organisations. I had my doubt about the success of the NEC in achieving this great objective. In any case, the existence of a new political organisation such as I had in mind would not conflict with the aspirations of the NEC. As for the Egbe Omo Oduduwa, I ruled it out of reckoning. The following is what I said about it, as recorded by Mr S. T. Oredein (*Pro tem* Secretary) in the minutes of this first meeting:

This was the only organisation which enjoyed popularity in the Western Provinces at present. The recent tour of its Administrative Secretary had given an adequate proof of its popularity, but it was not a political organisation. It did not profess to send candidates to the Legislative Council. Members even dreaded and considered it dangerous for the Egbe to set out to fight elections. The danger would tend to the destruction of the Egbe and its ideal.

Having eliminated all existing organisations, the logical sequence was that a new one should be formed. I stressed that any new party under which I would be prepared to work and serve must place a premium on action rather than on words. Furthermore, only people in whom we could absolutely trust should be invited to the membership of the new party at the early stages. I thought three things were indispensable to the success of the new venture. The first was what I have just mentioned—action. There had been a good deal of gaseous effusions on the part of Nigerian politicians in the past, so much so that it had often been said of them by our white administrators that our politicians could only bark but never could bite. It was enough, I said, if our new organisation could bite even though it did not bark. The second prerequisite was that there should be discipline, and consensus of minds on fundamental principles among those who were to constitute the foundation of the new organisation. It was only the possession of these attributes that would enable the new party successfully to meet the challenge of the new Constitution, and to beat back the onslaught of any opponents. The third was secrecy. Any new political party that was formed in any part of the country must reckon with fierce and unbridled hostility from Dr Azikiwe. If the existence of such a party was known to him before its ideals had been well entrenched in the minds of its founders, it would be the easiest thing in the world for him to nip it in the bud by means of his skilled and fierce propaganda. The new party, if formed, must not, therefore, be announced to the public, nor must its existence be mentioned beyond an absolutely trusted circle, until its founders were satisfied that they could withstand the onslaught of its foes from whatever quarters it might come. After a lengthy discussion, this meeting of eight resolved that a new political party should be formed and that its name should be 'Action Group'.

I then addressed this first meeting and subsequent meetings on methods of organisation. I suggested that the organisation of the Action Group should be based on the smallest possible units in towns and villages, to be known as the Local Committees. These Local Committees should be grouped at the Divisional Level into Divisional Committees to which the Local Committees would send representatives. The representatives of the Divisional Committees would in turn constitute the Regional Body of the Action Group. I outlined the four immediate tasks which the Group must undertake:

1. Organisation;
2. Drawing up a list of candidates for election to the House of Assembly;
3. Programme; and
4. Propaganda.

In regard to (3) above, it was decided that the following items should feature in the initial programme of the Group (and I now quote from the minutes of the first meeting):

(1) Reform of the civil service; (2) Police reform; (3) Education; (4) Social and welfare services; (5) Water supply; (6) Agriculture; (7) Labour; (8) Elimination of chieftaincy disputes and regulation of succession to chieftaincies; (9) Abolition of native courts (this was later reversed and in its place was substituted native court reform); (10) Reform of land tenure; (11) Local government reform; (12) North-Western boundary; (13) Industrialisation; (14) Review of 'The Ten-Year Development Programmes' (this was a programme launched by the Nigerian Government); (15) Town planning; (16) Transport; (17) Mines; (18) Communications; (19) Minorities; and (20) Self-Government for Nigeria now (this was later modified to self-government for Nigeria within five years after the introduction of the Macpherson Constitution).

Before the public announcement of its existence, nine secret meetings of the Action Group had been held between the 26 March 1950 and the 4 March 1951. During this period, three decisions which are worthy of note in the life of the party were made. The first was whether the Action Group should continue to function as a separate political organisation, or whether its members should dissolve it and transfer their activities to the Egbe Omo Oduduwa which was then contemplating the formation of a political wing.

After the fatal blow to the NYM in 1941, those who disagreed politically with Dr Azikiwe had no effective political platform from which to fight. Dr Azikiwe was himself without a party until he joined the NNDP in 1945. It was on the platform of the NNDP that he contested the election to the Legislative Council in 1946. When the Egbe Omo Oduduwa was inaugurated in 1948 and Dr Azikiwe launched a savage attack on it, most of the Yoruba politicians who disagreed with Dr Azikiwe rallied to the banner of the Egbe. Even Chief H. O. Davies, Q.C., now a faithful follower of the NCNC, was there at the beginning. But the Egbe was not a political party; and the NYM continued to sink more and more into ineptitude and impotence. Those of us who wanted political action never tired of making a search for a new organisation. I was one of the founders of the NEC in 1949, a member of its Central Executive and the Chairman of its Ibadan Branch. The NEC embraced all the nationalists in Southern Nigeria. When it was founded, Dr Azikiwe was away from the country. But the organisation died soon after his return. Those of my colleagues who were resident in Lagos organised the Area Council, on the platform of which the Lagos Town Council election of 1950 was fought by us against the NNDP led by Dr Azikiwe. When the idea of starting a new party occurred to me in 1949, and I began to make contacts, I had frequent discussions with the leaders of the Egbe Omo Oduduwa. It was curious to note that many of them were tired of politics which they regarded as 'a dirty game'. I persisted in lobbying them. If the new party was to make any appreciable showing at all during the regional elections it must make use of the organisation and branches of the Egbe Omo Oduduwa throughout the Western Region. Besides, party organisation does cost money; and the people to whom I looked for financial support were to be found at the head of the Egbe. I was under no illusion at all that if these leaders of the Egbe frowned on the new political project, I would either have to abandon it, or to think again. It was when they gave their blessing that I convened the first meeting at which the Action Group was founded. I was determined that the more elderly members of the Egbe should not be brought into the new party at the early stages; though their influence as well as their financial assistance was badly needed. But I kept them fully informed of my doings. About May 1950, the Egbe feared that the Action Group when fully launched might become its rival and might even eclipse it. The Egbe, therefore, decided to enter into politics and to have its own political wing. It called on those of its members who were organising the Action Group to abandon it and join the Egbe's political wing. At the third meeting of the Action Group held in my house on 4 June 1950, I brought this matter up. I was quite prepared to have the Action Group disbanded, leaving the Egbe free to start its own political wing. There were eleven of us present at this meeting, and the discussion on the issue was long. At one stage, it was clear that the majority favoured the dissolution of the Action Group. But in the end it was decided that the Action Group should continue to function. The view was firmly held that it would be dangerous and contrary to its declared ideals for the Egbe to engage in party politics. Accordingly, a Committee was appointed to meet the Central Executive Committee of the Egbe to argue the matter out and allay the fears of the Egbe. In the result, the Egbe reversed its former decision and agreed to remain a cultural organisation, giving itself freedom of action to back any political party whose policy and programme appealed to it in the Regional elections.

The second decision was made at the sixth meeting held at my house on 8 October 1950, at which only nine of us were present. I had felt regularly disappointed by the poor attendances at previous meetings. I had always invited as many as between 60 and 100 persons, and the highest attendance had been eleven. I had not merely sent out circular letters, but had made a great amount of personal contacts as well. As a result of the very poor responses, I had a feeling that our people were not ready for the new organisation. In the circumstances, I saw no point in continuing with it. I made my feeling known to the meeting and said that it would be advisable to wind up the Action Group. Mr E. A. Babalola, who attended the meeting for the first time, supported by Chief Sowole and Mr Ajasin, opposed my suggestion. They argued that it did not need a large number of people to get a great movement started. In fact the fewer men the better for the early smooth functioning of such a movement. All the other seven members concurred in this view, and I had no alternative but to agree that we should carry on. The very next meeting—the seventh meeting—was highly encouraging: it was attended by twenty-seven people.

It was at this seventh meeting that the third decision was made. I seized the opportunity of the relatively large attendance to reiterate some of the things that I had said at previous meetings. For about eight months, the new party had done nothing but talk. It was about time we put some of our ideas into action. I pointed out that time was running short, and we had not yet set up a Shadow Cabinet. This was due to the fact that very few people had attended previous meetings. I reminded my hearers that if we were to be masters of the new situation into which we were about to enter under the new Constitution, we must see to it that those who would man the new government were versed in the problems with which they would be confronted, and had a clear idea of the sorts of solution they would offer for them. At this meeting, the Shadow Cabinet was set up. Each member was placed in charge of a subject and was also appointed Chairman of a committee. The Shadow Minister together with the members of his committee was to study his particular subject as exhaustively as he could and to produce a policy paper on it.

When the Action Group was publicly inaugurated at Owo in Ondo Province on the 28 April 1951, representatives from twenty-two out of the twenty-four Administrative Divisions of the Western Region attended. I opened the inaugural conference with an address in which, among other things, I said

The aims and objects of the Action Group have not only been published as I said, but are contained in the Draft Constitution, copies of which have been forwarded to you. I will not, therefore, take your time by repeating them.

There are however two items in the aims and objects which I

222

should like to emphasise, since they are the very basis of the Action Group. I refer to items (1) and (3). The two are complementary and they read as follows:

(1) To bring and organise within its fold all nationalists in the Western Region, so that they may work together as a united group, and submit themselves to party loyalty and discipline;

(2) To prepare and present to the public programmes for all departments of government, and to strive faithfully to ensure the effectuation of such programmes through those of its members that are elected into the Western House of Assembly and the Federal Legislature.

The attainment of the two aims implies identity of adherence to basic principles, and identity of methods in the application of the principles.

If any group of people fails to agree as to basic principles and as to the methods to be adopted in applying those principles, it is impossible for them to work within the same fold, and to submit themselves to party loyalty and discipline.

The basic principles which have brought the members of the Action Group together are summarised in the following motto:

FREEDOM FOR ALL, LIFE MORE ABUNDANT

It is our belief that the people of Western Nigeria in particular, and of Nigeria in general would have life more abundant when they enjoy—

i. Freedom from British rule;
ii. Freedom from ignorance;
iii. Freedom from disease; and
iv. Freedom from want.

In our view, the rule of one nation by another is unnatural and unjust. It is maintained either by might or by the complete subordination, through crafty means, of the will and self-respect of the subject people to the political self-aggrandisement of the tutelary power. There can be no satisfactory substitute for self-rule.

Therefore, British tutelage is to be denounced without any reservation. In principle, it is indefensible. In practice, it has been characterised by extreme planlessness and disregard for the vital interests of the people.

After almost 100 years of British rule, our land is still riddled with unspeakable ignorance, disease, and want.

The basic principles which, therefore, have brought us together within the fold of the Action Group may be stated in the following words:

1. The immediate termination of British rule in every phase of our political life.

2. The education of all children of school-going age, and the general enlightenment of all illiterate adults and all illiterate children above school-going age.

3. The provision of health and general welfare for all our people.

4. The total abolition of want in our society by means of any economic policy which is both expedient and effective.

Having agreed on these basic principles, it becomes necessary to take the next step, namely to agree as to common methods in the application of those principles. This is a very important step; because even though people may agree as to principles, if they don't agree as to methods of application it would not be possible for them to work together.

It is in order to evolve these common methods that some members of the Action Group have been commissioned to prepare papers not only on government departmental subjects but also on the organisational problems of the Action Group.

It will be our duty at this conference to declare our irrevocable adherence to the principles already enunciated and to fashion out from the papers which are already submitted on various subjects what our common methods of application shall be.

Once we have succeeded in doing these two things, the fulfilment of our aims and objects is well-nigh achieved. All that we would need in addition would be persistence and consistency in the pursuit of our principles, and resolution and discipline in the execution of our common methods of application.

Only we must make sure about two things, namely: that our principles are just, and that our methods are practical. For nothing defeat their own ends so easily as unjust principles and impractical methods of approach.

These then are the ideals of the Action Group and the principles of action by which the party has been consistently guided during its brief ten years of existence. The Action Group has made a decisive impact on party politics and political thoughts in Nigeria, such as no political party before or after it has ever done.

It was the Action Group that for the first time in the history of Nigeria carried party politics and political consciousness to the rural areas and to the country's peasantry. It has provoked the establishment of rival political parties. The NCNC was converted into a political party with individual membership only after the Action Group had been publicly inaugurated. Before the Action Group, party politics such as there was (and this was confined to Lagos and Calabar) had been conducted on the basis of personal abuses and mudslinging. This ugly feature has not yet been wholly eradicated from our political life; but through the constructive efforts of the Action Group, it is diminishing both in scale and venom. In the regional elections of 1951, the Action Group was the only party that published policy papers as well as a manifesto. Dr Azikiwe himself condemned this innovation, and regarded it as an attempt on our part wantonly to deceive the voters. He was confidently of the opinion that policy papers were unnecessary and should never be published for the purpose of elections. It was when a party had won an election, he argued, that it should essay to declare and publish the details of the policy it would pursue in office. This was the NCNC stand, and we described it as a demand on the voters to give the NCNC a blank cheque. As for the NPC—it had no stand in 1951, and declared none. Indeed those members of the Northern House of Assembly who later declared themselves to be members of the NPC did so after the elections had been over. They had contested the elections as unorganised individuals. In the Eastern Region most of the members who were returned to the House of Assembly there did not contest the elections on any political platform, though the majority of them were manoeuvred into the NCNC after they had been elected. The result was that in 1951, for the Northern and Eastern elections there were no manifestoes at all from the NPC and the NCNC respectively. On the other hand the Action Group published policy papers on regional as well as on federal subjects. Whilst we confined our electioneering activities to the Western Region, we were fully conscious of the fact that if we won a majority of seats in the Western House of Assembly, most of our members would be elected to the Federal House of Representatives and three of them would be Ministers in the Nigerian Council of

Ministers. It was in accordance with our beliefs that those who would take part in the Federal Government as well as those in the Western Region should be fully seized of party policies on specific subjects so that they might be properly guided in their approach to and in their handling of such subjects.

At every election since 1952, we had adopted the same method of publishing both policy papers and manifesto. Our persistent efforts yielded dividend only during the federal elections of December 1959, when both the NCNC and the NPC for the first time emulated the Action Group (which was again first in the field in this regard) and published their own policy papers alongside their manifestoes. As a result, the last federal elections smacked much less of personal abuse and gutter electioneering tactics than was the case in previous years. Each political party strove more than ever before to win votes on the basis of the relative merits of its policies and programmes. In this respect, what I said in my inaugural address is of interest: it has unerringly served as a beacon of light to the Action Group, although it must be confessed that there were times when we were tempted to hit back at our opponents after the manner of their unwholesome style. In that address, I had said:

Our enemies and detractors are already at work. They are seeking to dwarf our stature in order to delude the public that they are taller than we are. They are also seeking to divert us from our noble and constructive courses into the barren land of petty strife and fruitless controversy.

It is . . . an evidence of weakness and utter demerit, for any group of people to attempt to commend themselves to the public by the negative process of belittling and condemning others.

It is not an easy matter to resist the temptation of being dragged down the drains of bitter recriminations and press war. But if we are to attain our objects we must resolve to pursue our course unflinchingly without paying the slightest heed 'to the envious, and the asses that bray'.

What our people want to know above all things else is not the defect or incapacity of this or that organisation, but the plans and programmes which we have for improving their lot and the relative merits of such plans and programmes.

Such plans and programmes we have; and what is more they are plans and programmes which could be put into execution within a period of five years.

Our line of action is therefore clear. Whilst our enemies and detractors busy themselves with abusing and decrying us, we should direct all the machinery of our publicity towards the propagation of the excellence and the relative superiority of our programmes and the suitability of the men who will be put forward to execute them.

The Macpherson Constitution did not envisage the emergence of politics on party lines such as the Action Group introduced on the eve of the elections under the Constitution. When the proposals for this Constitution were reaching their final stages, many of the senior British officials expressed alarm at the tremendous powers which were going to be transferred to Nigerian public men who were unpractised in the art of government. These officials feared that these powers would be misused, and maladministration and mismanagement of public affairs would ensue. These fears were allayed by Sir Hugh Foot, who pointed out that things would not be likely to work out as they had imagined. Powers would be concentrated in the hands of Nigerian ministers only if there were an organised political party system. In his view such a system was not likely to emerge for some years to come. In the circumstances, the senior British officials would still more or less have considerable control of governmental affairs even though certain powers were apparently vested by the constitution in Nigerian ministers. When these discussions were going on between Sir Hugh Foot and the senior British officials, none of them had dreamt or learnt (in spite of the Government's Intelligence Service) that a political machine of enormous and thundering strength was being assembled in my residence at Oke Ado, Ibadan. Or if they knew, they did not think that it would be capable of the historic performances which it later exhibited to the discomfiture of all the senior British officials, and in accelerating the advancement of Nigeria to its goal of independence.

As we have noted, under the Macpherson Constitution, there were three Regional Legislatures: Eastern, Western and Northern. Each Legislature served as an electoral college for

227

electing the members of the Federal House of Representatives, as well as for the election of Regional Ministers and Federal Ministers. But the nomination of candidates for election as ministers, and the appointment of such persons after being elected, were vested in the case of the Regions in the Lieutenant-Governors, and in the case of Nigeria in the Governor. The Lieutenant-Governors and the Governor had thought that it would be possible for them to exercise these powers in their discretion as provided in the Constitution. The Action Group proved them wrong. The elections to the Regional Legislatures were held at different times. The first to be completed were those of the Western Region with the Action Group having a majority of elected members. This fact was brought to the notice of the Lieutenant-Governor of the Region by means of written declarations duly executed by the Action Group members in the new House of Assembly. Nonetheless, the Lieutenant-Governor refused, or was inordinately tardy or reluctant to invite me to form a government. This attitude of his sparked off a political conflagration. We went to town in a big way, and I personally wrote a series of editorial comments entitled 'CRY HAVOC' in the *Nigerian Tribune*—a paper published in Ibadan and founded by me in 1949. A distinction was made between the letter of the constitution on the one hand, and the spirit or convention of the constitution on the other. It was prosaic and unimaginative, I argued, for the Lieutenant-Governor to think that the provisions of the constitution vesting him with power to nominate and appoint ministers could operate the way he liked. Ostensibly, the law cloaked him with authority in this regard, but in actual fact, it is the person or group of persons who commanded a majority of following and support in the House of Assembly who would exercise or decisively influence the exercise by the Lieutenant-Governor of that authority.

When this public outcry by the Action Group had gone on for some days, the Lieutenant-Governor, Sir Chandos Hoskyns-Abrahall, invited me to discuss the nomination of candidates for appointment as ministers. I went to his office accompanied by Chief Bode Thomas who was then the Deputy Leader of the

Action Group and Chief S. L. Akintola at that time only a member of the party's executive. Sir Chandos already had a list of his own nominees. We rejected all but one of his nominees and submitted ours to him which he readily accepted. The only nomination acceptable to us was my name, but the portfolio which he proposed to assign to me—that of Agriculture and Natural Resources—was not acceptable. I preferred Local Government which portfolio I held for three years. In this regard it is pertinent to point out that the Sardauna followed my example a few weeks later and Dr Azikiwe did likewise two years later: before they became Premiers in October 1954, they each held the portfolio of Local Government in their respective regions. The victory of the Action Group, in compelling recognition as the party in power in the Western Region, had salutary effects on the Lieutenant-Governors of the Eastern and Northern Regions. Without any ado, they invited the leaders of the majority parties in their areas for consultations on the nomination and appointment of ministers. The Governor of Nigeria, Sir John Macpherson, lost no time in following suit. At different times, he invited leaders of the three parties for consultations concerning the nomination of candidates as ministers in the central government. I do not know how Sir Hugh Foot himself felt on learning of what actually happened in Nigeria to debunk his theory. From what I knew of him, he would have nonetheless felt supremely delighted that a party system had emerged. Sir John Macpherson was the undoubted initiator and inspirer of the Constitution rightly named after him; but the versatile and adept architect of it was Sir Hugh Foot.

The same awesome fate which befell the Richards Constitution also overtook the Macpherson Constitution: they both came to a premature end. When the Richards Constitution was introduced by its great author Lord Milverton in 1946, he decreed for it at least a nine-year span of life, after which it should be reviewed. Lord Milverton (then Sir Arthur Richards) was a man of massive intellectual attainments and overpowering personality. He was astonishingly careless of public opinion. His motto seemed to be: 'Do nothing because of public opinion, but everything because of conscience.' In his maiden speech as Governor of Nigeria he had an injunction for his officials: 'Woe unto you when men shall speak in praise of you.' The Constitution named after him and the manner of its introduction were in many respects distasteful to Nigerian nationalists. But all our protests and criticisms meant little or nothing to the self-contained and oracular Lord Milverton. He had made his decree, and there was the end of the matter. But Sir John Macpherson who succeeded him in 1947 had different ideas.

There were three features of the Richards Constitution which as far as they went commended themselves to me. First, each Region had a Deliberative Assembly. This was a right step in the federalist direction. But I had thought that the Assembly should not only be Legislative but also that Nigerians should be given an opportunity at the executive level of trying their hands at managing their own affairs. Secondly, for the first time there was an unofficial Nigerian majority in the Nigerian Legislative Council as well as in the Regional Houses of Assembly. It was a grudging majority, first because it was slender and secondly because most of the unofficial Nigerian members were nominated and not elected. Nevertheless, an important step towards the realisation of Nigeria's political ambition had been taken. Thirdly, the Northern Region not only had a House of Assembly and a House of Chiefs, but also for the first time its representatives sat side by side with their fellow-Nigerians in the Legislative Council of the country. In spite of these relatively progressive measures, nationalists of Southern origin were not satisfied with the Richards Constitution chiefly because it merely aimed 'to secure greater participation by Africans in the *discussion* of their own affairs'; or to quote another variant of the same objective, 'to secure a greater *voice* in their affairs for the Africans themselves'; and partly because the system of nomination was largely employed in packing the Houses of Assembly and the Legislative Council with the favourites of senior British officials. For instance, out of the twenty-five unofficial Nigerian members of Nigeria's Legislative Council, only four were elected by the people by means of franchise limited by property or income qualification.

Sir John Macpherson clearly recognised the political ferment in the South, and quickly made up his mind to do something to meet the upsurge. He was at the same time keenly cognizant of the events which were then taking place in Ghana where constitutional advancement was well ahead of Nigeria's, and of the effect which this was bound to have on Southern Nigerian nationalists who then, as now, constituted the hard core of political agitation in Nigeria. Sir John Macpherson was an exceptionally ingenious administrator whose proficiency, considered strictly on an impersonal plane, was well-nigh perfect. He was a very shrewd judge of men and matters, and always meant well. But he was a man of strong prejudices and partial affections. These shortcomings not only made people doubt his good intentions, but also led him into paths of unpardonable error. Nigeria will, however, never forget the name of Sir John Macpherson. For he it was whose right judgment in 1949 and stubborn misguidedness in 1952 and 1953 created situations which favoured the lightning progress of Nigeria towards independence.

In 1949, Sir John Macpherson declared that the Richards Constitution should be reviewed—that was six years before it was decreed to be reviewed by Lord Milverton. After the review, the Macpherson Constitution came into operation in 1952. It was the ardent wish and indeed the resolve of Sir John that the Constitution fashioned under his auspices should last for at least five years from the time of its introduction. There was a story that Sir John once told Sir Charles Arden Clarke, former Governor-General of Ghana, that he expected the Constitution to last ten years. Sir Charles Arden Clarke was reported to have said that he would be surprised if the constitution operated successfully for five years. And how right he was.

Throughout the review of the Richards Constitution, the people of Nigeria declared that they wanted a federal constitution. But what was produced under the Macpherson Constitution was neither a unitary nor a federal constitution. I have already described it as a wretched compromise between the unitary and the federal system. There are those who have been more liberal and have described Nigeria under the Macpherson Constitution as an unusually tight federation. Whatever view people might hold on the nature of the constitution, the truth is that it proved in operation to be most insufferable and tantalising to the Action Group.

Within four months of its introduction, the Action Group discovered a number of very serious defects in the Constitution. Before mentioning one or two of these defects it must be emphasised that when the Action Group took office in the Western Region, it meant to govern and administer the Region in accordance with its declared policies and programmes. Unfortunately, however, there was not a single British official in the Western Region or in the Central Government who took us seriously. They thought that either we were crazy or we had only cunningly deceived the voters, by promising to embark in five years on the far-reaching (and indeed, according to our critics, fantastic) programmes contained in our published policy papers. We paid no heed to the criticisms, gossip, and discouraging remarks with which we were inundated. We were resolved to pursue our policies and make a success of them. If this were to be so our decision, as ministers, on any matter must be final and not subject to the whims and caprices of any other person who did not share our views and had no faith in our objectives.

The first defect which we discovered was this. The Minister was to administer the affairs of his Department (*not* Ministry) in association with the official Head of that Department. We had interpreted this to mean that the Head of Department would only advise the Minister in regard to matters pertaining to his Department, and that if the Minister after due consideration made a decision, the Head of Department would, like a good civil servant, willingly and submissively abide by such a decision. But we soon discovered in practice that our construction was wrong and that a Minister was expected to be a junior

232

partner in the departmental establishment. To us this was decidedly unbearable; and by means of threats of political action as well as incessant newspaper criticisms of these officials, we succeeded in compelling them to accept our interpretation. But it was an uphill task all the time. The second defect was a major one. It was provided that in matters to which the Executive Authority of the Region related the Lieutenant-Governor should accept the advice of the Executive Council, but that he was not bound to accept such advice if powers in respect of such matters or any of them were conferred upon him by laws in existence on the 26 January 1952. In other words, if the same matters were contained in laws enacted by the Regional Legislature after 26 January 1952, the Lieutenant-Governor would be obliged to act in accordance with the advice of the Executive Council, unless of course he felt impelled to reject such advice in the interest of public faith, public order and good government. This to us was a strange and iniquitous provision. It was never agreed to by the various conferences that considered the proposals for the Macpherson Constitution, nor was it brought to the notice of the public until we had discovered it. We felt that the people of Nigeria had been cheated and double-crossed by this provision. For since all laws affecting matters to which the Executive Authority of the Regions related were in existence on 26 January, a few days before my colleagues and I assumed office, it followed that until the new Government could re-enact all such laws, the Lieutenant-Governor would be free to act in his discretion in respect of such matters. In spite of this provision, we had thought that the spirit or the convention of the constitution rather than its letter would be observed by the Lieutenant-Governor. But we were mistaken.

One day in our Executive Council in the Western Region, certain appointments to the membership of a public corporation were to be made. My colleagues and I submitted certain names to the Executive Council, which after consideration were approved. The Lieutenant-Governor, Sir Hugo Marshall, who presided, then informed the Council that he would give thought to the names already approved and make up his mind whether or not to accept all or any of them. He would probably accept all of them, but he would like to turn the matter over in his mind before making a final decision. I was indignant and I told him that we had not been elected into the Executive Council merely to reinforce his team of official advisers. We had been elected by our people on a definite platform, and we had taken office in order to govern the Region according to our own light, advised from time to time by him and the other senior British officials in the Executive Council and in the Region. Sir Hugo Marshall was a highly seasoned and experienced administrator: always cool and unruffled. In a calm voice, and with a sort of mocking smile on his face, he told us that that was the law of the constitution and he had no intention of departing from it. I then informed him that in view of our experiences with the working of the constitution, we had already written to the Governor, Sir John Macpherson, who had already given us an appointment to discuss our problems with him. It was going to be an important item in our list of complaints that our Lieutenant-Governor had not been working in accordance with the spirit of the constitution. He had no objection to our meeting the Governor, but he thought it was an act of discourtesy that we should arrange such an appointment on matters affecting him and his Region without any previous intimation to him.

On 10 June 1952, all the Action Group Regional and Central Ministers accompanied by the Ministers without Portfolio met Sir John. He was in a fighting truculent mood, and was set for giving us a technical knockout before we even had a chance of attempting a blow. The Constitution had been made for the whole of Nigeria, he affirmed in a tone of finality, and he was not prepared to tolerate any attempt by only one section of the country to criticise or attack it, especially so soon after its introduction. No constitution however perfect could work, unless the people for whom it was made were prepared to give it a fair trial. Whilst the present constitution did not claim perfection, he considered it good enough for the present stage of Nigeria's political development. But it would appear that we had no intention to give it any trial at all. It was significant, he added, that whilst complaints against the constitution kept flowing in from us, none had come from the other Regions.

On being permitted to speak, I assured Sir John that we had no desire to be unnecessarily critical of or obstructive to the new constitution. It must be borne in mind that the constitution had been named (quite rightly I believed) after him; and it was in the interest of his own reputation as well as for the good of Nigeria that the constitution should work, and be workable to conscientious nationalists. It was interesting to hear that the other two Regions had made no complaints as we had done; but that was understandable. I likened him to the manufacturer of the new model of a car. Three customers bought one each of the new model from him. One of them only kept his new acquisition in the garage as a show piece: he did not know and had not yet grasped the ABC of how to operate it. The other customer used his own car very rarely: once in a blue moon for a joy ride. But the third customer was making an intensive use of his own car. Consequently, he was much better placed than the other two customers to discover at a much earlier date than they what defects there were in this new-model car. This was exactly the case with the Macpherson Constitution *vis-à-vis* its operation by the NPC in the North, the NCNC in the East and the Action Group in the West. Now, if the manufacturer of the car wanted to continue in business, and wanted to push the sales of the new model he must listen with patience and undisguised gratitude to the complaints of that conscientious customer who had been making real use of the car. And the moment the manufacturer was satisfied that the defects complained of were genuine, it would be his urgent duty to put them right not only in the car of the complaining customer, but in those of the other customers who had not yet discovered them. After this analogy the frigid and imperious mien which Sir John Macpherson put on when he first spoke, softened a little, and the discussions proceeded.

In addition to the two major defects already mentioned, four other complaints were made at the meeting. First, our understanding was that, however silent the Constitution might be on the point, the appointment of a Minister necessarily implied the existence of a Ministry. Officials in the Western Region had refused to accept our interpretation of the Constitution on this point, with the result that the Minister who should be the head of his Ministry was just an appendage to a Department presided over by a civil servant. Secondly, the attitude of the heads of Departments and senior officials (all expatriates) was forbidding and irritating. They professed no loyalty to the Regional Government and they gave none, simply because constitutionally they were servants *not* of the Regional but of the Nigerian Government. Thirdly, it was incomprehensible that the Governor should turn down our request for the appointment of parliamentary secretaries for the more important Ministries. Fourthly, there was an abhorrent and outrageous practice in the Western Region which we demanded must be stopped forthwith if Action Group Ministers were expected to continue in office. We had discovered that the Civil Secretary was in the habit of making regular secret intelligence reports on the Ministers collectively and individually. These reports, it would appear, were circulated not only to the Governor and Lieutenant-Governor but also to Residents of Provinces. I had made the discovery by accident. I was away from Ibadan on an official tour. I wanted information on certain matters and I asked the Resident in charge of the area to help me if he could. In error, he sent me a file which contained not the information I wanted but secret reports on Ministers. I read them and made notes, some of which I quoted in the hearing of Sir John Macpherson. We left him in no doubt that we bitterly resented a state of affairs in which the Civil Secretary or any other official with whom we were expected to work in harmonious association was made to spy on us and to write damaging or laudatory reports on us as he pleased.

On behalf of my colleagues, I appealed to Sir John to remedy the situations about which we had complained. He could do this either by means of executive instructions to the Lieutenant-Governor and his subordinate officials enjoining them to place a liberal rather than a rigid construction on the provisions of the constitution, or by amendments to the constitution itself. The Governor ruled the latter alternative out of consideration. The constitution had only run for five months and it was too early and preposterous to talk about amending it. We did not share Sir John's view, and we told him so. But he was insistent that there could be no question of amendments to the constitution at that stage. He would, however, consider our representations; but before making a decision on them he would like to consult the other Regions, and the Central Council of Ministers. We had a hint that Sir John did consult the other Governments in the Federation and that they all without exception condemned our move to modify or amend the constitution so very early in the day—less than six months after its inception.

At the meeting with him, Sir John made a promise to let us have an official record of the proceedings, and to communicate his decision to us after he should have heard from the other Governments. This promise has not been fulfilled to this day. After this minor crisis of 10 June 1952, the attitude of the Lieutenant-Governor and his officials changed for the better. I was inclined to believe that this was due partly to the realisation on their part that we were determined to have our way. I also presumed that it was not unlikely that Sir John was partly responsible for the change of attitude: he had probably applied some gentle but forceful suasion to the officials in question. We were, however, not satisfied; and because of this and of subsequent incidents which were more galling to us than those already complained of, we made up our minds to wreck the Macpherson Constitution as soon as a favourable opportunity offered itself.

In my inaugural speech at Owo I had declared the four basic principles which brought the members of the Action Group together. It will be remembered that first on the list was 'the immediate termination of British rule in every phase of our political life'. In another prepared address which I delivered at the Glover Memorial Hall, Lagos on 28 August 1951, I had said

The four freedoms enunciated by the Action Group have been extensively publicised. Our people must be free from British rule in order that they can tackle in their own way and in their own interests the problems of ignorance, disease and want. . . .

As our objective, therefore, we will seek by all effective constitutional means to terminate British rule during the five-year period of our tenure of office.

In December 1952 during the Second Annual Conference of the Action Group held in Benin City from 17 to 20 December, a resolution was passed fixing 1 December 1956 as the target date for Nigeria's independence. This was followed up by a motion tabled in the House of Representatives by Chief Anthony Enahoro, one of the leaders of the Action Group, and the most brilliant parliamentarian in Nigeria today, in the following terms:

That this House accepts as a primary political objective the attainment of self-government for Nigeria in 1956.

This motion constitutes the most prominent landmark in Nigeria's struggles for freedom. It marked the unmistakeable beginning of the end of British rule in Nigeria. It also turned out to be the most controversial, the most intriguing and the most explosive motion ever tabled in the annals of Nigeria's parliament. The Council of Ministers were sharply divided on it: the three Action Group Ministers (Bode Thomas, S. L. Akintola and Arthur Prest) together with His Highness Aderemi I, the Oni of Ife supporting it on the one hand, and the NCNC and NPC Ministers together with the Governor, Sir John Macpherson, leading a team of official members of the Council opposing it on the other. The Council of Ministers by a majority decided that the motion should be opposed, and that an amendment by the Sardauna of Sokoto deleting from the Action Group motion the words 'in 1956' and substituting therefor the words 'as soon as practicable' should be supported. Our four Ministers from the Western Region made their stand

238

quite clear. They would, contrary to the decision of the Council of Ministers, be bound to support the substantive motion and oppose the amendment. In such circumstances, they were well aware of the course of action open to them: to resign their membership of the Council, take their seats as ordinary members of the House of Representatives, and then speak in accordance with their conscience and the declared policy of their party.

The obscurantist attitude of Sir John Macpherson to this motion astounded and puzzled many people; but it was explicable on three grounds. In the first place, he regarded the new constitution with almost morbid fondness: he believed it was epoch-making (quite rightly); and he was very proud of it (justifiably). Consequently, he was very sensitive to any suggestion to modify or amend it. To speak of amending the constitution was to him intolerable enough; to talk of fixing a date for Nigeria's independence after less than fifteen months of its operation and to seek to get the date fixed to coincide with the allotted span of the life of the Constitution were to him beyond contemplation. In the second place, he had developed very strong prejudices against the Action Group as a corporate body for its impatience with the defects of the new constitution, and in particular against Chief Bode Thomas who with his penetrating legal mind and biting tongue had already become a harassing headache to him in the Council of Ministers. In the third place, at our Benin City Conference in December 1951, we had passed a resolution forbidding all our members from fraternising socially with Sir John. The reason we gave for this action was that we were satisfied that he was wilfully obstructing the political progress of Nigeria, and that his mischievous actions in certain matters tended to impair the unity of the country. Sources close to him indicated that he was more infuriated and agonised by the reason we gave for our action, than by the resolution itself.

The Action Group motion on self-government for Nigeria in 1956 was placed on the Order Paper for 31 March 1953. But it was the last on the list of seven motions for the day.

Since the sitting of the House was going to be adjourned *sine die* on the following day, it had obviously been calculated that the motion would not be reached and an imminent crisis might be averted or postponed for a long while. Early in the year, there had been a split among the parliamentary members of the NCNC both in the East and in the Centre. Those who declared allegiance to Dr Azikiwe in the House of Representatives were led by Dr K. O. Mbadiwe, whilst those who did not were led by Mr A. C. Nwapa, then Federal Minister of Commerce and Industry. On the morning of 31 March, Dr K. O. Mbadiwe approached me and solemnly promised the unstinted support of his followers to the motion on self-government. Of the six motions which were listed before the self-government motion, three were sponsored by Action Group members and the other three by NCNC. We had decided among ourselves that our three motions would not be moved. I explained this to Dr Mbadiwe and he also got his men to agree not to move their own motions as well. And so, contrary to the expectation of the Council of Ministers the motion on self-government became the only one left on the Order Paper and which its sponsor was prepared to move. After the Sardauna's amendment had been moved and seconded, we were taken completely by surprise by a dilatory motion in the following terms:

I beg to move that the debate be now adjourned.

This was moved by Alhaji Ibrahim Imam, then a member of the NPC, but now Action Group Leader of the Opposition in the Northern House of Assembly. I wound up for the Action Group on the dilatory motion. I spoke on the spur of the moment and concluded as follows:

We should be free to say our mind on this issue without being fettered, and the North should be free to say its mind without being fettered.

At division time we know by the look of things that we will be beaten.

But we are not afraid.

It will go on record that A, B, C and D once voted for freedom for their country and that E, F, G and H, once voted against.

240

That is all we are seeking.

But what do we find now?

We find that the Northern majority is not only being used in having their way, but is also being used in preventing the minority from having their say.

That is a situation with which we find it absolutely impossible to accommodate ourselves.

I should have thought, Mr President, that you would have ruled this motion out of order, and use your discretion in favour of allowing the original motion and amendment to be fully debated.

But you have already decided in favour of allowing a dilatory motion to be debated and voted upon.

There is no doubt in anybody's mind that when the division comes, the North will win the day, and this momentous motion would have been postponed indefinitely.

With a situation like that, as I said before, we are not prepared to accommodate ourselves.

We are prepared to be voted out any time, in a spirit of sportsmanship.

But we are certainly not going to submit to a situation in which we are being muzzled into the bargain. I would like to say, Sir, on behalf of the Western Region that we will not stay here to continue this debate.

As my colleagues and I were about to walk out of the House, Dr Mbadiwe signified to me the decision of his team to join us; but he would first of all like to say a few words in support of our stand. So we waited for him to have his say, and after he had done we all walked gallantly out.

When the motion for self-government and the amending and dilatory motions were being moved and debated, Dr Azikiwe was in the visitors' gallery. When we walked out, he was in the front of the House of Representatives waiting for us. There he ecstatically embraced and congratulated me. Soon after, an alliance between the Action Group and the NCNC was concluded. On the morning of this memorable 31st March, His Highness Aderemi I, the Oni of Ife, was the first to tender his resignation as Minister Without Portfolio. The three Action Group Federal Ministers submitted their resignations later in the morning. Thus the constitutional crisis which Sir John Macpherson had done all in his power to avert had occurred.

241

The reaction to the crisis of Oliver Lyttleton (now Lord Chandos), Secretary of State for the Colonies, was most satisfying to us. Within a few days of its occurrence, the Governor, Sir John Macpherson, left Nigeria for the United Kingdom, no doubt at Lord Chandos's invitation. During the third week of April Lord Chandos's Minister of State, Mr Henry Hopkinson had arrived in Nigeria. At a meeting which he held with the Action Group leaders on the 26 April 1953, he explained that he had come to Nigeria principally to attend the Defence Conference. But he had received the permission of Sir Winston Churchill, the Prime Minister, to prolong his stay so that he might know at first hand the circumstances surrounding the present crisis. We seized the opportunity to enumerate quite frankly the defects which we had discovered in the Macpherson Constitution before and after June 1952. Our delight knew no bounds when in a statement in the House of Commons on the 21 May 1953, the Secretary of State gave expression to the very heart of our complaints. He was reported to have said 'that Her Majesty's Government had regretfully decided that the Nigerian Constitution would have to be redrawn to provide for greater Regional autonomy and for the removal of powers of intervention by the Centre in matters which could, without detriment to other Regions, be placed entirely within Regional competence. . . . The work of re-drawing the constitution, having regard to the complicated problems involved, would inevitably take time. Her Majesty's Government would, however, wish to co-operate in this process as closely as possible with the leaders of the peoples in all three Regions, and as a first step proposed to invite representatives from each Region to London for discussions.' The Conference on the Nigerian Constitution, the first in a series of four to be held in five years from July 1953 to October 1958, opened in London on 30 July 1953 and closed about the 21 August of the same year. The following passage from paragraph 3 of the Report of the 1953 Conference is of interest:

The following terms of reference, agreed in a discussion between the Governor of Nigeria, and the leaders of the Action Group,

National Council of Nigeria and the Cameroons, and the Northern People's Congress, at a meeting on the 19th June, were accepted by Her Majesty's Government as the terms of reference of the Conference:

(a) The defects in the present Constitution.
(b) The changes required to remedy these defects.
(c) What steps should be taken to put these changes into effect; and
(d) The question of self-government in 1956.

In agreeing to the inclusion of (d) in the terms of reference the Secretary of State for the Colonies made it clear that this should not be regarded as in any way committing Her Majesty's Government to this proposition.

Lord Chandos was a Colonial Secretary very much after my heart: businesslike, clear-headed, firm and precise. He did not suffer fools gladly. Some Ministers there are who allow themselves to be made tools in the hands of their Permanent Secretaries. Not so with Lord Chandos. He was big and courageous enough to make up his own mind on any issue however vital and delicate. I adored him for his many good qualities, and in particular for the businesslike despatch and firmness with which he handled the 1953 crisis. I fell out with him, however, on one issue: whether Lagos should continue as part of the Western Region, or should be separated from it and declared a Federal Territory. I did not like the trap into which he led my delegation over the issue, nor the untenable argument employed by him in arriving at what, in the circumstances of Nigeria, was a sound decision.

The alliance between the Action Group and the NCNC was, as I said before, short-lived: it was reared in April 1953, and broke down on the issue of Lagos in August of the same year. From my own point of view, the achievements of the alliance whilst it lasted and even the very cause of its demise were, without exception, all to the good of Nigeria, and the means of providential help to the Action Group in solving some of the knotty problems which then confronted the Government of Western Nigeria. In the first place, the unity of Nigeria was saved by the alliance. The NPC had gone to the 1953 Conference with a proposal that Nigeria should be transformed into a confederation or a customs union in which each of the three Regions would enjoy a status slightly short of that of a sovereign state. The proposal was resisted by the Action Group–NCNC alliance, mightily backed by Lord Chandos. Then one morning at the Conference, the Sardauna, who had not until then uttered a word, broke his silence and declared that he agreed that Nigeria should continue as a federal union. He was cheered; and for his generous 'concession' in this regard Lord Chandos awarded Lagos to him as a Federal Territory! In the second place, and as I have pointed out in a previous chapter, as a result of the alliance Dr Azikiwe accepted federalism as well as its implications as being the most suitable constitution for Nigeria. The fact that he now shrinks from some of these implications, such as for instance the breaking of the North into more States, is another matter. In the third place, though as a result of the opposition to it by the NPC, it was not possible to get Her Majesty's Government to name 1956 as the year of Nigeria's independence, yet the demand of the alliance was met half-way when a declaration was made that in 1956 Her Majesty's Government would grant to those Regions which desired it full self-government in respect of all matters within the competence of the Regional Governments. The reactions of the Action Group and the NCNC to this declaration were different. We made it clear that whilst we were prepared to accept what was given, we were nonetheless disappointed that what was granted fell short of what we had asked for. Dr Azikiwe on the other hand hailed it as an offer of 'self-government on a platter of gold'. When in 1955 the Western Region Legislature passed a resolution expressing its desire for Regional self-government in 1956, Dr Azikiwe changed front and condemned the move. The grand finale of Dr Azikiwe's acrobatic display was that the Eastern Region under his premiership acceded to regional self-government at the same time as the Western Region. It was, however, left to my colleagues and me alone to defend the wisdom of accepting the offer of regional self-government whilst we continued to press for the independence of the Federation of Nigeria. In one of my many speeches in defence of my party's stand on the issue against Dr Azikiwe's attacks, I had said:

To my mind, the argument that regional self-government might induce complacency in Nigerian leaders has been effectively answered by the fact that after the acceptance of the offer of regional self-government a motion was moved, and unanimously passed, in the House of Representatives calling upon Her Majesty to grant self-government to the Federation of Nigeria in 1959. It is significant that the mover of this historic motion in the House of Representatives is the Deputy Leader of the Action Group, which has been the main object of attack in regard to this question of regional self-government. In his motion he asked the House of Representatives to instruct delegates to the forthcoming Conference to do all in their power to secure the grant of self-government for the Federation of Nigeria in 1957. An amendment substituting 1959 for 1957 which was sponsored by the NCNC and the NPC was accepted by him.

It is our belief that every ground won from British rule, no matter how circumscribed in space that ground is, is in accretion to our strength and courage in continuing the struggle for complete liberation. For instance, regional self-government will mean, in respect of matters within regional competence, the end of the Governor's so-called veto or reserve powers. It will also mean a severe restriction of the Secretary of State's power of interference in our domestic affairs. Above all, it was the immortal Aggrey who said: 'Ask for what you want; get what you are given; keep what you have got, and ask for more.' The people of the Western Region have done no more than to follow this sensible and practical advice of one of the greatest sons of Africa. But may I take this opportunity of assuring you that whilst we are keen in the Western Region to have self-government in regional matters this year, we are equally keen, and will not yield first place to anyone, on insisting that the Federation of Nigeria shall be independent by 1959, and that the Western Region shall be a component unit of that Federation.

The wisdom and farsightedness of the stand of the Action Group were vindicated by the following declaration on the independence of Nigeria made by Mr Lennox-Boyd in 1958:

The Secretary of State reminded the Conference that at the 1957 Conference he had said that if, early in 1960, the new Nigerian Parliament passed a resolution asking Her Majesty's Government to agree to full self-government by a date in 1960, Her Majesty's Government would consider the resolution with sympathy and would then be prepared to fix a date when they would accede to this request. *He said that since then there had been sixteen months' experience of Regional self-government in the Eastern and Western Regions,* . . . and the Conference had now agreed on the pattern of self-government for the Northern Region. All the Regional Governments would shortly have had experience in what he had called 'taking the strain of Regional self-government'.

. . . In the light of all these developments, and in response to the wishes of all the delegations, . . . he was authorised by Her Majesty's Government to say that if a resolution was passed by the new Federal Parliament early in 1960 asking for independence, Her Majesty's Government would agree to that request and would introduce a Bill in Parliament to enable Nigeria to become a fully independent country on the 1 October, 1960.

In the fourth place, because of the united strength of the alliance, the Commodity Marketing Boards for the purchase and sale of Nigeria's chief export products (cocoa, cotton, groundnuts and oil palm produce) which were then controlled by the Nigerian Government, were regionalised and all their accumulated surpluses were divided among the Regions on the basis of derivation. Furthermore, Dr Azikiwe and I insisted, in the face of stiff opposition from NCNC dissidents like Professor Eni Njoku, Mr Okoi Arikpo and Professor Eyo Ita, that allocation of revenue to the Regions should also be made on the principle of derivation. The effect of these two decisions was that the Western Region became possessed of large sums of accumulated funds and recurrent revenue. The problem with which the Action Group was already grappling before the alliance came into being, was where to find money for financing the capital and recurrent expenditure of its projected free universal primary education, free medical treatment for all children up to the age of 18, and other far-reaching programmes. In the fifth place, though the alliance was wrecked on the issue, the decision to declare Lagos a Federal Territory, sponsored by the NCNC and NPC against the Action Group, was good for the Western Region Government. Feelings ran very high when this issue was live and fresh, and sentiments were expressed in violent and provocative terms. I felt very strongly on the issue myself, but my feelings were not based on the mere sentiment of blood relationship between the indigenous inhabitants of Lagos and those of the Western Region. I happened to know what many people did not know, and that was that Lagos was a financial liability to the Western Region. For instance, of the total expenditure on medical services for the whole of the Region including Lagos, 45 per cent was spent on Lagos alone. Nevertheless, I fought for the continued merger of Lagos with the Western Region for two reasons. First, it is difficult, in the matter of revenue allocation based on derivation, to separate revenue attributable to the Western Region from that imputable to Lagos. Second, the scope for independent revenue through purchase or sales tax on imported goods is severely limited for the Government of the Western Region by the mere juxtaposition of the most populous and most prosperous parts of the Western Region to Lagos, which is the premier port and the busiest commercial centre in Nigeria. These two problems have been satisfactorily settled by the 1958 Constitutional Conference. In any case, anyone who knows something of the expenditure now being incurred on Lagos by the Federal Government, will readily agree that it was in the best interest of the Western Region that Lagos was severed from it in 1954.

Several accusations have been levelled against the Action Group: that it is a Yoruba organisation and an offshoot of the Egbe Omo Oduduwa; that it is a party with a Western regional outlook and following; and that it is a party which does not believe in the unity of Nigeria. Many overseas journalists and visitors have been made innocent purveyors of these accusations. They can be excused because they have never been in possession of the true and detailed facts about the Action Group narrated in this chapter, which are a complete answer to and a telling refutation of such accusations. It is true that when the Action Group was founded, it was meant to be a Western Regional political party. But it must be remembered that the party had as its primary objective the winning of the then approaching Western Regional elections. In any event, in view of the then existing political situation, it would have been crass folly for me to attempt to bring leaders of the other Regions into the fold of the Action Group at the early stages. Immediate success was essential to the survival of the new party. It was imperative, therefore, that I should make sure that those who were induced into the secret activities of the party were people whose political leanings I could vouch for and in whose loyalty to the new party I could absolutely trust. After the Ikoli/ Akisanya crisis of 1941, I lost complete touch with my few Ibo friends and colleagues: they regarded me with suspicion and I found it hard to trust them either. Furthermore, because I had dared to criticise Dr Azikiwe publicly, I had incurred the ire of many an Easterner. At that time too I knew very little of the Northern Region and its politicians. As a matter of generalship, therefore, I thought it wise to confine the activities of the Action Group to the Western Region until success had been achieved at the ensuing regional elections. If we won the elections in the West, and there was still no countrywide political party in whose leadership we believed, we would have no alternative but to launch the Action Group in the Eastern and Northern Regions. And this was what we in fact began to do before the end of 1952. It was difficult going to start with. But today, due to the assiduity of its leaders, the Action Group of Nigeria is a truly nation-wide organisation with branches in practically every town, village and hamlet in the country. It is in control of the Government of the Western Region, and it is the Official Opposition in the Eastern and Northern Houses of Assembly. After relinquishing the Premiership of the Western Region, I now lead in the Federal House of Representatives an opposition team which is drawn from the three Regions of the Federation. Since it was publicly inaugurated in 1951, the Action Group has been making steady and irresistible advances on all fronts. Indeed, the story of the Action Group is the story of a new Nigeria in its glorious and most admirable facets; and it is to this party that history will attribute the credit for setting Nigeria's feet on the path to freedom through carefully planned constitutional and constructive means.

CHAPTER 15

EIGHT YEARS OF OFFICE

WHEN the Action Group won the Western Region elections in 1951, we were quite definite as to the objectives which we were going to pursue both at the Centre and in the Western Region, and had fairly clear ideas as to how we would achieve them. We had all agreed to the four freedoms enunciated by me at Owo, and we were inflexibly resolved that nothing on earth should deter us from moving as fast as we ever could towards the ramified, variegated and complex goals distinctly set by them. The race before us was a historic and epoch-making one, and regardless of many obvious hazards we literally burnt with unquenchable ardour and enthusiasm to run it.

First in the list of our objectives was to free Nigeria from British rule by the end of 1956. The choice of this year was not arbitrary as many students and observers of Nigerian affairs have made it appear. The pendulum of my attitude to British administration in Nigeria had always oscillated between the middle-of-the-road and the left wing. From the time I returned to Nigeria in 1946 up to 1951 when the Action Group was inaugurated, I stayed permanently on the left. I was very much incensed by the conceit of a large number of young administrative officers who claimed to know more about the problems of my country than I did. The older classes of administrative officers were *sui generis*: extremely overbearing, static in their outlook, fossilised in their ideas, and irredeemable in their dislike for the educated Nigerian nationalists. To me, what the British administrative officers paraded as administration was sheer muddle and stagnation. When, therefore, these officials reacted unfavourably to the proposals for the Macpherson Constitution and said unkind things about Nigerian politicians,

249

most of us felt it was time they all packed up and left our country. We had no doubt in our minds that we could administer our affairs much more efficiently than they.

Having declared our desire to work the Macpherson Constitution with all its imperfections when introduced, and to improve it from within, we were resolved that it would be the last constitution for a dependent Nigeria. When it had run its five-year course, the next constitution must be one for an independent and sovereign Nigeria. Furthermore, we wanted to bring pressure to bear on Britain to agree to a target date for our independence towards which we should strive. Enough, in our view, had been said about 'independence for Nigeria within the British Commonwealth of nations' being the goal of British rule in Nigeria. We already knew the goal but we were anxious also to know exactly when we were scheduled to arrive at the goal. Under the Macpherson Constitution Nigerians would be appointed Ministers; so that when the newly appointed Ministers should have run their full term under the constitution, they would have had five years' experience of managing the affairs of their fatherland. That period in our view was sufficient for our apprenticeship under officials whom we did not rate as high as ourselves in most aspects of our public administration. Hence we decided on 1956 as the target date for Nigeria's independence.

From our standpoint, the obstacles between us and the attainment of our goal in 1956 were many and formidable, but by no means insurmountable. When the Richards Constitution was being reviewed, it was with infinite difficulty that the Northern leaders were made to agree to the introduction of a ministerial system for the Northern Region and the Centre. Any talk about bringing Nigeria to independence five years after the introduction of the new Constitution would horrify them beyond words. They would feel sore about such a proposal and would put up a stiff resistance to it. To us, however, it did not matter whose horse was gored, so long as the path of our great objective was indefectibly pursued. Most of the British officials who were strategically and powerfully placed in the country's administration had thought that the height to which the Macpherson Constitution had raised its Nigerian beneficiaries was going to prove so dizzy and catastrophic that nothing but Providence or sheer luck could save the situation. They would feel aghast, therefore, if they came to realise that we were really in earnest about our electioneering promise that we would agitate for self-government for Nigeria in 1956. There was no doubt in our minds that these highly-placed and influential officials would do all in their power to stage a rearguard action to prevent the accomplishment of our aim. There were also a few Southern Nigerians who felt the same way as the British officials.

The position was complicated by the mutual antagonism which existed between the Action Group and the NCNC, and their divergent methods of approach to the attainment of one and the same goal. When the leaders of the two parties were together in the NEC their slogan was SGNN (Self-Government for Nigeria Now); but when the NEC ceased to exist and they all regrouped under the banners of their opposing parties, SGNN was abandoned in favour of 'SGN in 1956'. There has been unending argument as to which party first declared 1956 as the date for Nigeria's independence. If the truth is to be told, it was the Action Group that first made the declaration at its Owo Conference in April 1951. It was not until August of the same year at its convention in Kano that the NCNC made a similar declaration. In any case, the problem which confronted us was not whether we were first or second in the field in fixing a target date for Nigeria's independence, but whether with the formidable forces against us, we could succeed in achieving our objective. From the pronouncements of its spokesmen it was obvious that the NCNC preferred extra-constitutional methods in agitating for self-government for the country. They constantly spoke of 'boycott of the constitution', of 'violence', and of 'the blood of tyrants being used to water the tree of liberty'. On the other hand, we of the Action Group abjured violence in any shape or form as a weapon in the fight for our country's liberation. We believe that whatever is won

251

by violence can only be kept by violence or at least by constant show of it. Besides, the use of violence, apart from doing grievous harm to a cause was in the prevailing circumstances of British rule in Nigeria uncalled for. There had never been a properly organised country-wide demand for independence which had been spurned or contemptuously turned down by Britain. We acknowledged the fact that Nigeria was a British creation, and right or wrong Britain was for the time being in administrative control of it. It was too much to expect her to abdicate that control simply because a demand to that effect was made by a number of detribalised politicians and journalists living in the urban areas of the South. Public opinion throughout the length and breadth of the country must be organised so that the people would prefer the rule of Nigerians by Nigerians. We were sure that world opinion as well as left-wing British opinion would be strongly on our side the moment we could show that the accredited representatives of the people of Nigeria did make a demand for independence.

With all these considerations in mind our methods of approach were meticulously devised. We would eschew violence or any action that would inevitably lead to it. Instead we would mobilise public opinion by means of our organisational machinery and of all available media of mass propaganda. In this connection, the Action Group and the NCNC were, in spite of themselves, at one. From time to time we threw poisonous darts at one another, but neither the one party nor the other wanted to be outdone in the fight for the country's freedom. One method of organising public opinion in favour of independence was decided upon at the Action Group Benin Conference in December 1952. After passing a resolution fixing 1 December 1956 as Nigeria's target date for independence, we also decided that all our branches throughout Nigeria should celebrate December 1st as Nigeria's day of liberation, until actual freedom was won on the same day in 1956. Such a celebration would help to arouse the people's passion in support of the chosen target date. Before 1 December 1953 when the first celebration was due, Her Majesty's Government had already declared that it would grant self-government to any Region which desired it; and in rejecting the demand for Nigeria's independence the only reason given was that Her Majesty's Government could not entertain the demand because more than half of the population of Nigeria wanted independence 'as soon as practicable' and not in 1956. The ball was back at our feet and we could not conscientiously blame Britain for failing to play. In actual fact, after the 1953 Constitutional Conference, excepting the occasional periods of our barren friendship with the NPC, we directed our campaign against that party as the enemy of Nigeria's freedom. It was unfortunate that in this campaign the Action Group was condemned at every turn by the NCNC. The reason given was that the Action Group campaign could only have the result of driving the NPC leaders into wanting to separate the North from the rest of Nigeria. The case of the NCNC and the plea of British officials were that we should take it easy with the NPC leaders. I thought this was a mistaken policy. Those who aspire to political leadership must on no account be sheltered from the hard knocks which a political career in a democracy inevitably entails. Besides, I am convinced that the separation of the North from the rest of Nigeria would of a certainty lead to economic disaster for the North. No sane Northern leaders, in my view, would ever try it, however much they may threaten to attempt it.

As part of our methods of approach we considered it a matter of paramount importance that those of us who were Ministers should command respect from British officials in Nigeria, and from overseas visitors from Britain and elsewhere, by our undoubted mastery of the subjects under our respective charge. We were determined to exert every ounce of energy in our being to demonstrate to our detractors that more often than not it is opportunity that makes the man; and that given that opportunity the African can hold his own in the art of efficient and stable government. Above all, as soon as we thought it judicious to do so we planned to table a motion in the House of Representatives where the accredited representatives of the people would present their united demand to our British overlords.

The 1953 self-government motion was filed by Chief Anthony Enahoro without previous consultations with the party. He asked for my imprimatur, and I gave it on my own responsibility. It was after the text of the motion had been published in the newspapers that the other leaders of the party knew about it. There was a sharp controversy within the party as to whether the motion should be proceeded with or withdrawn. From the very start I knew that the majority of the leaders and of the rank and file of the party supported the motion, and I made up my mind to be firm. Those who favoured a withdrawal criticised Chief Anthony Enahoro for acting impetuously in the matter. I stood by him like the rock of Gibraltar; and it thus became my turn to be castigated for acting on such a momentous and grave issue without any previous consultations with my colleagues. My defence was that the policy of the party on the issue was irrevocably settled: the year 1956 had been proclaimed by us and we had even gone to the extent of fixing a specific date in that year. The present motion did no more and no less than to reflect our declared and well-known policy. In the circumstances, I considered it superfluous to hold further consultations with my colleagues on a matter on which the stand of the party had been settled beyond the slightest shadow of doubt. In reply to my argument two further points were raised. Firstly, it was pointed out that from the look of things the motion might precipitate a constitutional crisis. If that happened, we would need the backing of the Obas in the Western Region; but they had not been consulted. To me, this was a serious point and was well-taken, but I and a few others undertook to contact the Obas without delay and secure their support. It was to their credit that the Obas readily gave the support sought. Secondly, it was urged that it would have been much wiser if we had taken steps to carry the NPC with us on the issue of a target date before tabling a motion on it. Those of us who supported the motion felt that the best thing to do for the rapid political advancement of Nigeria was to provoke the Northern leaders out of their cast-iron shell of ultra-conservatism. If we waited for their good time, we would never go forward at our desired pace.

As we planned for Nigeria's independence, we were fully conscious that freedom from British rule does not necessarily connote freedom for individual Nigerian citizens. I and most of my colleagues are democrats by nature, and socialists by conviction. We believe in the democratic way of life: equality under the law, respect for the fundamental rights of individual citizens, and the existence of independent and impartial tribunals where these rights could be enforced. We believe that the generality of the people should enjoy this life and do so in reasonable abundance. The most detestable feature of British administration was that the governed had no say in the appointment of those who governed them. A Nigerian administration by Nigerians must be erected on the general consent and the united goodwill of the majority of the people. In my view, there can be no satisfactory alternative to this. At the same time I fully recognise that the healthy growth of a democratic way of life requires the existence of an enlightened community led by a group of people who are imbued with the all-consuming urge to defend, uphold and protect the human dignity and the legal equality of their fellow-men. But to us it was not going to be an easy task. Right there with us in the Region outside Lagos, democratic practices were unknown. At the local government level, many Obas and Chiefs were autocrats with legislative backing. Native Courts, where justice was expected to be administered in accordance with customary usages, were dens of corruption, and the instruments of tyranny and oppression. In most parts of the Region people had already become restive and were ready for a revolt. As things stood we knew on which side we should be: the popular side, the people's side. But we wanted to try, if we could, to carry the Obas and chiefs with us. For them it was going to be a sudden transformation from ancient to modern. But it was a transformation which must be brought about if the institution of chieftaincy was to survive the break-through of the flood of progressive trends which had been dammed for some time by the British administration in the country. High on our list of priority then was democratisation of Native Authorities (now known as Local Government Councils), regulation of succession to Chieftaincies, and Native Court reform. At first we had intended to abolish the Native Courts. But in view of the needs they served in remote rural areas which could not then be equally effectively served by the small number of available magistrates, we preferred reform to abolition.

With regard to the other freedoms—freedom from ignorance, freedom from disease, and freedom from want—we knew that we would encounter towering problems of an intractable character when our objectives came to be related to the means —that is money and manpower—for attaining them. We were not certain yet about where the money would come from, nor of the amount of co-operation which would be forthcoming from the British officials who then monopolised the higher rungs of the civil service where policies were formulated, and from which level their implementation would be directed.

We had promised our people that we would introduce before the end of our five-year term: (1) free universal primary education for all children of school-going age; (2) free medical treatment for all children up to the age of 18; (3) one hospital for each of the twenty-four Administrative Divisions in the Region which did not yet possess one; (4) improvement in agricultural technique and higher returns for farmers; (5) better wages for the working class; (6) improvement of existing roads and bridges and the construction of new ones; (7) water supply to urban and rural areas; and so on and so forth. From information which had reached us from authoritative sources, the officials with whom we were to associate in executing these policies neither believed in nor had sympathy for them. Apart from administrative impediments, we did recognise that there were also financial hurdles of a mountainous height to be overcome. But we were determined to blast our way through them all, and compel the force of any adverse circumstance to serve our will. We had put in long and hard preparation to meet the

256

challenge of the new constitution; we had evolved elaborate plans which, with such modifications as inside knowledge of governmental facts and figures might dictate, were ready to be launched at a moment's notice; and what is more, we had an abiding, flaming faith in the soundness and practicableness of our plans. We regarded ourselves as crusaders in a new cause, and as eminently qualified for the pioneering role which we had imposed upon ourselves. At the same time, we meant by example to compel our counterparts in the other Regions to join in the marathon race which we had pledged ourselves to run.

In November 1951, even before the five Lagos members for the Western House of Assembly were elected, and having won a majority of all the eighty seats in the House, we assembled our ministerial team. Two of them had to be dropped and replaced by two others when we lost all the Lagos seats to the NCNC. We divided the team into two: those for the Centre and those for the Region. As the leader of the party, the obvious place for me was the Council of Ministers which was at that time a superior body constitutionally to the Regional Executive Councils. As we have noted in a previous chapter, all bills passed by a Regional Legislature must receive the blessing of the Council of Ministers before they could become law. I made my preference clear to my colleagues. The issue was given a full dress debate. The only place where our policies and pro-grammes had a chance of being made effective was the Region where we would be the party in power. If we were to ensure success for these policies and programmes, the leader of the party himself who was the moving spirit behind all these plans, must be on the spot to take charge and direct the operations. By the behest of the party, therefore, I was to remain in the Region as the chief exponent and executant of the party's ideals, until independence for Nigeria was achieved in 1956. We were so obsessed by the belief that Nigeria would attain indepen-dence in 1956 that I was emboldened to make the following assertion in my presidential address to the Action Group Con-ference in Benin City in December 1952:

Now that our freedom is not far off, we must begin to look beyond our boundaries for future allies and friends.

The Macpherson Constitution did not provide for the operation of a party system at the Centre. Each Region was to send four Ministers—three of whom would be from the House of Assembly and would hold portfolios, and one from the House of Chiefs and without portfolio. (The Eastern Region had no House of Chiefs then and so all its four Ministers were drawn from its House of Assembly but one of them represented the Southern Cameroons and was without portfolio.) There were also a number of officials in the Council together with the Governor who presided over its deliberations. Since the elections in the three Regions had been won by the three major parties, it followed that the Council of Ministers would consist of three incompatible political entities. It was a fashion which is still very much in vogue for the NCNC not to see any good in anything that the Action Group did and, less often, vice versa. It was also a fashion, now in wider currency than ever before, for the NCNC to come to the defence of the NPC whenever the latter, for any good reason, was criticised by the Action Group. Besides, we of the Action Group did not trust the official members of the Council to play a healthy role: we feared that they would love to play Nigeria's mutually antagonistic parties against one another. In the circumstances, there was very little hope of pushing any of our party's policies through the Council of Ministers, but we meant to try. Our grand strategy however was that we should use the Council of Ministers much more as a battle ground for the improvement of the Constitution than as a forum for the formulation of policies. To this end, our central team was carefully chosen. Our team of three was led by Chief Bode Thomas who was then my deputy. Chief Thomas was an exceptional character in a number of ways. He had a rare gift of intuition which bordered on the prophetic. Whenever we had acted in accordance with his warning and advice we had been the happier for it; but on the few occasions that we had rejected them in deference to the force of logic we had regretted our indiscretion. He was a

258

brilliant lawyer with a quick and acute perception of abstruse legal technicalities. He had a peculiar temperament which alternated with perfect ease between alluring, persuasive calm, and a roaring tempest. We all adored him for his unique endowments, and had no doubt in our minds that in the Council of Ministers he would successfully construe some of the provisions of the new Constitution the way we wanted them to operate.

With Chief Bode Thomas at the Centre was Chief S. L. Akintola—also an able lawyer. He is a breezy, affable character who cannot be ruffled easily, if at all. His peculiar gift consists in his capability to argue and defend two opposing points of view with equal competence and plausibility. This quality backed by his sense of humour and his capacity for nuances made him an insoluble puzzle to our opponents. He and Chief Bode Thomas employed their talents well. Sir John Macpherson in one of his farewell speeches, described Chief S. L. Akintola as 'a master of ambiguities'. And in a bitter complaint which Sir John once made to me, it was clear that Chief Bode Thomas had become a constant and inescapable wasp beneath his vest. The third in our central team was Chief Arthur Prest—yet another lawyer and formerly an officer in the police force. He is a very clever person, but he was politically unpredictable. If he was held in leash he could almost move mountains. I depended on Bode and SLA to keep him on the right track, and they did. Inside one year, under the indefatigable leadership of Chief Bode Thomas, the three of them had given such construction to the Macpherson Constitution that Sir John himself had to wrestle with himself to recognise the natal identity of his own constitutional offspring.

When I took charge in the Western Region on 6 February 1952, I made a careful survey of all the advantages and disadvantages of my new venture, and tried to count them one by one. The advantages I discovered were few in number but inestimable both in their contents and potentialities. First, the people of the Western Region are enlightened and prosperous relatively to those of the other Regions. They live in large communities, and almost half of the population are concentrated in towns each with a population of 20,000 or more. If their goose was scientifically tended, I mused, it would lay the golden eggs; and, in any case, the siting of amenities would not present the same problem as in places where the population is scattered in villages and hamlets widely separated from one another by several miles. Second, my team of Ministers was unexcelled. It was a team of which any head of government anywhere in the world would be proud. It was a well-knit, highly disciplined and fanatically loyal team. Each of them knew his subject well. It may look invidious to single out one or two for special mention where all are deserving of praise. But I cannot help mentioning three of them, because of the deep and lasting impression which they made on my mind. There was Mr S. O. Awokoya: exceedingly competent, scholarly, haughty. He was in charge of education, and it was his assignment to ensure the launching of our free primary education scheme by January 1955. There was Mr E. A. Babalola, the Minister in charge of Works: a rugged, dynamic man with a rigid school-master's mentality. At any given time, he knew what was to be done and how to get it done. To him a time-table was a time-table, and it was made to be religiously adhered to both in the school and in the execution of public works. And there was His Highness Aholu Jiwa II, the Oba Akran of Badagry, whom I always fondly refer to as the Aga Khan of Badagry. He is more or less an absentee ruler of his domain: a quiet man with an unimpeachable sense of duty. His portfolio in 1952 was Development, and he had an astonishing grasp of its multifarious problems. My third advantage was that I had unshaken faith in God that the mission entrusted to me would be a success. My colleagues too without exception shared this faith.

The disadvantages on the other hand, were numerous, but counted for naught in the face of the state of mind which we adopted towards our historic and noble assignment. Only some of them need be mentioned in addition to those which were already explicit in the problems to which I have adverted in the earlier part of this chapter. The people of the Western Region may be divided roughly into two groups: the Yoruba and the non-Yoruba. The Yoruba are a fastidious, critical and discerning people. They will not do anything in politics merely to oblige a fellow Yoruba. If the Yorubaman is satisfied that your policy is good and will serve his self-interest, he will support you no matter from which ethnic group you hail. A large number of them were members and supporters of the NCNC at the time that we took office. As a matter of fact, I held the view that if in 1951 the NCNC had been as well-organised in the rural areas as we were, it would have stood a good chance of winning the elections. The non-Yoruba elements were rabidly anti-Action Group, because they were anti-Yoruba. For years they had been fed with Dr Azikiwe's propaganda that the Yoruba hated them, and for that reason had diverted all the good things of the Region to their own section of it. Furthermore, the vast majority of them erroneously believed the false propaganda that the Action Group was a Yoruba organisation. Consequently, of the twenty members who were elected there in 1951 only four were members of the Action Group; and even these four were elected on their own personal merits rather than on the acceptance by their electors of the Action Group policy or leadership. I had no illusion at all about the problem which confronted me in this regard. A large section of the community whose affairs I was to administer had no faith in my party; and this meant a good deal in a society such as ours where people can be insensate and unreasoning in their likes and dislikes.

Besides, I had to reckon with the Obas and Chiefs who were very jealous of and extremely sensitive about their traditional rights and privileges. In spite of agitation here and there against this or that Oba or Chief, the institution of Obaship and Chieftaincy was still held in high esteem by the people. But the traditional rights and privileges which the Obas and Chiefs wished to preserve were antithetic to democratic concepts and to the yearnings and aspirations of the people. To make a frontal attack on these rights and privileges would be the surest way of bringing a host of hornets' nests about our ears. To compromise with them, on the other hand, would mean death to our new party. The problem which faced me, therefore, was that whilst I must strive to harness the influence of the Obas and Chiefs for our purposes, I must, at the same time, take the earliest possible steps to modify their rights and abrogate such of their privileges as were considered repugnant, to an extent that would both satisfy the commonalty and make the Obas and Chiefs feel secure in their traditional offices.

Above all, the level at which we had to start to provide for our people those modern amenities which we had promised them was very low indeed—much lower in many cases than in the Eastern Region with which the Western Region had always engaged in healthy competition in such matters. Three instances are enough. The roads in the Region were in a most sorry state —much worse than in the Eastern Region—and only 178 miles of them had been bituminous-surfaced through the instrumentality of the outgoing Regional Administration. There were 38 hospitals with 939 beds in the Region. Only 15 of these hospitals were built and run by the government; the rest were private and missionary. In the Eastern Region, on the other hand, there were 55 hospitals, 20 of which were owned by government—with 3,097 beds. The hospital beds worked out at 235 per million of population in the Western Region and 590 per million of population in the Eastern Region. The same story goes for education. Whilst about 65 per cent of the children of school-going age were attending primary schools in the Eastern Region, only about 35 per cent were doing so in the West. Besides, as against 105 secondary grammar schools in the Eastern Region there were only 25 in the West. In other words, per million of population, there were only 6 secondary schools in the West as compared with 20 in the East.

It was in full recognition of these and other handicaps not related here that my colleagues and I took office. Rather than their damping our enthusiasm, these handicaps had only helped to steel our hearts. We had made revolutionary promises to our people and the expectations of the majority of them had been heightened. Any obstacles that stood in our path, therefore, must be removed at all costs: for it was by so doing that the stuff of which the Action Group professed to have been made would be practically demonstrated.

As I said before, we actually assumed office in the Western Region on 6 February 1952, and the Budget meeting of the House of Assembly began twelve days after on the 18 February. As the new government, it was our duty to pass a budget which had been prepared by officials long before we assumed office, and indeed at the time when we were still busy with electioneering. It would neither be wise nor politic to reject the whole of the budget. But we decided that, in passing it, we should make it bear the stamp and the impress of some aspects of the Action Group programmes. The principles by which we were to be guided in considering the estimates were enunciated by me in a ministerial statement in the House on 20 February 1952; that was the day before the debate on the Second Reading of the Appropriation Bill began on the 21st. I said:

In our study of the Estimates we have been guided by three principles which I very earnestly commend for the consideration of this House. The first principle is that, save in the case of those Departments which cater for the educational, economic, health and social needs of the people, there should be no increase in establishment except in so far as such increase is due either to re-organisation which makes for the re-distribution of a number of staff into the three Regions or to the inclusion of Lagos in the Western Region. I do not pretend, Mr President, that this particular principle is fool-proof; but it is a good working basis. The second principle is that wherever practicable, increase in establishment should be governed by the policy of Nigerianisation.

And the third principle is that as far as possible expenditure on services which tend to the welfare, and health and the education of the people should be increased at the expense of any expenditure that does not answer to the same test.

In strict pursuance of these principles, we did a few things which were unprecedented in the annals of public administra-

263

tion in any part of Nigeria, and which served as shining objects of emulation to the other Governments in Nigeria for a long time after. We made provision of £80,000 in the estimates for the award of 200 post-secondary scholarships tenable in British and American universities and in the University College, Ibadan. No provision at all had been made in the estimates for scholarship awards. It was the first time ever that such a large number of scholarships were provided for and awarded in one year by any Government in the country. The Nigerian Government up to then had not awarded even as many as 20 scholarships annually. We also made provision of £25,000 for recreational facilities. Only a sum of £950 had been provided in the draft estimates. We reduced the proposed establishment of administrative officers, and rejected those items of expenditure which we considered obviously wasteful. We also introduced what we called a 'frigidaire policy'. It was part of our election promises that the key posts in the civil service of the country should in due course be filled by Nigerians. When the Macpherson Constitution was introduced there was no plan anywhere outside that of the Action Group's for accelerating what is generally known as Nigerianisation of the civil service. In our view, British officers were being brought into the country to perform jobs which could be competently discharged by Nigerians.

But appointment into the civil service was neither in our control as politicians, nor even within the competence of the Western Region Government. Fortunately for us at that time, and for a long while thereafter, an oversea officer was paid an inducement allowance in addition to the basic salary attached to his post, known as 'expatriation pay'. In the estimates which we were considering, every post had 'expatriation pay' attached to it. If a Nigerian was appointed to the post, he did not draw this pay, but if an oversea officer was appointed, he did. As a means of accelerating the pace of Nigerianisation of the civil service in the Western Region, we decided that 'expatriation pay' in respect of all new posts and of all posts which were vacant should be frozen, and that the amount of money thus

264

frozen would be released by the Western Region Government only after it had been satisfied that there were no Nigerians with the requisite qualification to fill the posts to which the pay was attached. This policy and the phrase with which it was christened were well received throughout the country, and with jubilation by Nigerians in the civil service. As was expected, the 'frigidaire policy' did not go down well with the overseas officers serving in and outside the Region. It took some time before we and the British officials grew to like one another. By and large, we never got on well with the older classes. As for the younger and more resilient ones, the relationship between us and them became cordial: as time went on they proved themselves loyal and responsive and sympathetic to our aspirations; and we did not hesitate to repose our trust in them.

The 1952/53 draft estimates provided for an estimated surplus of £101,000; but after we had dealt with it in the manner which I have described, we were able to show an estimated surplus of £128,000. The Opposition led by Dr Azikiwe did not think much of our efforts; but like all political parties, we lustily sang our own praise.

By May and June 1952, most of the policy papers which we published before the elections had been embodied in Sessional Papers and Bills. When we assumed office, there was in existence a Five-Year Plan of Development and Welfare for the period 1951/56. The Ten-Year Plan to which I referred in the last chapter had been revised and broken into two quinquennial periods—1946/51 and 1951/56. The revised 1951/56 Plan covered the whole of Nigeria, and each Region was provided for under it. We took what appealed to us in this Plan, but otherwise we did not work in accordance with it. There were certain financial allocations to the Western Region under this Plan made by the Colonial Secretary under the Colonial Development and Welfare Act. These allocations were made to be spent on projects approved by the Secretary of State. We did not want to do anything that would deprive us of the funds available to us under the Act. So when the Secretary of State suggested, and the other Governments agreed, that the 1951/56 Plan should be terminated and another one commencing from the 1st April, 1955 should be introduced, with the proviso that the outstanding allocations under the Colonial Development and Welfare Act in respect of schemes under the 1951/56 Plan were carried forward in favour of the Governments concerned, we readily agreed. We then produced what amounted in our case to a revised and consolidated Five-Year Plan, entitled 'Development of the Western Region of Nigeria 1955/60.' Other governments in Nigeria did likewise, but their plans were not as well-thought out and comprehensive as our own. In 1958, the Colonial Secretary again suggested that the 1955/60 plans should be terminated in favour of a Three-Year Plan for 1959/62. We refused to accept this suggestion, though the other governments did. Our Region was already self-governing; we had been shabbily treated in the new allocation of Colonial Development and Welfare Funds (North £3¾ million; East £2¼ million, and West £½ million), and we had enough funds of our own to execute our plans. In November 1959, we introduced another Five Year Plan entitled 'Western Regional Development Plan 1960/65'.

In the course of my eight years of office, I gave my personal attention to the formulation of every major policy, and the execution of practically every important programme. It was the greatest pleasure of my life to watch the Region grow from a little acorn into a promising oak. But there are certain matters which were particularly dear to my heart, and to which I devoted the closest personal attention. In our under-developed society, I placed the utmost premium on (1) education, (2) health, (3) economic development, and (4) democratisation of local government (Native Authority) councils. I have reasons for my predilection for these subjects.

As I said before, we believe in the equality of all men, and in the liberty of the individual. I believe that every citizen, however humble and lowly his station in life, has a right to demand from his government the creation of those conditions which will enable him progressively to enjoy, according to civilised standards, the basic necessities of life as well as reasonable comfort and a measure of luxury. In other words, every citizen, regardless of his birth or religion, should be free and reasonably contented.

It is often overlooked that there are two vital and inescapable stages in life wherein all men and women, however great or small, and however rich or poor, are equal: at birth and at death. Through these two events, Nature herself is incessantly imparting to us a lesson which is also vital and inescapable and which mankind ignores at its peril, namely that all men and women should be treated as equal, both as political and economic beings. For this reason all laws, measures and programmes introduced by government must be framed so as to give equal treatment and opportunity to all. Various forms of government—absolute monarchy, oligarchy and autocracy; and different economic devices—feudalism and *laissez faire* capitalism, have at one time or another been practised by man in defiance of this principle. But in the fullness of time these devices have crumbled because they are evil. From the very start, therefore, I have always had before me the supreme objective of a welfare state which is denoted by our motto of 'Freedom for all and life more abundant'. At the same time, I do recognise that this objective will be realised only if the state is prepared to step into the breach to help the needy, especially the young ones, both to discover and develop their talents or natural bents.

Whilst man is the highest of all known creation, he is nonetheless susceptible to the influences of environment and heredity. Under these influences alone, what is known as natural capacity differs between one man or woman and another. In other words our talents, and hence our chances for equality of development, differ. But whether a man's talent is one, and another's are five, each of them should have equal opportunity for developing what he has. Furthermore, environmental and hereditary handicaps or advantages are factors which can in the one case be eliminated, and in the other maintained and enhanced, in a society where the government recognises that its duties are to all its citizens without exception. The converse is of course true. In a society where the principles which I have tried to adumbrate are ignored or are indifferently or half-heartedly observed, the initial handicaps or advantages of environment and heredity will respectively be increased or diminished. The duty of a good government is, therefore, clear. In vesting it with authority the populace have acted jointly and as equals. It is not open to the government to prefer the members of its own hierarchy or some of the members of the community in the provision of amenities. It must devote identical interest to the welfare of all citizens, and it must display special concern for the afflicted and those whose talents are in danger of being buried or destroyed. If there are those who are retarded by environmental and hereditary handicaps, they should, under a welfare administration, attract special attention and assistance from the government. In other words, in order to achieve equality of opportunity, the amount of attention and assistance required from the government is bound to vary as between one citizen and another. Broadly speaking, the poorer or less fortunate the citizen, the greater the attention he requires from the government; and the richer or more fortunate the citizen the less.

Because of all this, I attach the greatest importance to the subjects which I have previously mentioned. The provision of education and health in a developing country such as Nigeria is as much an instrument of economic development as the provision of roads, water supply, electricity, and the like. To educate the children and enlighten the illiterate adults is to lay a solid foundation not only for future social and economic progress but also for political stability. A truly educated citizenry is, in my view, one of the most powerful deterrents to dictatorship, oligarchy and feudal autocracy. The last two are very much present with us in most parts of Nigeria; and the fulminations of some Nigerian political leaders do strongly suggest that the possible emergence of a dictator could not be entirely ruled out, unless the citizens are sufficiently educated to know their individual rights and to cultivate enough courage to resist any encroachment on those rights. Education in the true sense of the word does more. It gives the citizen a correct and wider perspective of the things of this world, and makes him a good neighbour to his fellow-men.

To provide health services is to combat those diseases in Nigeria which are wasting human resources and are a drain on the productive potentialities of our people. 'Mens sana in corpore sano' is the motto of a famous institute of psychology. Indeed, an educated and healthy individual is in my opinion the strongest single factor in the economic and social advancement of any nation. Rightly or wrongly, godless materialism has been equated with communism. The professed aim or end of communism is social justice for all citizens. 'From each according to his ability, and to each according to his need' is a socialist tenet which is now of unrestricted application in many of the so-called capitalist countries. So that the means to the end of social justice for all in the economic sense, or of a welfare state, need not be brutal, bloody and godless; provided of course an early step is taken to combat and eradicate or at least seriously undermine and weaken the imperialism of ignorance, disease and want wherever it holds sway. When the Action Group came into being there were three imperialisms reigning side by side and in concert in Nigeria. They were the imperialism of ignorance, disease and want which I have just mentioned; British imperialism; and the imperialism of local caesars who flourished under the aegis of British imperialism. It would be idle, naïve and dangerous to imagine that the only enemy to be destroyed in order to usher in freedom and life more abundant to our people is British imperialism. My colleagues and I have never been under such an illusion. On the contrary, I have always stressed the point that unless we work hard and in the right direction, when Britain abdicates sovereignty over Nigeria, she would leave behind the other two imperialisms, whose reigns could be poignantly grinding and oppressive. Apart from taking good care of their education and health, therefore, it is the urgent duty of the government to take steps to enlarge the productivity of all our citizens. A considerable and continual growth in the wealth of the Western Region in particular, and of Nigeria in general must be assured. This is not enough. Government must also ensure that the wealth which is from time to time produced is distributed justly and equitably to those who have contributed to its creation, and as a matter of humanity to those who through ill-health, physical incapacity, or other causes are unable to produce anything.

But man does not live by bread alone. His education, health and material comfort would be meaningless and insipid unless the atmosphere in which he lives and has his being is conducive to the development in him of self-reliance and freedom from fear. Such a healthy and ennobling atmosphere can only exist in a democratic society. In Chapter 13, I quoted from the Minorities Report Churchill's definition of liberal democracy. It would be presumptuous, and an affliction to the reader for me to attempt to improve on Churchill's lucid, functional and practical definition. This much I wish to add in order to illustrate what had gone on in my mind before and during my eight years of office, and what still dominates my political outlook. There can be no alternative to a democratic way of life, if the aim of the government is the physical, mental and spiritual welfare of the people. It has been said that democracy is liable to abuse, especially in an unsophisticated society; and that through the instrumentality of democracy the wrong type of people may be thrown up as the government of the day. The question is: who are to judge the type of persons who should be appointed to rule a particular people? The answer is: the people themselves. If their estimation of what is good does not accord with that of the minority elements among them, the latter group can only wait and hope, and continue to advocate what they believe to be good until, if they are indeed right, the majority swing to their side. I fervently prefer the inconveniences of democracy to the inarticulate and fearful material comfort of a dictatorship, even granting that such comfort ever comes the way of the majority under a totalitarian system.

'When the disciples are ready, the master will appear' says the mystic: an eternal truth which is applicable to politics as it is to mysticism. It is the readiness and the yearnings and aspirations of the people that will determine the calibre and character of those who rule them. In a society of rogues, honesty will be at a heavy discount; and that is as it should be. The task of a great and humane reformer is to win support both by precepts and by examples. His reward may be the realisation of his dreams in his lifetime, or after. More often than not he will earn the condemnation of those whom he essays to serve, if they are not yet ready. The pragmatist will always identify himself with the changing moods of the people—however unedifying; but the idealist will strive to make them see a wider vista—to dream great dreams and to attempt lofty flights. In other words, the idealist-pragmatist reformer will strive to make the people ready. If he imposes himself on them against their will, he is a spoliator and not a reformer.

The point has also been widely canvassed that the best form of government for a backward people such as ours is benevolent dictatorship. The very phrase 'benevolent dictatorship' is a contradiction in terms. Man in his earthly nature is an animal. If he is elevated to a position where he could feel unfettered by and above the sanctions and conventions jointly imposed by his fellow-men, he would prove to be the savagest of savage animals. It goes without saying, therefore, that if absolute power is vested in any man, the chances are ten to one that he will use it to the detriment of his fellow-men and for his personal aggrandisement.

The beauty and the essence of democracy, in spite of its known and admitted imperfections, lie in the checks and balances which it provides among the members of a community. By means of these devices, no one citizen is in a position to lord it over his fellow-citizens, or to deprive others of their fundamental rights. In a democracy, everyone however high or low is enjoined to live his life and conduct his private and public

271

affairs so that he does not constitute himself a nuisance or a bugbear to his fellow-men. If any citizen takes it upon himself to disregard the checks and balances provided by the laws and the usages of the land, or flouts the restraints imposed upon him in the interest of the common weal of the society in which he lives, he at once exposes himself to the never-failing sanctions which the society, through their elected parliament, has prescribed for the enforcement of mutual respect and of reciprocity of rights and duties among all citizens. What applies to the individual citizen also applies to the government. The group of representatives or agents of the people known as the government owe as much duty to the individual citizens as the latter do to them. If these agents become a nuisance to the majority of the citizens, they must, like any individual citizen in a similar plight, regard themselves as subject to the sanctions which society has laid down for dealing with their case. They are liable to be removed at periodic intervals, and any attempt on their part to stultify the wishes or sanctions of the people is fraud of the worst kind.

In my view, therefore, democracy exists only when the people are free, periodically and at their will, to re-elect or remove those who have been elected by them to administer their affairs. It is when this freedom exists that man can grow into the self-reliant and fearless creature that God intends him to be. But the moment a single person or a group of persons contrive to put themselves in a position where they become a law unto themselves, and are not amenable to the arbitrament of the people under their jurisdiction, they become a menace to their fellow-men: the governed lose their self-confidence, self-reliance and self-respect, and they live in an atmosphere of dread and spiritual hopelessness. There is, however, a Jewish proverb which every despot must always remember: 'When the tally of bricks is too heavy, then comes Moses.'

As I said before, by June most of our policy papers had been embodied in Sessional Papers and Bills. These were laid on the table of the House of Assembly during its meeting which started on 14 July 1952. All the Sessional Papers were fully debated by the House of Assembly and were unanimously passed. The House of Chiefs passed them without debate. The Local Government Bill which I regarded as my magnum opus, and which I described as the 'Charter of Freedom', together with other Bills were passed into law. The financial requirements of all these measures were clearly shown, and on the aggregate they came to a mighty sum. By way of illustration, the estimated capital costs for education and health alone amounted to £10 million, whilst the recurrent expenditure on the same items was expected to go up by about £3 million during the 1954/55 fiscal period. As against these, the total revenue available for capital and recurrent expenditure in 1952/53 was only £4·79 million. Where would the required money come from? That was the question. And it was a question which had to be tackled with speed and success, if we were to redeem our promises to the electorate. I decided to do everything possible to save money on approved capital estimates. I placed an embargo on expenditure on a number of building projects such as staff housing. I ruled that government staff, whether white or black, must go and hire houses wherever they could find them in Ibadan. I applied for a grant from the Cocoa Marketing Board, to meet part of the capital expenditure on education. My argument was that reserves accumulated from the marketing of cocoa belonged to farmers in the Western Region. The new education scheme would benefit people living in the rural areas more than those in the urban areas. The scheme was, therefore, a legitimate project for financial assistance from the Cocoa Marketing Board. When my application was turned down, I threatened that I would agitate for the Cocoa Marketing Board to be controlled by the Western Region Government instead of by the Nigerian Government. It was wrong that the people of the Region should starve educationally whilst they had huge sums of money belonging to them lying unused in the hands of some misguided custodians. My threat went unheeded.

I then had a brain-wave. The capital expenditure on new schools could be considerably reduced if buildings with permanent foundations and ordinary mud walls were erected instead of completely permanent ones. I made careful investigation and I was informed that such semi-permanent structures would cost only about a third of the estimates for permanent ones, and that they would last at least 50 years. I took the view that the duty we owed to the present generation of young people would have been amply discharged if we were able to provide for them school buildings which would last 50 years. In any case, even if we erected permanent buildings, their architectural styles would probably be out-of-date in 50 years' time, and would be due for reconstruction in any case. Accordingly, I brought a memorandum to the Executive Council, and we decided that semi-permanent school buildings should be erected. This would reduce the capital expenditure on our education programme from £9 million to £3 million. When the technical people in the Works Department were apprised of our decision they were flabbergasted. They told us that they could neither handle nor supervise the type of buildings we had in mind. I convened a meeting of contractors to explain our proposition and problem to them. They turned up; but only Nigerian contractors promised co-operation, and actually helped in erecting these buildings. European contractors thought it was beneath their professional dignity to handle our type of semi-permanent buildings.

But the problem of finance for education and health and for our other projects had not been solved. We decided to impose a levy of 10/- on all adult male taxpayers. At my request, the Lieutenant-Governor Sir Hugo Marshall convened a meeting of the Senior Administrative Officers (called Residents) in charge of Provinces, in order to inform them of our decision and to secure their co-operation in plucking the goose without too much squeaking. Some of them thought 10/- was too high; but it was made quite clear that this was the lowest levy we could impose if our schemes were to be implemented. When a resolution seeking the approval of the Legislature for this tax levy to be imposed with effect from 1 April 1953 came before the House of Assembly, the Opposition (still led by Dr Azikiwe) was up in arms. They denounced the 10/- levy and suggested 2/6d instead. In a society where the majority of the people could not understand why a government which could mint coins and print paper money should be levying a tax on its subjects the NCNC suggestion was received with widespread acclamation. A fierce and ferocious agitation against this tax measure, mainly instigated by the NCNC, followed in certain parts of the Region.

The time-lag between this tax measure (1953) and the actual introduction of the educational schemes (1955) on account of which it was imposed, made the government very unpopular. The NCNC seized the opportunity to din it into people's ears that they had been led up the garden path, and that the capitation levy had been imposed for purposes other than those which the people were made to believe by the government. The courage of the Action Group leadership in the face of the attendant public obloquy was severely tested, but we remained as undaunted as ever. The NCNC opposition called on the government to resign; but instead I went to the House of Assembly to obtain a vote of confidence on the government's tax policy. I always have the feeling that if the Residents and the Administrative Officers under them had been enthusiastic about the levy, and had shared our faith in the schemes for which it was intended, they would have been more discreet and tactful in the way they put it across to the people, and the violent nature of the agitation in the initial stages would have been averted. My colleagues and I intensified our campaign throughout the Region to explain the benecfient purpose of the levy to the people. Sporadic violence and rioting ceased; but the Government remained unpopular. The measure of this unpopularity was shown by the defeat which we suffered in the federal elections of November 1954. We won 19 seats; the NCNC 22; and one seat went to an independent candidate who campaigned on a purely anti-tax platform. The actual votes cast were more revealing than the narrow defeat which the number of seats won by us indicated. Of the total votes cast we scored only 35 per cent (147,301 votes); the NCNC

53 per cent (218,473 votes), and the *ad hoc* anti-tax parties and independents 12 per cent. The NCNC's renewed demand that we should resign because of these results was ignored, and we pressed on with our schemes. We also imposed a purchase tax on cocoa, and oil palm produce. Other avenues of raising revenue such as an entertainment and cinema tax and a lottery were explored. As a result of all these exercises we increased our revenue in the 1953/54 fiscal year by about £1½ million. In respect of our water supply projects we applied to the Federal Government for a loan of £1 million which was granted. In addition, I had in the meantime succeeded in saving about £750,000 on capital expenditure.

But all these did not amount to more than chicken-feed in the face of our gargantuan requirements. All the same we proceeded with the implementation of our programmes on a scale permitted by the funds at our disposal. If we were to work to our target of starting the free primary education scheme in January 1955, expansion of teacher training must commence in January 1953. This was done, and for a start we made use of hired houses. Free medical treatment for children up to 18 years of age was introduced in 1953; and all our other schemes were also introduced on a skeletal scale. The real miracle occurred, however, when as a result of the alliance between the Action Group and the NCNC the Commodity Marketing Boards which were controlled by the Federal Government were regionalised, and allocation of revenue was made mainly in accordance with the principle of derivation. By means of the former, an accumulated reserve of over £34 million was transferred to the Western Region, and as a result of the latter our revenue rose from £6·39 in 1953/54 to £13·20 million in 1954/55. The initiative for both of these measures came from the Action Group; and whilst Dr Azikiwe later regretted his art and part in them, I had no cause to. Since the introduction of these financial measures, our revenue has been on a steady increase. The system of allocation of revenue has been revised, and it is now based not mainly on the principle of derivation, but on a combination of several principles which favour less developed areas of the Federation than the Western Region. In his Report of the Fiscal Commission of July 1958, Sir Jeremy Raisman commented in this connection as follows:

Starting from the base of 1958/59, it will be seen that our scheme may be expected to provide increasing revenue in each year for all the Regions save the West. There is a case for some check in the rate of expansion of Government services in the West in view of the favourable treatment which the Western Region has enjoyed under the present allocation system.

But the fall from £15·88 million in 1958/59 to £15 million in 1959/60 forecast by the Raisman Commission did not materialise. The revised estimated revenue for that year which was the last fiscal year with which I was connected was £20·13 million.

During my eight years of office, apart from being Leader of the Party in power from February 1952 to September 1954 and Premier from October 1954 to December 1959, I also held specific portfolios at different times: Local Government from 1952 to September 1954; Finance from October 1954 to March 1955; Economic Planning from October 1954 to November 1957, and Chairman of the Region's Economic Planning Committee from 1955 to December 1959. The achievements of the Western Region Government during these eight years are truly phenomenal and remain the object of emulation by the other governments in the Federation, as well as the subject of special mention and constant praise by overseas visitors to Nigeria. I will give a summary of only some of them here.

My aim throughout my tenure of office has been to establish and maintain a sound and democratic government in the Region. We have succeeded in doing this owing to the good sense and patriotism of our people and the loyal and devoted service of all members of our civil service, expatriates as well as Nigerians. We have ensured the participation of our Chiefs in the work of the Regional Legislature by establishing a House of Chiefs, and in the House of Assembly we have adopted the well-tried parliamentary practice obtaining at Westminster. We have maintained law and order throughout the Region; and on the few occasions when breaches of the peace have occurred, we have restored order speedily.

In the sphere of local government we inherited in 1952 a system of Native Authorities with Obas and Chiefs enjoying a position of dominance, and the Administrative Officers 'holding their hands'. In its place we have established democratic local government councils: the Obas and Chiefs take their places side by side with elected Councillors in the statutory ratio of at least 3 elected Councillors to not more than 1 Oba or Chief; and the Administrative Officers are confined to their proper role of advisers and inspectors. We passed the epoch-making Local Government Law in 1952, and since then a total of 226 Councils has been established. When I moved the second reading of the Local Government Bill in 1952, I stressed the new features of the reforms which it sought to introduce. Under the new law, we would at the local government level rule ourselves through the agency of the traditional institutions which we had evolved for ourselves. These traditional institutions would be moulded and modified from time to time in accordance with the popular will of the people. The Obas and Chiefs would henceforth be the agents of their own people and answerable to them, and not the delegates of the Lieutenant-Governor or of the Resident as before. The importance which I attach to local government was emphasised in the following passage (quoted from my speech on the second reading of the Bill):

The importance of local government in any political set-up cannot be over-emphasised. It is the foundation on which the massive and magnificent superstructure of state, Regional or central government is erected. It is the training ground in political awareness and civic responsibility for a much larger number of public-spirited citizens than can ever have room to operate on the Regional or national levels. Its day-to-day doings directly affect the lives of those who live within its jurisdiction, for better or for worse. Indeed, it is the most effective agency by means of which the Regional or state government ministers to the basic needs, welfare and general well-being of the citizens.

We realised that Local Government Councils, if they are to

succeed, must have efficient staff. Accordingly, we introduced the Unified Local Government Service, with its own independent Board, which is responsible for the appointment, posting and discipline of its members. The training of local government officers has also been vigorously pursued. Like all human institutions, the new Local Government Councils have undergone strains and stresses. A very small number of them have fallen by the wayside. But on the whole they have justified our expectation. Some of them which have proved themselves worthy of it, have been granted financial autonomy. To promote competition among councils for efficiency and probity, I awarded a shield annually to the best council of the year. The Minister of Local Government also gave a cup to the next best Council of the year. In 1954, we systematised succession to chieftaincies by means of the Chiefs Law, thus minimising the acrimonious disputes which had hitherto bedevilled appointment to a vacant chiefship. In 1959, we passed a law to establish a Council of Obas and Chiefs which must be consulted in matters of discipline relating to any Oba or Chief.

Justice is an important element in good government and we have, therefore, striven to ensure that a sound judicial system is established throughout the Region. We have more trained judges and magistrates per million of population than any other Region in the Federation. We have made provision for a self-contained Statute Book, embodying all laws in force in the Region, other than Federal Laws, thus eliminating references to English legislations. We have learnt, on good authority, that this is the first time that such a scheme has been carried through by any dependent territory in the British Commonwealth. We, alone of all the Regions in Nigeria, have produced a revised Statute Book for our Region and we have also introduced a system of law reporting.

As regards Customary Courts (formerly Native Courts), a completely new system and structure has been introduced. Among its many progressive features are the establishment of a special independent body for the appointment of court members, the regulation of all procedure by rules of court, the conferment of a right of representation by legal practitioners in certain grades of court, the removal of general powers of review by administrative officers, and the simplification of channels of appeal which lead directly or indirectly to the higher courts. Finally, all Customary Courts have been divested of jurisdiction to try criminal offences against unwritten law, and criminal jurisdiction has instead been conferred in respect of statutory offences. Undoubtedly, this last development is the first step of its kind in British territories in Africa.

In the field of public finance, perhaps the greatest achievement of the government during my time has been, as I already indicated, a steady annual increase in public revenue coupled with the strictest control of public expenditure. The result is a state of buoyancy and solvency throughout the period of my regime which has enabled the government to devote the bulk of its expenditure to development projects. As I said before, our recurrent revenue rose from £4·79 million in 1952/53 to £20·13 million in 1959/60. This has been achieved largely as a result of our economic development programme. Under our 1955/60 Five-Year Programme we planned to spend £105 million; but in actual fact we did spend a little more than this amount, and without external borrowing save the £1 million which we had borrowed from the Federal Government in 1952. The execution of this development programme has brought about a substantial increase in the real income of the people, a consequential rise in their standard of living, and an enlargement of their taxable capacity. As regards expenditure, by pruning all unnecessary items of expenditure and keeping every programme under constant review, we have succeeded in channelling public spending to the most utilitarian ends. Our total expenditure, comprising of recurrent and capital expenditure, rose from £4·67 million in 1952/53 to £30·45 million in 1959/60. The wisdom of our spending is shown by the fact that 31·8 per cent is devoted to purely economic projects, 41·5 per cent goes to social services and general administration claims the remaining 26·7 per cent. The importance which I attach to education in particular is reflected in the fact that, of the total expenditure of £51·688 million on social services throughout the period of my regime, education alone takes £39·363 million.

In the field of economic planning, I gave pride of place to the development of agriculture. Nigeria is an agricultural country, and no less than 95 per cent of its population engage in agriculture. But their methods of farming are to say the least unscientific. I believed that if the standard of the people was to be raised as quickly as possible the efficiency and productivity of the farming population must be increased. This could be done in several ways: by the introduction of scientific farming methods, and of marketing and storage techniques; by the general enlightenment of the farming classes and the improvement of their health; by the control of pests and diseases, and the conservation of soil fertility. In order to achieve these ends, the government must expand its extension services considerably, so that new knowledge and techniques might be taken to the farmers on their farms. Many an educated Nigerian does not like an agricultural career. Nevertheless, the agricultural extension workers of the government rose from 77 in 1952 to 478 in 1959.

Our biggest source of wealth was cocoa and oil palm produce. But the fact that we were dependent on two main crops only makes our economy shaky and precarious. All the same we were determined to make the best of what we had whilst we explored every avenue for diversifying our economy. Cocoa, oil palm produce and rubber thus became the subjects of intensive research. Advice was made available to farmers who were engaged in these crops on planting, cultivation, regeneration, crop harvesting (tapping in the case of rubber) and processing. In this connection, new high-yielding and disease-resistant seeds or seedlings were from time to time provided by the government for the farmers. By way of illustration, under the Rubber Improvement Scheme, whilst only 90 or so seedlings of high-yielding clones were distributed in 1958,

300,000 were distributed in 1959 and the figure will rise to about two and a half million by 1960. Over six million seedlings of the high-yielding Amazon variety of cocoa were available for planting by farmers in 1959. When we assumed office in 1952, black pod and capsid were dread diseases to cocoa. Today they have been completely overcome. Not only are farmers instructed in the best ways to deal with these diseases, which do grave damage to cocoa, but also they are assisted with loans to purchase chemicals and spraying equipment. By the end of 1959 28,500 farmers had been trained in black pod control measures, and 32,453 in pest-control measures against capsid. Through the Western Region Finance Corporation, the loan finance currently available to farmers has reached the level of £$\frac{3}{4}$ million. The government has also provided subsidies in respect of purchases of planting materials, or, in partnership with the Marketing Board, in respect of chemicals required by farmers for combating pests and diseases. Farmers who produce food crops have also received special attention from the government. New disease-resistant and high-yielding seeds have been introduced to them. They have been given advice on cheap modern farming technique and on the storage and marketing of their products. They have also been given loan assistance at the very low interest of 5 per cent per annum; and this without any security from them save their bona fides and the crops on their farmlands. In 1959 alone £176,000 was given out as loans to farmers producing food crops and to fishermen. Apart from helping individual farmers in the manner already described, one of the last acts of my regime was the establishment of thirteen co-operative farm settlements and three farm institutes under the auspices of the government. Here young educated persons are taught and made to practise the science and technique of modern farming, with a view to their standing on their own as successful co-operative farmers after a short period of pupillage. Under this scheme ten additional farm settlements were to be established every year for the succeeding five years.

Through one of its agencies, namely the Western Nigeria

Development Corporation, the government is also assisting plantation development; and a great deal of progress has been made in this field. By 1958 the Corporation already had six plantations of its own, covering 20,517 acres. In partnership with Co-operative Societies and Local Government Authorities, it has eleven plantations covering 8,468 acres. The crops grown include rubber, cocoa, oil palm, citrus, cashew and coffee. Plans were made for expansion and the establishment of new plantations which would bring the total acreage to about 56,000 acres in 1960.

The aim of my Government since 1952, however, has been to promote the growth of secondary industries in the Region *pari passu* with agricultural development. The pursuit of this aim created some tricky problems for me at the early stages. In the economic sphere, the dominant note of my regime was that the government must ensure a never-ceasing expansion in the economy and wealth of the Region, and an equitable distribution of each additional unit of wealth. In this connection I refused to be wedded to any particular ism. I had declared at Owo that one of our guiding principles should be 'the total abolition of want by means of any economic policy which is both expedient and effective'. The emphasis, as far as I am concerned, has always been on the words 'expedient and effective'. From time to time, the point has been keenly urged by a very influential body of people in the party that the Action Group should declare itself a socialist party. My own view, which is shared by many, is that what matters is not the label which a party bears, but the policy which it actually pursues either in office or opposition. In any case, in the circumstances of Nigeria, it would be reckless and lead to economic chaos to adopt a rigid socialist policy, or drink the cup of undiluted capitalism. For the rapid development of our country, we need foreign capital as well as managerial and technical know-how. At the same time, the admission of foreign capital into the country must be well-regulated, if our future is not to be mortgaged for the satisfaction of present needs. I firmly believe that the motive force behind private enterprise can be made to serve socialist ends by means of state participation in industries, and of legislative control of the activities of certain classes of industrial undertaking. Downright state ownership of all the means of production would create for us more problems than we set out to solve. My attitude to foreign investment in the fields of industry and plantation is that such investment should be made in partnership with indigenous capital supplied by the government or any of its agencies or by Nigerian businessmen.

As I said before, the need to diversify our economy through the establishment of secondary industries is realised. But it is also realised that the development of agricultural technique and the increase in the farmers' productivity is bound to lead to a situation in which fewer men than before are required to produce all the food we need. It is the responsibility of the government to see to it that those who are thus displaced from the farmlands are gainfully employed in other occupations. To this end, not only has the government facilitated the growth of private enterprise in the industrial field by removing all those obstacles that tend to inhibit economic growth and by providing basic services (including the establishment of industrial estates), but it has also entered the field of industrialisation through its agencies, the Development Corporation and the Finance Corporation. On its own, the Development Corporation has financed, and managed, three projects including a rubber factory which produces crepe rubber. In partnership with overseas investors and industrialists, it has invented funds in nine undertakings including the gigantic West African Portland Cement Company Works (which has a capital of £4½ million) at Ewekoro on the Abeokuta–Lagos road. By 1960, it is estimated that the Corporation will have invested more than £3 million in large-scale industrial enterprises alone.

The Finance Corporation is the Government agency for making loan finance available to Nigerian entrepreneurs who have sound industrial and commercial projects in hand but are short of capital to start or expand them. The total industrial loans at the disposal of the Corporation for 1955/60 were estimated at £407,000; those for 1959/60 alone amount to about £150,000. The scope of the activities of the Finance Corporation extends to equity participation in local business, and between 1957 and 1959 it invested £279,000 in shares and equities.

We have fostered the growth of the Co-operative Movement in the Region in every way. The Co-operative Bank was established in 1953 with a capital of £1 million. A Co-operative College has been planned and the number of Co-operative Societies has risen from 564 in 1953/54 to 926 in 1957/58. Their activities cover producer, consumer, thrift, credit, crafts and other aspects of the Movement.

One aspect of economic development which we vigorously pursued is the provision of basic services. We recognised from the outset that there must be electric power, a good and reliable water supply, and efficient means of communication, if economic development is to be well founded. The Electricity Corporation of Nigeria which is a Federal set-up was not up-and-doing enough for our purpose. But under the law no other agency could generate electricity without a licence from the Federal Government. This was an intolerable handicap. We, therefore, fought and succeeded in getting a provision inserted in the Constitution that a Regional Government or its agency could generate electricity without obtaining a licence from the Federal Government. The result of this provision was a change of attitude on the part of the ECN. After due negotiation, the Western Region Government granted the ECN a loan of £1·3 million free of interest for a number of years, in order to speed up the provision of electric power in the Region both for domestic and industrial purposes. It is planned that by 1962 electricity should be available to all the principal towns in the Region. The pilot scheme, which is now in operation in some smaller towns and villages, is expected to provide the information and experience upon which to base a region-wide rural electrification programme. Since 1952, several towns have been supplied with pipe-borne water. Rural water supplies have also been developed in many places in the Region and experiments are proceeding with borehole supplies.

As regards roads and bridges, the position was, as I said

before, most unsatisfactory when we took office in 1952. Roads were bad and were also badly maintained, whilst bridges were narrow and were becoming inadequate for the volume of traffic that they were expected to carry. We therefore embarked upon the strengthening, widening and re-surfacing of the most important roads, and the rebuilding of bridges. Local Authorities were encouraged by means of generous grants to construct new feeder roads. The result is that apart from Trunk Roads 'A', which are the Federal Government's responsibility, there were by March 1959 1,600 miles of bituminous-surfaced roads in the Western Region as against 178 miles in 1952. In the middle of 1959 and in response to the clamour from different parts of the Region, I got the legislature to approve a capital expenditure of £2·5 million for a special Road Development Programme, so that by 1960 the total mileage of bituminous-surfaced roads in the Region (excluding Trunk Roads 'A') will be about 2,200 miles.

The labour policy of my Government was the most enlightened in the whole of the Federation. At a time when the governments of other Regions were paying their workers as little as 2/4d per diem per worker, the Western Region Government decided on a minimum wage of 5/- for workers with effect from 1 October 1954. This was raised to 5/6d with effect from the 1 April 1959. My colleagues and I believe in a national minimum wage, but we have advocated this cause in vain during the past eight years. It is not disputed that the costs of living in the three Regions are more or less the same: slightly higher and slightly lower in the East and North respectively than in the Western Region. As a direct result of our wage policy and of other services which increase their real incomes, both the morale and efficiency of our workers have risen considerably, and are now the highest in the Federation. The machinery for consultations between the representatives of workers and of the government has operated smoothly and satisfactorily throughout my period. The result of all this was that there was not a single strike by workers in the employ of the government during my tenure of office.

As has been mentioned, we launched a universal free primary education scheme in 1955, which has been so firmly and successfully established that everyone now takes it for granted, despite initial predictions of failure by many well-meaning persons. Apart from financial handicaps, we also had initial planning difficulties. We decided that the new schools should be so sited that no child would have to travel more than two miles by the shortest route to get there. We depended almost wholly on Nigerian teachers who were elevated to the status of Education Officers for that purpose, and partly on a number of loyal British administrative officials, to get the siting properly done. The work of siting commenced before the enrolment of children. We had calculated, in accordance with the census data compiled in 1953, that only 275,000 children would be eligible for enrolment. But in actual fact almost half-a-million children enrolled. Many villages and families had not been counted during the census enumeration. All previous sitings for schools had to be revised with the speed of summer lightning towards the end of 1954. Our Nigerian teachers rose to the occasion; and our united efforts have been amply rewarded. The primary school population has risen from 429,542 in 1953 to 1,037,388 in 1959.

The figures for secondary education are equally impressive. Our policy was to provide secondary education for at least 10 per cent of the pupils who have successfully completed their primary school course and in consequence, many secondary grammar schools have been opened. The total is now 139 instead of only 25 in 1952. In addition, there are 363 secondary modern schools in the Region providing places for over 50 per cent of the primary school-leavers. Thus while there were 6,775 pupils in secondary schools in the Region in 1952, our secondary school population in January 1959 stood at 84,374. This is far larger than the combined population of all the secondary schools in other parts of Nigeria. We recognised the pre-eminent place which teacher training must occupy in our educational programme. The number of teacher training colleges has doubled since 1952 and we had about 11,000

287

trainees in them in 1959. We have also improved the salary scales and employment conditions of teachers considerably since 1952 in order to retain good men in this important service. We resolutely tackled the problem of technical education. If our development programmes are to succeed we need skilled labour. In order to produce the requisite number of technicians, skilled workers and managers, therefore, two technical schools were opened. In addition, the existing Trade Centre at Sapele in Urhobo Division has been considerably expanded, and five more are being established. The provision of post-secondary scholarships tenable in Nigeria and overseas has soared; over 1,200 were awarded during my time.

As regards medical and health services, the government has fully implemented its policy of establishing at least one hospital in every Administrative Division in the Region, and has proceeded to provide hospitals for some of the more important towns. Ten such additional hospitals had either been completed or were in the process of completion by the end of 1959. A number of mobile dispensaries take hospital and other medical facilities to remote parts from bases in Ibadan, Abeokuta and Benin Provinces. For the riverine areas, touring launches do the work of mobile dispensaries, and ambulance launches take patients to hospitals. Grants have been given to Local Authorities to enable them to provide Rural Health Centres in their areas, and there were 14 such centres in 1959 as against only 1 in 1952. From 1952 to 1959 the number of dispensaries has risen from 200 to 365 and that of maternity centres from 122 to 239. A big expansion in these fields was launched on the eve of my departure from the Region. The government's policy of providing free medical treatment to young persons up to eighteen years of age, which is unique and without a parallel in Nigeria, has been maintained.

In order to ease the general shortage of houses in the Region, particularly in large urban areas and to encourage house ownership, the government established the Western Housing Corporation. The Corporation has set up a 350-acre housing estate at Bodija in Ibadan with well-drained roads and modern sewage disposal. More than 200 houses had already been constructed there by 1959—less than one year after its inception. Another 750-acre estate is being laid out at Ikeja; of this, 200 acres are earmarked for industrial estates and the remainder will be residential. The Housing Corporation also grants loans to borrowers who want to build their own houses. Loans totalling about £380,000 have been granted on mortgage to borrowers by the end of 1959. Members of the public are encouraged to deposit their savings with the Corporation against future housing transactions: more than £12,000 has been so deposited in the short time since the facility became available.

In the sphere of public relations, we advanced beyond recognition from the puny efforts of the Public Relations Department which we inherited in 1952. We have carried enlightenment and entertainment to remote areas through the Government Free Cinema Scheme, and through the publication of a weekly paper (*Western News*) and a monthly illustrated magazine (*Western Nigeria Illustrated*) both of which are objective and non-partisan. In 1959 there were in use 40 cinema vans and 6 cinema barges. We established our own film production unit, and one of its outstanding achievements is the 85-minute film in colour which covers all aspects of our self-government celebrations and the visit of Her Royal Highness the Princess Royal. Of all the governments in Africa, the Western Region Government is the largest film producer, having the largest government cinema audience as well.

Our Nigerianisation policy is the boldest and the best in the whole of the Federation. Even when we did not have the power directly to influence Nigerianisation, we had initiated the brilliant device of the 'frigidaire policy'. We have not looked back since then. Our post-secondary scholarships were mainly geared to our Nigerianisation policy. We were determined that there should be no lowering of standards, and there has been none. Many of our scholars have returned to take their places in the public service of the Region; and a large number of Nigerian civil servants have been given the facilities of in-service training; with the result that at the time of my departure the number of Nigerians in the higher rungs of the civil service in the West was 1,275, that is 75 per cent of the total actual strength of senior officers as against 18 per cent in 1952.

My last act in the Western Region was the provision of a television service which is the first of its kind in the whole of Africa. Television service is a complicated project. But it was one of the boldest conceptions in the Action Group's endeavour to bring the latest in entertainment and, above all, enlightenment to the people of the Region. Owing to technical difficulties the scheme is at present limited to the Ibadan and Ikeja areas of the Region; but it will in course of time be extended to the other parts of the Region. When the official transmission of the Television Project was launched at the end of October 1959, it proved to be the crowning climax of the achievements of the Western Region Government under my direction, and it once more proclaimed and confirmed the Action Group as the 'pacesetter' in the Federation of Nigeria.

Before I left the Region, I took the opportunity of a meeting of the Legislature in November to make a valedictory address to the two Houses. Nothing, in my humble opinion, could be more fitting as a finale to this chapter than extracts from that valedictory speech. On 3 November 1959, addressing the House of Assembly, I said, among other things, these words:

Eight years are a short period in the life of a legislature. . . . But the eight years since January 1952 have been packed with deliberations, decisions and actions of an exceptionally momentous and memorable kind.

The government and the opposition do differ quite naturally, most often very strongly, on the merits of the achievements of the government and of the Legislature of this Region since 1952. But there can be no conscientious dispute as to the facts of those achievements.

In the course of our journey, the government and the Legislature have erected a number of truly brilliant and imperishable milestones. These have been a credit to us.

When the battle for 1956 as a target date for Nigeria's independence raged fiercely in 1953, it was our Legislature alone that passed resolutions in support. By means of resolutions unanimously passed in this honourable House and in the other place, we were, by a long stretch, first in the field in opting for Regional self-government which eventually served as the precursor to national independence, and as the most powerful instrument for accelerating the advent of Nigeria's freedom.

When we first assembled here in January 1952, with the exception of a few members we were all new to a parliamentary life as distinct from extra-parliamentary political activities. There were cynics as well as well-meaning people who thought and predicted that we would make a mess of our great and historic assignment.

It would be pretentious to suggest that we had not made mistakes, but which earthly institution is free from these unavoidable human frailties? Indeed we have made our mistakes. But on the whole it is correct and incontrovertible to say that the Parliament and government of this Region have conducted themselves and the affairs of the Region in strict accordance with the best traditions; with credit to ourselves, honour to our Region, country and race; and glory to God.

It is the duty of the government resolutely to govern the people under its jurisdiction according to its light and judgment. On the other hand, it is the duty of the opposition to express its views candidly in opposition to any government measure which in its view is not in the best interest of the people. Criticisms have been made in this House, especially during the consideration of Bills, that the government does not often give regard to opposition views. The truth is that it is neither politic nor wise for a government to submit or appear to submit in the open, on major issues, to the opposition. It must be clearly recognised, however, by those who have learnt anything about the running of a government that in the private counsels of a Cabinet and the Government Party, the SPIRIT of the opposition is always present. It is present to warn the government of the day against acts and measures which might give the opposition the cudgel with which to whip the government and attract the majority of the people to its side. . . .

The aim of a good government is the welfare of the entire people under its jurisdiction. In pursuance of this aim, it is impossible for a government to please everyone. As long, however, as the government is satisfied that any given policy, measure, programme, or legislation, will rebound to the greatest good of the greatest number of the citizens under its charge, it should be inflexible in its path. This indeed has been the guiding principle of the government which I have headed since 1952.

Under God's guidance, dominated in our thoughts, counsels and actions to do the best we ever can for all our people, and occasionally restrained by the SPIRIT of the opposition, I am satisfied that my government and this honourable House have done exceedingly well for this Region. We have set a pace and a standard unequalled and unsurpassed in the annals of our great country.

Since 15 March 1957, when I declared my intention to leave Regional politics for good for the Centre, some friends and admirers have wondered why I have chosen to relinquish the certainty of a Regional Premiership for the probability of a Federal Prime Ministership. My attitude on this issue, however, is clear and unequivocal. I have never had any doubts that the place for the leader of a nation-wide political organisation is the Centre. When my party won the Regional Elections in 1951 we decided that I should lead the team in the Western Region because we realised then that it was only at the Regional level that Party policies and programmes could be put into effect. We had the burning desire to demonstrate to the world Nigerians' capabilities in the art of government, and to establish, through our performances in the Western Region, a firm basis for the accelerated advancement of the country as a whole towards independence. With the attainment of self-government by the Western Region in 1957 and the irrevocable promise of Independence for Nigeria on 1 October 1960, our objectives have been realised and my assignment in the Western Region is completely discharged. From December this year, it is at the Centre that I will exhibit my political activities, playing there such role as Providence may from time to time entrust to my party and to me.

I have come here this morning, therefore, to take my bow on this exalted stage, to the audience before whom I have performed, these eight years past.

The undoubted, outstanding and epoch-making successes which have characterised my regime have not been achieved single-handed. I have owed these successes to God's abiding grace and mercy, and to the co-operation of all my colleagues without exception. I take this opportunity to pay public tribute to my cabinet and Parliamentary colleagues for their patriotism, public-spiritedness and devotion to duty; and for their unwavering loyalty to the noble cause of our great party and to my leadership.

However much one may dislike the methods of some individual opposition members, the fact remains, and I hereby publicly and gratefully acknowledge it, that under the leadership of the Honourable Dennis Osadebay, the opposition has made worthy contributions to the healthy growth of parliamentary democracy in this Region.

As I leave this honourable House certain things give me great satisfaction and confidence as to the future of this Region. Firstly, I am leaving behind a team of ministers whose competence and sense of duty are undoubted; a fair-minded and proficient Speaker, and a body of legislators whose patriotism has never been in question. Secondly, the team of ministers is going to be led by a colleague whose wise counsels and advice have been of great help to me in my conduct of the affairs of this Region. Thirdly, our civil service is exceedingly efficient, absolutely incorruptible in its upper stratum, and utterly devoted and unstinting in the discharge of its many and onerous duties. For our civil servants, government workers and labourers to bear, uncomplainingly and without breaking down, the heavy and multifarious burdens with which we have in the interest of the public saddled them, is an epic of loyalty and devotion, of physical and mental endurance, and of a sense of mission, on their part. From the bottom of my heart I salute all of them. Fourthly, our police force is impartial and efficient and is capable of maintaining law and order, and of speedily coping with any breach or attempted breach of it. Fifthly, we have a judiciary which is independent and impartial in every sense of the word, and a thoroughly upright, knowledgeable and fearless Public Service Commission. Sixthly, the economy of the Region is in a very healthy state, and the finances of the government are sound and buoyant.

I want to end this valedictory speech by paying special tribute to the Obas, Chiefs and people of the Region. It is the loyalty, patriotism, obedience to constituted authority, and sense of civic responsibility on the part of the vast majority of them that have made the governmental regime and era with which my name will for ever be associated in this Region such a supreme and completely satisfying success.

CHAPTER 16

SOME REFLECTIONS

WHEN Nigeria becomes a self-governing nation on 1
October 1960, it will have made history. Her road to freedom
has been strewn with a large assortment of verbal diatribes
from Nigerian nationalists, and unnumbered administrative
blunders on the part of our British overlord. But it has been free
from violence and bloodshed. 'Hard words don't break bones',
said a British official; and our denunciations and invectives
against British imperialism over the years have broken none.
At the same time, the defects in British administration have
turned out to be a blessing in disguise. For if British rule had
been less inept than it was, the opportunity for Nigerians to
demonstrate that they are quite qualified to manage their
own affairs would have been correspondingly reduced.

Two things have combined to make the transition from
colonialism to sovereignty so smooth and peaceful in Nigeria:
constructive nationalism or constitutional agitation on the part
of Nigerians, and liberalism on the part of the British government. Nationalism in a colonial territory is perforce characterised by two seemingly contradictory features: the constructive feature as well as the negative. Because of the political and
other disabilities suffered by the indigenous inhabitants of a
colonial dependency, the natural tendency is for them to place
much greater emphasis on the negative feature, and to give
scant attention to the constructive aspect of their struggles for
liberation. This ought not to be so, and has not been the case
in Nigeria. Anti-imperialism, which is coterminous with
negative nationalism, sees nothing good in foreign rule; and
collaboration with the colonial power in any measure, however
desirable for the common good, is condemned as an act of

294

treachery. In an uncontrolled rage, the slave, who is relatively ill-equipped for the purpose, makes a physical assault on his master; he is badly mauled in the encounter, and there is a consequent prolongation of his period of enslavement. Constructive nationalism or constitutional agitation, on the other hand, demands almost stoic self-restraint and discipline; an objective appreciation of historical and contemporary trends, and an overpowering desire to ensure that the journey to freedom does not bring more discomfort to the masses of the people than is absolutely necessary, and compulsively dictated by the prevailing circumstances at any given time.

During Nigeria's glorious march to freedom, there have been occasional but unsuccessful attempts to deflect her from the constructive path. The last of these attempts was made in 1957. During the Nigerian Constitutional Conference of that year held in London, Nigerian leaders had unanimously demanded than the attainment of independence for Nigeria should be fixed for a date in 1959. In the course of discussions at the conference, it became crystal clear that the arrangements for the transfer of power, even if Britain was prepared to make such transfer immediately, could not be satisfactorily completed before the end of 1959. A demand for a date in 1960 was accordingly made. But the British government was not prepared to commit itself. There was a feeling of sharp disappointment amongst the entire Nigerian delegations. Some of the delegates held the view that Britain was determined to drag its feet indefinitely on the issue of a target date for Nigeria's independence. I did not share this view. Since the 1953 Conference, when self-government in 1956 was guaranteed to any Region that wanted it, I have ceased to nurse any doubt about British sincerity on the question of early independence for Nigeria. Consequently, before the 1957 Conference opened, I was able to say in an address to a meeting of Nigerian students in London:

Now that all the leaders and people of Nigeria are unanimous on a target date, it appears to me safe to assume that Her Majesty's

295

Government will find no difficulty at all in granting our ardent and legitimate request. . . .

There are three other important grounds for this assumption. Firstly, world opinion is now very strong against, and very critical of, imperialism of whatever guise and character. The advocates of this opinion are growing larger in number and stronger in influence every day, with the result that colonial rule is fast becoming anathema to the imperialists. Secondly, the peoples of Nigeria are more articulate and more resourceful than ever before, and their agitation for self-rule is now sustained and without respite. Thirdly, there has been a revolutionary change of outlook on the part of the British people themselves. . . . The colonies have ceased very largely to be the sources of cheap labour and cheap raw materials. And the experience gained from those colonies which are now free has shown conclusively that sooner or later a so-called colonial territory will attain to independence. In these days of violent ideological conflict, and of a progressive swing in the balance of military power, there seems to be a general feeling among the British people that it is better to let the colonies go when relations are still cordial than to hold on until anti-British feelings become so exacerbated that friendly association between the mother country and its former colonies becomes badly prejudiced or completely alienated.

When the British government refused at the 1957 Conference to fix a date in 1960 for Nigeria's independence, my colleagues and I were disappointed but not unduly shaken. Indeed, we were quietly heartened by the statement made by Mr Lennox-Boyd. Though he did not say so in so many words, the inference was obvious that if all went well in Nigeria, the year of independence would be 1960. That was our impression, and my colleagues and I held firmly to it. The Sardauna of Sokoto and Sir Abubakar Tafawa Balewa appeared to have gathered the same impression. The Action Group and the NPC were poles apart on other issues, but we stuck together on this score. At a private meeting of Nigerian leaders we combined to oppose the suggestion that the constitution should be boycotted in order to bring it home to Britain how envenomed we had been by the refusal of the British government to concede our unanimous request. Public discussions as to whether or not the constitution should be boycotted were provoked in Nigeria and among Nigerians abroad. If things were not to get out of hand, it was imperative that the traditional good sense of our people should be re-asserted and upheld. My colleagues and I promptly joined issue with the advocates of boycott and non-cooperation. In my presidential address to the Action Group Congress held in Lagos on 12 July 1957, sixteen days after the conference, I said:

The history of subject peoples which have eventually become free and independent has demonstrated that one or all of three different methods have been employed by them for the redemption of their liberty. They are: violence; non-cooperation; and constructive or constitutional agitation. It is, I think, in the interest of Nigeria that we should examine and evaluate each of these methods publicly now.

Throughout the period of our political subjection we have wisely and quite rightly eschewed violence as a suitable weapon for the redemption of our lost freedom. Violence never settles anything right: apart from injuring your own soul, it injures the best cause. It lingers on long after the object of hate has disappeared from the scene to plague the lives of those who have employed it against their foes. Besides, these are days when all civilised peoples of the world are striving with might and main to outlaw violence in any shape or form in the settlement of disputes between man and man. The mere fact that they have not quite succeeded in their noble venture is no invitation to us to attempt what is palpably destructive of all that is best in the hopes, aspirations and endeavours of mankind. We would be extremely foolish to contemplate it, much more to use it. . . .

Since the close of the London Conference, some people have advocated non-cooperation and what they described as the boycott of the constitution. They have called upon all the ministers and legislators to resign their posts and seats in the cabinet and legislatures. This, in my humble and considered opinion, is a counsel of destruction and despair. The consequences of such a course of action are obvious. Non-cooperation or boycott of the constitution as advocated would automatically lead to the suspension of the constitution. This would generate bitterness on such a scale as might in turn lead to the outbreak of disturbances and violence in different parts of the country. The inevitable result would be the complete disruption of our society and a total collapse of all the large-scale development programmes on which we have embarked. All this

297

would culminate in chaos, poverty and utter discomfort for the masses of our people.

It required a superman like Mahatma Gandhi, who enjoyed unquestioning leadership throughout the length and breadth of India successfully to lead a non-cooperation non-violence movement in India. Quite apart from the fact that there is no Gandhi today in Nigeria, even the illustrious Mahatma Gandhi himself was unable to restrain the violent elements in India from engaging in acts of terrorism of which the Mahatma strongly disapproved. But then there is nothing in this country since we entered the new phase in 1947 to compare even remotely with British acts of oppression and high-handedness in India in the first quarter of this century.

. . . I am happy to note that the vast majority of our people do not at all favour a course of action which is certain to put their lives, property and future prospects in jeopardy without any just cause whatsoever. The weapon of non-cooperation or of boycott of the constitution is the last resort. It is never used, and was never in fact used in India, where there are chances that the weapon of negotiation might still succeed.

We of the Action Group have pledged ourselves, as a matter of fundamental principle, to employ the weapon of constructive agitation, and this weapon alone, in our fight for political liberation. This is the weapon of spoken and written words in the service of a just and noble cause. It is the weapon of psychological offensive whereby world opinion and indeed British opinion may be skilfully organised against continued British rule. It consists also of the employment of such constitutional powers as we possess at any given time to encroach and impinge upon the remaining preserves of British rule with a view to forcing it into retreat and complete surrender. It is a weapon which requires considerable thought, planning, organisation, and careful timing as well. But its advantages are tremendous. You achieve the same objective of political liberation whilst you maintain at home orderly progress and increased prosperity among the citizens. Furthermore, constructive agitation, in the present war-tired and violence-surfeited world, has the knack of evoking considerable sympathy and active support from the nationals of the tutelary country as well as from those of the other parts of the free world. It is a weapon which has worked well in this country in the past. It is the only one which has the chance of keeping Nigeria together as a united country. It is above all a weapon of peace, a weapon of love, and it is through such a medium that God comes more readily on the side of those who fight in a just cause.

There are people who say that they prefer to reign in hell rather than serve in heaven. We all know that this is the attitude of a fallen angel who is eternally denied re-admission into paradise. It does not appear to me that our relationship with Britain warrants such an extremity of desperation. We are right now on the threshold of paradise, where we will reign with other members of the Commonwealth of Nations. After sixty years or so of journeying, we only require three years to go to arrive there. We must not do anything rash to send us several years back from the gate of heaven.

The contribution which the protagonists of boycott and non-cooperation made to the early grant of independence to Nigeria is not to be discounted or minimised. It must have been brought home vividly to the British government that if the apostles of constructive nationalism were discredited by undue delay on Britain's part to accede to the wishes of the people of Nigeria, political extremism would be enthroned and the friendship of Nigeria would be forfeited for good. It must also be put down to their credit that in spite of their tendency in that direction, the anti-imperialists never went so far as to create a state of violent disturbances in our agitation for freedom.

The view has been expressed in some respectable quarters that the peaceful attainment of independence by Nigeria has its disadvantage. Our struggles for independence have produced no martyr—no single national hero who is held in reverence and affection by the vast majority of the people of Nigeria. It is believed that we need such a hero to keep together the diverse peoples of our country, after the British government shall have withdrawn its cohesive influence on the 1 October 1960. A George Washington, a Gandhi or a Nehru is required to infuse a sense of oneness and of common nationality in the peoples of Nigeria; and the lack of such a leader, so the argument goes, would be likely to militate against the future solidarity of the country. I don't think that this will necessarily follow. Nigeria has won her independence without a George Washington simply because the manner in which Britain has handled our agitation for freedom is totally different from her cold and contemptuous attitude to the American Colonies. I have no doubt that the good sense with which we attained independence will keep us together as a free and united people. There is a strong desire among the diverse elements in the country to remain together; and if the need ever arose this overpowering desire would produce an Abraham Lincoln who might not have to invoke the force of arms to re-establish and re-seal for all time the unity of Nigeria. Any observer of recent political development in Nigeria will agree that, having regard to the sensible and statesmanlike manner in which we had tackled our problems in the past, there can be no fears as to the future of the country. Nigeria will have her full share of the strains and stresses that beset all modern states; but she will survive them. The important point to be borne in mind is that all the leaders of opinion in Nigeria are unanimous in their determination to keep the constituent units in the country together. As for the younger generations, they just cannot contemplate a Nigeria different in boundaries and smaller in size than the one which Britain bequeathes to us on independence. Every sane Nigerian today shrinks from giving even a fleeting thought to an alternative to one Nigeria. For it is not difficult to imagine the catastrophe that would be attendant on the disintegration of the country. Such a tragic event would be preceded by bloody disorder and consummated in chaos. It would take several years—perhaps several generations—for any of the units emerging from such a disintegration to maintain good government at home, or enjoy even the semblance of prestige abroad.

Apart from the united resolve of Nigerian leaders to keep the country together, there are two important factors which, if fully employed, will make for the permanent and harmonious unity of Nigeria. The first is the acceptance and the practical unfoldment of federalism, with all its implications, as the only suitable form of constitution for Nigeria. I have already dealt with this *in extenso* in Chapters 12 and 13. The second is the pursuit and the preservation of a democratic way of life in the conduct of our governmental affairs. Any departure or continued falling short at any level from this form of government might gravely threaten the unity of Nigeria and weaken her influence in the comity of nations. In view of what I have said before, any deterioration in the corporate existence of the country would be bound to provoke a counter-movement, the form and extent of which I would not now dare to predict. Government by tyranny or dictatorship is maintainable only by the use of force and by various acts of repression and oppression against those who disagree with or are critical of the tyrant or dictator. One of the lessons which history has repeatedly taught, however, is that, however repressed it may be, mankind cannot permanently attune itself to the base and inhuman conditions of a dictatorship. Sooner or later (and in these modern times it is now sooner than later), those who have been repressed, suppressed and tyrannised over make an adamant and irrepressible bid for their liberation. The degree of the intensity of this counter-action would, to a large extent, depend on the degree of the low depravity of the situation which it is sought to remedy. Russian communism, with its diminishing human degradation, is a logical sequel to the gross and infernal excesses of tsarism. In all its long history Russia has never known democracy. And it will be long after those generations which knew the tsarist days have died off before liberal democracy could ever have a chance of rearing its head among the Russians. The point must be stressed, however, that Russia is not a good example for aspiring dictators. Nor is Nigeria, on independence, likely to provide a fertile soil for more than a very limited period for the flourishing of autocracy at the federal, regional or local level. In our case we are fortunate that on the eve of independence, Britain has, at our demand and with our active co-operation, planted in our soil the sturdy plant of democracy. Those who have contributed to the achievement of this end will, I am sure, not relax their vigilance and efforts in the proper nurture of this new and glorious plant.

After independence, Britain will have no right to interfere in our affairs. Whatever association or co-operation there is between Nigeria and Britain would have to be voluntary. But it will not do for Britain and her friends in the Western democracies to say anything which would harmfully affect the activities of those who have dedicated themselves to the sacred task of guarding the existence and fostering the sturdier growth of our young plant of democracy. Similarly, it would be an act of bad faith for her to encourage, by tacit or other means, any group of people who might wish to contrive the destruction or sterilisation of that plant, on the pretext that a nondescript plant of African origin and of better efficacy is more suited to Nigerian soil. I make these points because there is a new-fangled theory now being propounded with erudition and gusto in the countries of the so-called Western democracies. The proponents of this theory hold the view that it is inappropriate and hardly fair to expect a newly emergent African nation to practise democracy as it is known and practised in the countries of Western Europe and the United States of America. Every mortal blow that is struck by an independent African nation at the vitals of democracy is rationalised by these theorists as the African's peculiar method of adapting democratic usages to his barbaric and primitive environment. The denial of fundamental human rights, the destruction of the rule of law, and the suppression of opposition have been brilliantly and felicitously rationalised. The outrageous declaration by an African leader that a one-party system is in accord with the democratic way of life has been ably defended by these spokesmen of the Western democracies.

Two things strike me forcibly in this strange and apologetic attitude of the Western democracies towards the debasement of the great ideal of democracy. The first is this. The nationals of these imperial powers, for a number of reasons which are well known, have always had a feeling of superiority towards the peoples of their former colonial territories. When these colonial peoples attain to freedom, though they are discharged from the bondage of political subjection and inferiority, they are regarded as nominally equal in status to their former masters. But only nominally. For it would appear that in their heart of hearts the white peoples, especially those of the Western world, still regard an African society as a group of inferior races, notwithstanding that they are politically independent.

In this connection, the British people are the worst offenders. They are never tired of expatiating, to the point of nausea, on the length of time—the number of centuries—it took them to evolve from feudalism to democracy. This is an indisputable historical fact, and British contributions to human civilisation are acknowledged. But our British friends overdo the story when they try to make it appear that the height which they have now reached and keep to can only be effectively scaled by their fellow English-speaking peoples. One brilliant English writer has said 'politicians should never read history books; and should cultivate short memories. Many owe their downfall to misguided attempts to translate the lessons of the past into current policies. . . .' In one sense this is cynical advice, and in another it is a wise admonition. We must read history books, and do more than merely read them: we must learn, mark and inwardly digest what we have read. We must do all this if we would avoid a repetition of the costly mistakes of the past, and benefit from the accumulated wisdom of the ages. But we must not in the process allow the facts of our national history, however noble and peerless, to occupy our minds to the extent of making us feel superior to other peoples. Specifically, the British must stop imagining and propagating the erroneous view that their achievements in the art of democracy are beyond the reach of others, or that the slow and painful course of their evolution must in other cases be strictly followed. It must always be remembered that we are now living in an age in which all that is good and bad on our planet is indivisible. Under existing conditions, late-comers have the singular advantage of benefiting from the experiences and accomplishments of older nations.

The second is a deliberate, subconscious or unwitting confusion between the ideal on the one hand, and the methods by which the ideal is realised in practice on the other. The ideal of democracy is not liable to modification or distortion, even though mankind has invented different methods for its realisation. In a democracy, the government must rule with the consent of the governed. The governed are inalienably entitled at periodic intervals to give this consent to the same or a different set of people who form the government. The expression of such consent must be free and unfettered; and must on no account be stultified or rigged. Furthermore, the consent must never be obtained by duress, threat or intimidation; by undue influence or fraud. These are the principles which underlie the ideal of democracy. Wherever these principles (or any of them) are tampered with or abrogated the resulting situation is anything but democracy. We all know that whilst these principles are solemnly observed in India, Britain and the United States of America, for instance, the methods of their application differ as between these countries. So the methods could differ in any African nation. But it is an affront to the African race to suggest that they are incapable of applying these principles.

Democracy and a one-party system of government are, in my opinion, mutually exclusive. Under a one-party system, the party in power arrogates to itself the right to be the only ruling party for all time. All other parties, therefore, which differ from or are in opposition to it are either suppressed or absorbed. At subsequent elections, if there are any, the consent of the people cannot be said to be genuinely sought and freely given, because there is only one choice open to the electorate. Human nature is not susceptible to mass regimentation. Wherever there are two or more persons, divergence of opinion is bound to exist. Besides, there is, more often than not, more than one side to every question of national importance. The people are entitled as of right to be given the chance to examine all sides of the problems confronting them, before expressing their majority will at the polls. Such an examination, however, will be possible only where people who hold different shades of opinions are allowed to organise themselves into parties if they wish, and are also free to explain their respective points of view to the electorate, who are the final arbiters as to which of the contending parties should be given the mandate to govern for any ensuing statutory period.

In acting as the apologists for those who destroy and discredit democracy, the spokesmen of the Western democracies do grievous harm to that noble ideal which they profoundly cherish, and which they are prepared to defend with their lives (as they have done in the past) if its practice in their homelands is at any time threatened. Communism is by reason of its birth a revolutionary and aggressive tenet. It is a legitimate reaction of the extreme left to the tyranny of narrow-minded and callous rulers of the extreme right. For centuries the masses of the people have groaned under the remorseless heel of a privileged few; and every attempt by them to assert their wishes was mercilessly suppressed and punished. On the other hand, democracy by its very nature is not a militant doctrine which can be imposed on others by means of violence and subversion. Free and unfettered consent can only be obtained by persuasion. But this is no reason for allowing a counterfeit imitation or a complete reversion of a great ideal to circulate as genuine currency. Communists have laid down dogmatic methods for the practice of communism. Any deviation from the methods thus promulgated, even where the ideal is still being faithfully pursued, is condemned and denounced as deviationism. There are no dogmas for the practice of democracy; and democrats cannot and must not censure any nation on the ground of deviationism. But they must at least have the courage and honesty to insist that a flagrant departure from the ideal of democracy is not an acceptable variant of the most beneficent and ennobling form of government which mankind in all its long and chequered history has evolved.

As we enter into independence, the thought that must be uppermost in many Nigerian minds is how best to organise and administer the affairs of our country and to cultivate the goodwill and friendship of our neighbours, for the welfare and happiness of our people, and the general good of mankind. In this connection, it is essential that our defence and foreign policies should be rational and enlightened, and our development programmes at home sufficiently bold and comprehensive to satisfy the immediate and pressing needs of our people. I regard defence and foreign affairs as complementary: the one is intended to discourage or resist external aggression, and the

305

other to cultivate external friendship. In determining what our defence and foreign policies should be, we must first of all settle in our minds which of two types of politics we prefer: power politics or welfare politics.

In the interest of our people, we must never cast as much as a glance in the direction of power politics. In this nuclear-, rocket- and dollar-dominated world we have no ghost of a chance of making any mark at all in this field. The paraphernalia of this type of politics are in themselves bewildering: a mighty array of armed forces whose claims must take pride of place in the disposal of public finances; territorial ambition; an arrogant and blustering attitude in international affairs; well-staffed and luxurious embassies in the more important countries of the world; a foreign policy that is motivated by cunning, chicanery and bad faith; an overpowering desire, stemming from sheer insensate national aggrandisement, to outwit, outshine or humiliate the other nations of the world; and so on and so forth. This kind of politics will not do Nigeria any good. It would bring miseries to our people at home, and notoriety to our nation abroad. Monies which could have been spent in catering for the welfare and prosperity of our people would have to be diverted to diabolical and fruitless channels. In any case, we are too late in the race and we just have not got the resources to indulge in it.

We have all heard a good deal of that summit where Britain, the U.S., Russia and France love to meet. From all accounts, it is a very chilly and precarious rendezvous. The foothills of the summit are comparatively obscure; but there is no doubt that it is quieter and safer there. 'He that is down need fear no fall.' Nations which indulge in power politics have brought perpetual fear and heartache to their people. The underdeveloped ones like Egypt have left their people to wallow in the mire of poverty, ignorance and disease as well. It is my submission that Nigeria should regard power politics as a poison, and should eschew it as such. If we choose welfare politics it will be well with us. In a developing country with slender means, such as ours, welfare politics and power politics do not mix. A choice must be made between butter and bullets: we cannot have both, as they have managed to do in the U.S.A. and Britain.

In view of the consideration which I have outlined, our defence policy should aim at doing no more and no less than maintaining and modernising the Queen's Own Nigeria Regiment in its present size and strength. There has been a great clamour in recent times for the enlargement of our army and navy (such as we have), and for the establishment of a strong air force. Whom are we arming against: ourselves or our neighbours? It is often overlooked that these things cost a lot of money. Nevertheless, it is my candid view that as much of these demands as are from time to time considered compatible with the preservation of our territorial integrity should be met. But we must not set out to build up these forces for mere national aggrandisement, or as an instrument for maintaining a totalitarian regime in Nigeria. The Dominican Republic spends 50 per cent of its total annual revenue on the armed forces in order to bolster up Trujillo's dictatorship. This will not do for Nigeria. Any government that does not enjoy the goodwill of the people should resign: it must not utilise the people's money for the purpose both of their enslavement and starvation. At the moment, we have no need for considerably enlarged armed forces. Our people are peace-loving; and our immediate neighbours are friendly. No territorial claims have been made to our soil, and present trends suggest that no such claims are likely to be made in the foreseeable future. I am sure that we on our part have no evil designs on our neighbours either. Reports that one of our neighbours is making attempts to subvert constituted authority in Nigeria must not be discounted. But the surest way to frustrate such attempts is the prosecution of sound domestic policies which redound to the general well-being of our people.

There are many temptations in the world today which beset the paths of new nations. Some big nations, intent on cultivating new spheres of influence, and on widening the areas of their ideological empire, dangle all sorts of bright and attractive objects before their eyes. Those nations which have fallen prey to such advances have, so far as the general good of their people are concerned, been lured to their doom. With a welfare state as our shining goal, therefore, it should be possible for us in Nigeria to tread the path of sane diplomacy. We will be in illustrious company if we do.

We have declared repeatedly that, after independence, Nigeria will remain a member of the Commonwealth of Nations. I believe also that, in view of our own indigenous monarchical institutions which we have solemnly pledged ourselves to preserve, Nigeria may remain a monarchy. The point on which there is divergence of opinion among Nigerian leaders is the nature of the tie and friendship which we would like to see subsist between Nigeria and Britain. In my considered opinion, a realistic foreign policy for Nigeria should be governed by a close and conscientious friendship with Britain. The sort of relationship which I want to see exist between Britain and Nigeria, is the kind that exists between Britain on the one hand and the countries of Canada, Australia and New Zealand on the other. It is a relationship among sister nations. There are many things which we do not like about British rule. But if the truth is told, there are also many good things which we have gained by our pupillage under that rule. In any case, after independence, wise diplomacy lies only in forgetting the grievances of the past, and working for the things of the future.

Close friendship with Britain does not mean that we will blindly approve and support whatever Britain does. Indeed, it does mean that we are free to disagree with her, and even criticise her as pungently as we ever could, whenever the circumstances of any issue demand, in our honest judgment, that we should do so. Britain has no greater friend in this world than Canada. But when Sir Anthony Eden bungled the Suez Canal issue, Mr Lester Pearson, Canada's then accredited foreign affairs spokesman, did not hesitate to castigate him. Again, close friendship with Britain does not mean that we shall necessarily be hostile to those who fail to see eye to eye with her. Indeed, we shall be free to acquire our own independent circles of friends and acquaintances. But it would be a negation of the sort of friendship I have in mind for us to enter into alliances or pacts which are prejudicial or inimical to British interests, and vice versa. If there is a conflict, however, between our interests and British interests—and this is not an unlikely eventuality—then failing a satisfactory compromise, our interests must prevail, whatever the consequences. Again, under no circumstances should we compromise the racial dignity of the African peoples in particular and of the coloured peoples in general; nor must we do or say anything at any time which would make us seem the docile satellite of the British or any government. We are a sister country to Britain and it is as such that we should behave and expect to be treated.

There are two distinct ideological camps in the world today: the Western democracies and the communist bloc. For reasons which I will presently give, my preference is unhesitatingly and unequivocally for the Western democracies. No nation in the world is absolutely good or absolutely evil. There is still a colour-bar in the Western democracies. Negroes in America are still being discriminated against, and can still be lynched with impunity. For her part Britain is still guilty, as before, though in a decreasing order of magnitude, of injustice to the black peoples in East and Central Africa. But such evils as are committed in the countries of the Western democracies towards the weaker peoples of the world are not only fast diminishing, but are being constantly subjected to strong and sharp criticisms in those countries by their nationals, without any risk to their lives or personal freedom. If you did likewise behind the iron curtain you would not live to fight another day.

The world in which we live is still very far from perfection. We have got to take it as we find it and, like conscientious and honest people, strive to contribute towards its peace, progress and happiness. From time to time, things will happen which in his judgment one individual considers to be wrong. Whether the individual is right or wrong in his judgment, he has an inherent and inalienable entitlement to entertain such opinion and to express it. The question is where, as between the Western bloc and the Eastern bloc, can a man freely exercise his natural right to hold and express any opinion, subject to such restrictions as may be laid down by laws enacted by the freely elected parliament of the land? The answer is obvious: it is in the Western bloc. As has been abundantly shown, we in Nigeria have won our freedom mainly as a result of unrestrained organised public opinion against the continuance of British rule. In our struggles against British rule we have enjoyed the support of many Britons as well. Besides, in the Commonwealth of Nations a member nation could hold and express any views it likes. But that is not the way it is done in the communist community of nations.

In the present world context, when atheistic materialism is threatening to destroy or stifle all that is best and noblest in man, neutrality in international affairs, whether passive, positive or independent, is an unmitigated disservice to humanity. My own analysis has led me to the conclusion that neutrality, as the basis of the foreign policy of certain nations, is no more and no less than the projection, conscious or unconscious, of the deep-seated prejudices which those nations have had towards some of the countries of the Western democracies. But I must urge that in our foreign relations, we must forget the past and work for the future—the great future of our land and of mankind. As between contending forces, we should have enough courage to make up our minds, independently of any outside influence, as to which side is relatively right and which side is relatively wrong. Having made up our minds, we should have the honesty to pronounce our view and stand. To pretend that neither of two diametrically opposed ideological camps is right or wrong, especially if we occupy an influential position in the assembly of nations, is to encourage evil-doing, and to damp the ardour for well-doing. There is a divine injunction as well as an attendant sanction which nations like individuals must never ignore. God Almighty, speaking to us through one of his prophets in Revelation III, 15–16, says to the neutrals:

310

I know thy works, that thou art neither cold nor hot: I would thou wert cold or hot. So then because thou art lukewarm, and neither cold nor hot, I will spue thee out of my mouth.

There is a policy which appears to be in vogue amongst some of the developing countries of the world. In their quest for financial and technical assistance, they adopt the tactics of wooing the nations of the two blocs at the same time, in the hope that in the anxious bid for new supporters or converts, they (the developing countries) would get the best of two worlds. I consider these tactics to be both disreputable and dangerous. Disreputable in the sense that it amounts in my view to diplomatic double-dealing. If we want help from more than one nation, by all means let us seek it. But it is immoral to play two opposing forces against each other in the process. It is this kind of diplomacy that is responsible for the fall of many nations in the past; for the many wars and incalculable miseries which have afflicted mankind; and for the tormenting fears and the mortifying distrust among nations, which the world is now witnessing. The tactics are dangerous because acts of double-dealing—whether diplomatic or otherwise—never pay in the end. There are times when even the greatest tactician in diplomatic cunning is outclassed in his own game. It is then that he discovers that all that he thought he had gained is but loss, and that what is left of national honour and dignity is but the shadow of an illustrious past that is gone for ever, or of a potentially great future that will never come.

A good deal has been said and written about pan-Africanism. No one has as yet precisely defined what it means. The phrase has been indiscriminately used to denote government of the whole of Africa—the United States of Africa; or an All-African nationalist movement. I am firmly of the opinion that it is visionary now and for many years to come to labour for the emergence of a United States of Africa, or even of economic co-operation (such as exists in Western Europe) among all the countries of Africa. It is unrealistic in the extreme to expect that African nations which have only recently won their independence from foreign rule would be willing to surrender or

311

even diminish their sovereignty in the pursuit of what is quite plainly an *ignis fatuus*. Apart from the impracticableness of the proposition, any serious attempt to bring about political union among the states of Africa is sure to engender suspicion, distrust and disharmony among those states. Economic and cultural association among the states of Africa, such as has brought into being the European Common Market is, as I have hinted, no less fanciful than political union. Such an association presupposes, by and large, common economic problems, and a similarity of political institutions and of social and cultural patterns, amongst the participating countries. Whilst most of the countries of the Western zone of Africa have many things in common, the same is not true of all the countries of Africa.

Two instances may be cited to illustrate the points which I have just made. The first instance is Egypt. It is true that, physically and geographically, Egypt is in Africa. But apart from the fact that her entire political heart is in the Arab world, she has never regarded herself as having any social and cultural affinity with the black races of Africa. The United Arab Republic, the pet creature of Nasser, which has one foot in Africa and another in the Middle East, is the very antithesis of a workable African community. With his undisguised totalitarianism, and his territorial ambitions in Africa and the Moslem world, effective co-operation with Nasser, in any field at all, would be possible only if the black races of Africa were prepared to remain as satellites in Egypt's orbit, as Syria now is. Besides, there is no similarity in substance in the economic and social problems of Egypt and ours. The second instance is South Africa together with other such countries in Africa. In South Africa, the Central African Federation and Algeria, the white settlers are in the minority, but they insist on dominating the indigenous African majorities. It is far-fetched to imagine that there is any real community of interests between the black races of Africa and these domineering white settlers.

As an all-African nationalist movement, pan-Africanism can be a most potent organisation if its membership is confined to black Africans and to those nationals of Africa, whatever the colour of their skin, who believe in the absolute equality of all races. In this sense, pan-Africanism should aim at giving active support to all dependent African peoples in their struggles for liberation. It should by constitutional means do all in its power to exterminate from the face of Africa the practice of racial discrimination and superiority, such as exists in South Africa, the Central African Federation and East Africa. If the aims and objects of pan-Africanism are limited in this way, and are not extended to the pursuit of a pan-African Government, the movement is decidedly on the right path, and Nigeria should give to it her fullest possible backing.

To sum up. On independence, Nigeria should do everything in her power to foster co-operation among all the countries of West Africa in economic and cultural matters. She should fearlessly champion the cause of the oppressed peoples in Africa and other parts of the world. She should take her place in the Commonwealth of Nations, and should not hesitate to make clear beyond any shadow of doubt her attitude towards the ideals for which the Western democracies stand. In so far as is compatible with her honest convictions, national interests, and her legitimate obligations as a loyal member of the Commonwealth of Nations, she should maintain cordial relations with all the other nations of the world, and do her best to promote peaceful co-existence between the Western and Eastern blocs. She should stand immovably for what Mr Macmillan calls 'peace with justice', and should make her voice heard at all times in this noble and imperishable cause.

In the fields of internal development our prospects for the future are good. In population Nigeria is the largest country in the whole of Africa. Its forty million inhabitants are fast growing in political consciousness and enlightenment. As I said before, in January 1955 free universal primary education was introduced in the Western Region, and a similar scheme was partially introduced in the Eastern Region in January 1957. The Northern Region government, so far as it lies in its power, is making a big drive to catch up with the South in the matter of education. All the governments of the country have considerably stepped up the number of awards for secondary and post-secondary scholarships, with the result that several hundreds of Nigerian boys and girls are now studying as government scholars in secondary schools at home, and in higher institutions of learning both in Nigeria and abroad.

The country possesses incalculable natural resources: we have coal and lignite; we have iron ore, lead, zinc, tin and its by-products; petroleum has been discovered in a number of places in commercial quantity; limestone, which is the basic raw material for the production of cement, abounds in almost inexhaustible quantity in different parts of the country. A large reserve of uranium has been discovered. So far, only a small fraction of our mineral resources has as yet been explored or discovered. We have cotton, cocoa, oil-palm products, rubber, timber, citrus, all of which at present form the basis of our wealth. We can be self-sufficient in the production of our foods.

Our human and natural resources are great potentialities which, if properly organised and deployed, will bring prosperity and orderly progress to our nation as well as contribute to the contentment of the world in general. I make bold to assert that the prosperity, strength and the influence which a nation possesses depend on the following factors:

(1) a large population which is enlightened, disciplined, nationalistic and loyal enough to make any requisite sacrifice, be it of money, time or even life, for the cause of the fatherland;

(2) the possession of natural resources in considerable measure, and the intensive exploitation of such resources for the benefit of the nation and humanity at large;

(3) a large pool of master-minds or experts in every walk of life who, out of a sense of mission to the nation and humanity, are determined to ensure maximum results in their respective callings.

It must be admitted that we are at present deficient in some of these essential factors. Our teeming millions are still far from being sufficiently enlightened. A public opinion strong and healthy enough to discourage irresponsibility and rascality in public life still has to be developed. A sense of civic responsibility on the part of the generality of our people is still to be

314

cultivated. Our natural resources, to which reference has been made, have little or no value for our people unless we apply to them, for their exploitation, a vast supply of capital, a strong and large body of technicians as well as persons with managerial skill.

Our immediate duty therefore is two-fold. First we must do everything in our power to create conditions in all parts of Nigeria which will be favourable to the admission of foreign capital and technique. But in the interest of ourselves and of the foreign investor himself, certain conditions must be stipulated for the admission of foreign investment. First, the foreign investor should undertake to train Nigerians in modern industrial and business techniques with a view to their taking over, at an early date, the operation and management of the ventures concerned; secondly, he must be prepared to admit Nigerian capital into partnership with his own, such capital being provided either by the government or any of its agencies, or by Nigerian private businessmen; and thirdly, he must agree that if the interests of Nigeria so dictate, he will readily and voluntarily surrender his shareholding in the venture concerned on payment to him in full of the prevailing market value of his shares. The second is that all the governments of the Federation of Nigeria should take immediate steps to increase and re-orientate their scholarship awards so that many more of our boys and girls may be enabled to go abroad to acquire those techniques and skills which are required for the rapid development of our country.

In the past few years, all the governments of Nigeria have launched development programmes under which several millions of pounds are being spent for the economic development of the different parts of the country. With the full implementation of these programmes, the national income of the country as a whole will be increased and the general standard of living of our people will rise.

But in order that our independence may be worthwhile, it is urgent and imperative that we should plan on a much bolder and grander scale. To this end, the governments of the Federation must avail themselves of the services and advice of all the talents which Nigeria and nations friendly to her can provide. Nigeria has in her all the makings of greatness. But we would be deluding ourselves if we imagined that size, population and natural resources, which are nothing but latent factors, are all that are required to boost us into a position of eminence and leadership. On the contrary, it is the amount of patriotism, unstinted effort and wisdom which we apply to the exploitation of our vast resources, and of the just and equitable distribution of the results of such exploitation, that will determine the measure of our greatness and happiness as a people.